GRAND THEFT AND PETIT LARCENY
Property Rights in America

Mark L. Pollot

Foreword by
Bernard H. Siegan

PACIFIC RESEARCH INSTITUTE FOR PUBLIC POLICY
San Francisco, California

The Pacific Research Institute is a nonprofit organization that advocates individual liberty through the fundamental principles of free markets, private property, and limited government. PRI focuses on current public policy issues and promotes a better understanding of those issues among opinion leaders in government, the media, academia, and the business community. For futher information on the Pacific Research Institute's programs and publications, please contact:

Pacific Research Institute for Public Policy
177 Post Street, San Francisco, CA 94108
(415) 989-0833   FAX (415) 989-2411

ISBN 0-936488-44-1

Printed in the United States of America
1   2   3   4   5   6   7   8   9   10

Library of Congress Cataloging-in-Publication Data

Pollot, Mark L., [date]
Grand theft and petit larceny: property rights in America / by Mark L. Pollot.
p. cm.
Includes bibliographical references and index.
ISBN 0-936488-44-1
1. Right of property—United States. I. Title.
KF562.P65 1991
346.7304'2—dc20
[347.30642]   91-12545
                                                               CIP

Research and Editorial Director: *Steven Hayward*
Director of Publications: *Kay Mikel*
Index: *Bonny McLaughlin*
Cover Design: *Richard Lee Kaylin*
Printing and Binding: *Edwards Brothers, Inc.*

Valid public goals cannot be legitimately achieved through illegitimate means, however efficient and effective those means may be at reaching the desired goal. This applies as much to those situations in which governmental bodies acquire what amounts to an interest in private property through the exercise of (what Justice Holmes once called) the "petty larceny of the police power" as it does to violations of the equal protection or speech guarantees of the Constitution. "Robbery under the forms of law" is the result when the government exercises its otherwise lawful power to condemn without paying constitutionally mandated compensation on the grounds that it is merely regulating the use of property. ... The uncompensated taking of property cannot be legitimized by resorting to claims that the public good is served thereby. The power of eminent domain, with its accompanying obligation to pay compensation for property taken, was given specifically to allow government to take property for the public good. When regulation is the method by which the taking is achieved, it is no defense to a uncompensated taking to say that the government has not taken much, or that the owner of the property has some economically viable use left in the property when the government finishes regulating it. The Constitution forbids petit larceny as much as grand theft and it does not distinguish between the taking of some property, and the taking of all property.

M. Pollot, Remarks to the National Federal
Lands Conference, November 1990[1]

CONTENTS

ACKNOWLEDGMENTS

I would like to thank many people for their assistance, but naming them all individually would take many pages and would run the risk of leaving out people whose assistance was invaluable. For this reason, I will name only Sandra and Christopher, without whose patience and understanding my task would have been much more difficult. I would also like to express my appreciation for those people who, although they did not participate in writing this book, fought the battles in the trenches that made it possible to have hope for the restoration of some measure of protection for this most important civil right.

FOREWORD

Freedom and abundance are essential to improve and enhance the human condition. These are also the major reasons for securing the right of property. In the absence of protection for this right, there can be little freedom for the individual and little abundance for society.

This is the great lesson of modern times. Millions of people repudiated communism in large part because it prohibited the exercise of economic freedoms. They knew, for example, that life was much more meaningful, comfortable, and convenient in West Berlin, Taiwan, and South Korea than in the adjoining communist societies of East Berlin, China, and North Korea. As numerous studies show, nations that protect the right of property along with other freedoms achieve much greater material progress than those that do not.

Nor can a nation be free if government has the power to confiscate or diminish private property. As Alexander Hamilton stated, a power over a man's subsistence amounts to a power over his will. How many people possess the courage to oppose or even criticize officials who have the authority to deprive them of their property?

The framers of our original constitution, the Bill of Rights, and the Fourteenth Amendment believed in these ideas and sought to secure them. With respect to property, each of these documents does little more than apply to government the seventh commandment: "Thou shall not steal." While owners must not use their property harmfully, they should otherwise be able to use it in their own interest, which individually or in the aggregate constitutes the public interest.

The takings clause in the Fifth Amendment (private property shall not be taken for public use without just compensation) is the Constitution's primary guarantee for ownership. As Mark Pollot explains in this book, it represents one of the basic commitments of a free society—that government will largely let people alone to further their own destinies.

Nevertheless, in this land of the free, the property right has often had to give way to capricious and oppressive regulation.

Mr. Pollot presents a study of how poorly the property right has faired in this country—to the great disadvantage of the nation. He reveals the day-to-day legal problems of producers in our society; how political and judicial processes, in defiance of constitutional meaning, have increased the risks of ownership and investment. Unless the judiciary provides protection, legislators have the power to deprive owners, investors, lenders, builders, and developers of their property. Public pressures often direct elected officials toward this end. Who, then, will build the houses, apartments, supermarkets, and industrial complexes?

The United States Supreme Court has for much of its recent history treated the right of property as of secondary importance, not giving it the high priority accorded speech, press, religion, travel, and privacy. In the Court's decisions prior to 1922, the Court strongly protected the right of ownership, generally securing any use that did not constitute a nuisance.

In 1922 in *Pennsylvania Coal v. Mahon,* the Court retreated from this rule and imposed a balancing test that considerably enlarged the meaning of harm, and thereby gave much more deference to the powers of government. While an owner's protection was reduced, it still remained at a high level. But the entire premise of property protection was severely limited in the 1926 case of *Euclid v. Ambler,* which upheld the constitutionality of zoning. In that case, the Court minimized individual rights and instead moved sharply in the opposite direction, to protect the authority of the state.

It held that "before [a zoning] ordinance can be declared unconstitutional [it must be shown to be] clearly arbitrary and unreasonable, having no substantial relation to the public health, safety, morals, or general welfare." Moreover, anyone challenging a zoning ordinance had the burden of showing its unconstitutionality. Notwithstanding the separation of powers, the Supreme Court had largely abandoned its constitutional responsibility in this area.

The courts maintained the *Euclid* position on land use regulation for more than fifty years, until the 1980s when a perspective more favorable to individual rights appeared. *Keystone Bituminous Coal Assn v. De-Benedictis* and *Nollan v. California Coastal Commission* ruled that a land use regulation will be upheld only when it (1) serves a legitimate state interest, (2) substantially advances that interest, and (3) does not deny an owner "economically viable use of his land." Under *First English Lutheran Church v. County of Los Angeles,* an owner is entitled to compensation if government regulation deprives him of all use of his land even for a temporary period. In the 1992 case of *Lucas v. South Carolina Coastal Council,* the Court held that denying an owner all economically beneficial and productive use of land requires payment of compensation unless the prohibited use constitutes or would cause a nuisance, as defined at the time the land was purchased.

Pursuant to these holdings, the protection of property again seems to be a meaningful constitutional guarantee. The Supreme Court once again accords reasonable, not maximum, deference to government. Mr. Pollot argues persuasively that the freedom and abundance of this nation demand no less.

One of the joys of teaching is the opportunity to advance understanding and scholarship. There is great satisfaction in knowing that an excellent student has achieved prominence in his profession. It is with great pride that I introduce the first major book of my former student Mark Pollot.

Bernard H. Siegan
Distinguished Professor of Law
University of San Diego
July 1, 1992

INTRODUCTION

THE FORGOTTEN CIVIL RIGHT

> *Some books are written for the pleasure or the zest of it.*
> *Other books are written as a painful duty, because there is*
> *something that needs to be said and because other people*
> *have better sense than to say it. It has not been a pleasure*
> *to write this book but a necessity. Nothing is more certain*
> *than its distortion.*
>
> Thomas Sowell[1]

Unwilling Sacrifices

The town of Bolinas is situated in Marin County on the northern coast of California. Whatever charm the small community of 1500 inhabitants may possess is marred by the presence of numerous dilapidated structures. Still, its residents guard its location jealously, going to extremes to keep outsiders from discovering the town. As fast as CalTrans, the state's transportation agency, can erect highway signs pointing the way to Bolinas, some of its residents lead midnight raids to remove them. Bolinas has achieved such notoriety from this behavior that at least one radio station in the San Francisco bay area aired commercials during June and July 1991 in which a fictional salesman lamented that if all customers were as smart as his equally fictional customer the salesman would "still be hiding road signs in Bolinas." Such notoriety has not changed the behavior of Bolinas citizens.

Phyllis spent many summers in Bolinas with a close friend, a permanent resident of the town. When she met and married Charles Gilbert, then a young teacher of handicapped children, Phyllis introduced him to the town and together they bought unimproved property in Bolinas on which to build a home to which they would eventually retire. Because Phyllis was then pregnant with their first child, the Gilberts could not afford to build immediately. When the new baby was born with major medical problems, creating expenses for which the Gilberts had no insurance, their plan to build was again postponed.

Fourteen years passed before they finally saved enough money to build their home. On the day in 1969 that the sewer permit—the first of many governmental approvals needed before a home can be built—arrived by mail, Phyllis was told that her mother had died and her father had suffered a heart attack. Again the plan to build foundered on unforeseen shoals, but the Gilberts did not give up on Bolinas. In 1972, three years later, Charles and Phyllis again were ready to build and were again thwarted, this time not by an impersonal fate bringing personal tragedy but by legal and administrative chicanery amounting to theft of their property.

Taking refuge in state statutes, the City of Bolinas declared a moratorium on new water-meter hookups in 1971, ostensibly because of a water shortage. The move effectively put a halt to new construction in Bolinas; without a water permit, no building permits could be issued. When the Gilberts found out about the moratorium, they went to the Bolinas Community Public Utility District to put their name on a list for water connection, but they were not allowed to do even that much. Every attempt they made to apply for a water permit was refused until 1975. Even after they were given an application and had filed it, the district did not act on it for twelve years. When the district finally did act, it denied the application.

The Gilberts were not the only people denied the right to build their homes. In 1976, they joined an association of Bolinas property owners composed of people who were also barred from building homes because of the water moratorium. (Of course, the community cheerfully continued to accept the association members' tax payments.) One woman had been able to drill a well on her property that would have met any water need generated by her proposed home. The well negated the sole rationale offered by Bolinas for refusing to allow her to build. She awoke one morning to find that persons unknown had filled the new well with cement. Another association member was told that any house built on his undeveloped property would be burned down before it was completed. No homes were built.

The building moratorium has lasted for nearly twenty years. If any question remains as to whether the true reason for the moratorium was a shortage of water, it cannot survive the following facts. During the moratorium, between 1972 and 1983 alone, water consumption by existing residents of Bolinas increased by 70 percent. After the moratorium was instituted, Bolinas built two reservoir storage facilities that increased the town's water storage capacity by 1100 percent. At the same time that the new reservoir was built, the district voluntarily relinquished a right it held to divert water from Pine Gulch Creek in times of heavy usage. At least one Bolinas official now argues that the city gave up that right because the city had been diverting the water illegally and had decided now to comply with the law. Nobody appears to have contested that water use while it was going on, however.

Notwithstanding the increased water supply, not one property owner who did not already live in Bolinas was permitted to construct a home. The city denied property owners the right to build their homes in Bolinas despite the fact that those people agreed to take steps to ensure that there would be enough water to support their homes.

The Gilberts and other property holders have tried to get relief from both federal and state courts, but so far their attempts have been rebuffed. Indeed, one court—in a move calculated to hamper any attempt by association members to press their claims that the city's actions unjustly deprived them of their property—has threatened the owners' legal representative, the Pacific Legal Foundation, with sanctions that could total as much as $600,000. During the past year, the trial court judge (in a ruling that accepted a federal magistrate's recommendation) stated that he would allow Pacific Legal Foundation to present evidence as to why a sanction should not be imposed. As he said later in an interview with the *Marin Independent Journal,*

> Before penalties are imposed, the attorneys will have a chance to provide testimony and evidence on why they shouldn't be fined, according to the ruling by U.S. District Judge Spencer Williams. "We don't want the courts to be used for this type of harassment," Williams said Thursday in a telephone interview. "But we want to be absolutely sure when we assess the sanctions, which we will."[2]

Initially, the court intended to impose sanctions on both the foundation and the individual attorneys. Later, the court dropped its plans to sanction the individual attorneys, but only with obvious reluctance.

In viewing this unsavory episode in judicial history, one gets the uncomfortable feeling that the courtroom of the Queen of Hearts is none too far away. Fortunately, the U.S. Court of Appeals for the Ninth Circuit subsequently issued an opinion in the case that reduced the chance that the sanctions will be upheld. Nevertheless, more than two years after the Gilberts finally retired, more than thirty-five years after they purchased their property, and approximately nineteen years after the district initiated its water moratorium, the Gilberts' property remains empty and unusable.[3]

Charles and Phyllis Gilbert are by no means isolated casualties of governmental excess. Their experience is shared by thousands of others on an almost daily basis across the United States. In New York City, for example, the Ziman family purchased a single-family house that had been converted by prior owners into small apartments. The Zimans bought the house for $280,000 in 1984 with the intent of reconverting the building into a single-family residence in which they and their children would live. Four months *after* they bought the house and began proceedings to change the house back to its original character, the city enacted an ordinance that prevented them from reclaiming the house. The ordinance left the Zimans and their two children, a son and a daughter, living in two rooms with a total floor space of approximately 350 square feet, barely larger than the average hotel room.[4] Two years later, they were able to reclaim only an additional 350 square feet.

The city was unsympathetic to the Zimans' plight. In its view, the Zimans "should have known" that the law might change after they bought their house. Six years later, after spending enormous emotional and other resources to challenge the ordinance in court (including approximately $100,000 in legal costs), they won the right to make their house their home when the New York Court held that they qualified under an exemption of the newly revised law. In the meantime, two of their tenants, both single men, occupied apartments at a monthly rent of less than $200 each, which was a minuscule portion of market rentals and was far less than the cost of maintaining such apartments.[5]

In Santa Monica, California, 89-year-old Lena Schnuck owned an eight-unit apartment building and lived in a split-level apartment in that building. In 1987, she suffered a stroke that obliged her to give up her split-level apartment because of mobility problems caused by the stroke. The Santa Monica rent control board refused to allow her to occupy the only single-level apartment in her own building unless and until the apartment's tenant either voluntarily left the apartment or seriously breached the lease in some manner. This action not only denied Lena the apartment she needed to live a life that approached independence but also gave the tenant a life estate in the property that the tenant had not purchased. Despite her medical condition and limited resources, Lena had to institute a court action to regain her own property—a case that may or may not succeed.[6] Elsewhere in the same state, the California Coastal Commission insisted that owners of existing homes donate portions of their property to the state in return for its allowing residents to build a revetment needed to keep their homes from being swept into the ocean.[7]

In one of the most unfortunate cases involving an individual citizen, John Poszgai, a Hungarian immigrant in his fifties, was sentenced to three years in prison and subjected to a $202,000 fine for cleaning up seventeen acres of land without the government's permission—and for refusing to believe that the government had the authority to require that he obtain its permission to clean the land.

The property that Poszgai had purchased and cleaned had been the site of an unofficial town dump. Unfortunately for him, the property met the federal government's highly technical definition of a wetland, although nobody who looked at the site—other than a regulatory body or an expert consultant—would readily have identified it as such. In fact, after the cleanup, Poszgai's attorney, Paul Kamenar of the Washington Legal Foundation, accompanied a reporter for *Audubon Magazine*, a publication of the Audubon Society, to the site. Looking around, the reporter appropriately asked where the wetland was.

The cleanup operation involved, among other things, removal of approximately 7000 old tires, restoring a clogged, intermittent stream to a free flowing condition, and covering over the degraded site with *clean* soil. When he was told that he needed a permit to continue the operation, Poszgai was outraged and refused to believe either that the property was a wetland or that such a requirement could be imposed on him.

Admittedly, Poszgai was abrasive, even obnoxious. Poszgai was determined not to accept the wetland description, even after being told repeatedly that the land was a wetland subject to being regulated. He was unquestionably obvious in his disregard for the regulators. Many supporters of the government's action point to Poszgai's behavior to justify his prosecution as well as the sentence meted out to him. Still, a three-year jail term and a $202,000 fine for an action that threatened neither health, safety nor, for that matter, environmentally sensitive or important land is an excessive price to pay for irritating the government.

In a crowning touch, when responding to Poszgai's petition to the Supreme Court, the Solicitor General for the United States rather sheepishly admitted the following: A photograph introduced by the government at trial to prove a fact necessary to find a violation of the law (a connection with interstate commerce) did not actually prove that fact, contrary to what the prosecutor told the jury.[8] A connection to interstate commerce is required before the federal government can exercise jurisdiction over land under the Clean Water Act. Instead, the government argued that the court could take judicial notice of that fact, a patently false claim. Judicial notice of an essential element of a crime, that is, acceptance of the truth of a fact necessary to find a person guilty of the crime without proof, is *never* proper.

The Civil Rights in Property

The pleasure I ordinarily derive from writing and from the intellectual stimulation of exploring history and law was singularly lacking when I wrote this book. As important as I believe property rights to be, writing this book has been particularly difficult because of the circumstances that compel its production. Writing about the daily violation of civil rights is not a comfortable position in the best of times. It is even less so when those violations are carried out in the name of achieving important social goals with which, in some instances, I agree. What I do not and cannot agree with is the premise, accepted by many, that it is either necessary or desirable to sacrifice individuals' rights to reach those goals, however important they may be.

Unlike Thomas Sowell's book, *Civil Rights: Rhetoric or Reality,* which examined of the nature of civil rights generally and the less-than-legitimate use of the very concept of civil rights by various interest groups, this book is about one civil right in particular or, perhaps more accurately, one class of civil rights: the rights of individuals to acquire, own, use, and enjoy property. For simplicity's sake, I will use the term "property rights" throughout this book to describe this class of rights. However, as was recognized by Supreme Court Justice Potter Stewart, "Property does not have rights. People have rights."[9]

The rights of people to acquire, own, use and enjoy property may themselves be viewed as a subset of a larger class of rights, the economic liberties. These liberties have been virtually stripped of all protection and their existence almost forgotten since the U.S. Supreme Court decided *The Slaughter-House Cases* in 1872. Their violation has occurred at the hands of people with unquestionable goodwill as often as by those with illegitimate goals. While there are far too many people in this latter group, the greater tragedy occurs when people of good intention willingly violate rights or, worse, simply refuse to recognize them, in the name of some higher good. This violation is even more tragic because it is easier to guard against villains than against truly well-meaning people. Worse, the well-meaning often provide the rhetoric and the legal and political devices that the less well-meaning can, and do, use to devastate rights with virtual impunity. In fact, the devastation of property and economic rights is often carried out with the active cooperation of those who were intended to be the very guardians of rights: the courts.

An individual's rights to acquire, own, and enjoy property have been recognized as being among the most fundamental of civil rights and as being the foundation of all other civil rights. Those who framed and ratified the Constitution and Bill of Rights (whom I'll refer to collectively as the Framers) regarded those rights as natural liberties that preexisted and were independent of the Constitution. The Framers considered the protection of property rights to be one of the primary purposes of government. The belief of these early Americans that these rights should be protected was partly moral; that is, it was based on a philosophy that held that individuals have natural and inalienable rights in their property and that those rights cannot legitimately be encroached upon except in the most limited of fashions. But the Framers' belief in the need to protect the rights of individuals in their property was also based on a profound pragmatism. They considered private ownership of property to be the foundation on which safety, security, and prosperity existed. Other countries in eastern Europe that have for decades been hostile to the very notion of private property and private economic enterprise have now realized that they need such rights.

We should not be surprised that the Framers concluded that protection of private property yields practical benefits. The new government was devised by people intimately acquainted with both philosophy and the lessons of history. Their own experiences and the experience of history demonstrated to the satisfaction of these early Americans that private ownership of property together with other liberties provide the key to long-term prosperity and security. They understood that private ownership of property provides incentives that maximize creativity and initiative. To find support for this view they had to look no further than the demise of the feudal system. The collapse of feudalism led to the spread of property ownership from the nobility to the common people and to the rise of a merchant class, which in turn resulted in widespread prosperity in England and Europe.10 Our own experience over the years also reinforces the notion that protecting property rights leads to more efficient use of resources and to greater and more widespread prosperity. Failure to protect property rights wastes resources and, ironically, has its greatest adverse impact on minorities and the disadvantaged.

In this book I will explore the dimensions of the debate over property rights, consider the importance of those rights in the modern world, and suggest a practical strategy for restoring property rights to their proper place in the constitutional scheme.

Part I discusses the nature of property generally, plus the history of the debate over the protection of rights generally and property rights specifically up to the time of the framing and ratification of the Federal Constitution and the Bill of Rights. My principal focus will be on development of the Anglo-American view of property rights and on the purposes underlying the provisions of the Constitution and Bill of Rights for protecting property. This analysis requires a brief discussion of issues of constitutional interpretation and the condition of constitutional government among the various states at the time of adoption of the Constitution and Bill of Rights.

Part II explores the initial level of protection afforded property rights by courts and the gradual decline in the protection of those rights by the same courts over time. It also examines the sharp increase in the invasion of property rights at all levels of government resulting from the influences of a smothering bureaucracy and the pressures brought to bear by various interest groups. In this exploration I will try not only to divine the direction the law has taken since adoption of the Constitution and Bill of Rights but also to understand the reasons for the deviation and the effects that this deviation has had on various aspects of American life. Part II also challenges modern courts' claims that they can find no property rights principles of general application to guide them as they consider legal questions brought before them.

Finally, in Part III, I offer suggestions for a practical strategy to restore property rights to their proper place in American society.

As will be seen, the spectrum of rights that can be lumped under the rubric of "property rights" is potentially very broad. It includes the entire realm of economic liberties and constitutional protections that had been designed to ensure respect for those liberties. These constitutional protections include not only the two most obvious constitutional provisions—the due process and just compensation clauses of the Fifth Amendment, and the due process and equal protection clauses of the Fourteenth Amendment—but also the contracts clause in Article I, Section 10 of the Constitution; the privileges and immunities clause of Article IV, Section 2; and the privileges and immunities clause of the Fourteenth Amendment, among others. However, to keep this look at property rights manageable, I have tried to confine myself to examining property rights in the context of the just compensation clause of the Fifth Amendment. I will examine particularly the application of that clause to regulatory conduct.

I have two reasons for limiting my discussion in this manner. First, the just compensation clause may be considered the principal and broadest property-protecting clause of the more than twenty property rights and economic liberties-related provisions in the Constitution. To the extent that there are property rights in a contract, for example, the just compensation clause must be read to provide substantive protection for contracts against federal intrusions (the contracts clause itself applies, by its terms, only to the states).* Second, to ensure doing justice to the topic, a discussion of the

---

* In saying this, I do not forget the due process clause. In fact, this book discusses it at some length because it plays a major role in the protection of property rights. But its role has been limited by modern courts largely to providing procedural protections, however substantial they were intended to be, whereas the just compensation clause provides more substantive protection. As the reader will discover, I believe that a great deal of the present difficulties in takings jurisprudence results from the problems that courts have had in distinguishing between these two clauses.

broader realm of economic liberties is more appropriate for a separate treatment.[11]

Modern Threats to Property Rights: Growth of the Regulatory State

Direct threats to property rights, in the sense of an unrestrained exercise of raw governmental power in physically seizing a property, are virtually unheard of in the modern United States outside the criminal law arena. The principal situation in which property rights questions arise today is one in which some government agency purports to regulate the ownership, use, or disposition of private property, thereby substituting a label for the exercise of physical power.

The growth of governmental regulations affecting property or other economic rights has been nothing short of phenomenal since World War I. The depression of the 1930s and World War II served merely to further accelerate the rate at which the government has intruded into private life.[12] In 1990 alone, the federal government issued more than 63,000 pages of new, revised, and proposed administrative regulations. This figure does not include new and amended federal legislation or court decisions that judicially amend laws that the courts are purporting only to be interpreting. Neither does it include state and local ordinances and regulations nor state court decisions, which add to, and sometimes confound, the federally imposed regulatory burden.

The volume of regulation does not tell the entire story. Its scope is equally staggering. Virtually every aspect of our daily lives is subject to regulatory management. What goods or services we may buy and from whom, how we may buy them, and what price we must pay are all directly or indirectly controlled by some government agency. What activities we may engage in and with whom; the colors of our homes; and even the manner in which individuals may mow their lawns, sweep their sidewalks, clear dead leaves from their property, or cook in their back yards may be dictated or affected by some governmental body. Many California regulatory jurisdictions, such as the South Coast Air Quality Management District, propose to regulate lawn mowers and leaf blowers in the name of protecting air quality. One California court upheld the right of a regional air quality management district to regulate backyard barbecues in the name of protecting air quality despite the questionable quality of the science used by the involved agency in promulgating the regulation.[13]

The individuals or agencies responsible for exercising such control are certain to have little understanding of our personal needs. Their ability to understand the long-term effects of their actions is minimal at best. Yet, despite their power to affect our lives, administrative officials are not held accountable in the same manner that we insist that elected officials should be held.

The threats to property rights and economic liberties posed by the dramatic expansion of regulatory activity at all levels of government are exacerbated by the development of public relations techniques that obscure rather than clarify issues, growing budget deficits, and voter-imposed limitations on spending and taxing. Spending and taxing limitations prompt governmental bodies to impose program costs (for which voters are not willing to pay taxes) on the last persons to make use of their property in any given community. California's Proposition 13, which rolled back property taxes in California and placed severe restrictions on reraising such taxes, is perhaps the most famous and imitated such voter-imposed limitation. Its passage stimulated the invention and development of exactions, dedications, and developer fees as a means of avoiding the results of the taxing limitation.

Growth of the regulatory state also poses a threat to rights because the regulatory arena has the greatest potential for breaking down the constitutional division of powers among the branches of government that are essential to the preservation of rights and liberty. Administrative agencies combine all the features of the legislative, executive, and judicial branches in one body—the combination most feared by the Framers of the Constitution and their contemporaries. Agencies promulgate regulations (a legislative function), interpreting statutes in the process (a judicial function). They enforce statutes and their own regulations (an executive function), determine whether regulations have been violated, and assess sanctions against the purportedly offending party (judicial functions). Many agencies even have officials designated as "administrative law judges." If, as is now often the case, the courts abandon their constitutional role as guardians of rights and defer to the judgment of regulatory agencies in all their various functions, then the constitutional system as originally devised is radically altered.

Paying the Price: The Cost of Abandoning Property Rights

Why bother to expend energy to protect property rights? The answer is straightforward. In the battle over whether property rights will be protected, more is at stake than vindication of an abstract philosophy, the reduction of personal frustration and hardship, or even attainment or nonattainment of personal or national prosperity. The failure to protect this constellation of constitutionally protected rights from encroachment—in the name of governmental efficiency—or to attain a particular goal, however laudable, has other unfortunate and possibly disastrous effects that must be avoided.

For example, the most important function of recognizing and protecting property rights is the role that the protection of those rights plays in preserving other rights reserved in the Constitution. It is this value to which Supreme Court Justice Potter Stewart referred when he observed that there is a "fundamental interdependence ... between the personal right to liberty and the personal right in property."[14]

It takes only a moment's reflection to comprehend the essential vulnerability of other personal rights and liberties if one's property is subject to virtually unlimited regulation by the state. The chilling effect that fear of retaliation against one's property has on the exercise of other civil rights cannot be overestimated. No other civil right ever need be subjected to a direct attack when its protection can be nullified by the simple expedient of regulating an offending or unpopular party's property. This is particularly true where property rights are nominally respected but are subject to only the most cursory of judicial scrutiny in practice, as presently occurs. In such circumstances, which provide a comforting illusion of security, individuals' other civil rights can be abrogated by basing the regulation of their property on some superficially plausible pretext with the regulators knowing that the court will not meaningfully scrutinize the government's conduct.[15]

Property owners who must go before an administrative agency to exercise their rights to use their property are acutely aware of these problems. They know the power of the agencies to affect their property and their economic well-being, and they know they must exercise caution to avoid offending any member of that body. That degree of unrestrained power also invites political corruption. Property owners who know that their rights to use their property are subject to the virtually unrestrained whims of a local regulatory body—whose decisions will not be given serious scrutiny by a court—will contribute heavily to campaigns by that body's members in hopes of obtaining favorable consideration.

Not one of the personal stories recounted in this introduction involves people in a business in which they or their business or project must regularly appear before an administrative agency. This is not because there are no such episodes; it is because people who must regularly appear before agencies refuse to let their stories be told for fear of retaliation by those agencies.

It is equally clear that a virtually unrestrained property regulation system can be directly used as an instrument of discrimination. Land use and planning devices such as large lot zoning and imposing multiple conditions on use permits can be used to increase the cost of housing or doing business so that minorities, people with lower incomes, and other disadvantaged individuals can be virtually excluded from commercial and residential life in desirable areas. Such mechanisms can also serve as anticompetition devices, keeping new and competitive businesses out of an established area to the detriment of consumers, especially low- and moderate-income consumers, many of whom are minorities. Such uses of the land use planning power are all too common and are wholly illegitimate.

Worse, a failure to fully protect any class of constitutional rights in the name of achieving some social goal its proponents see as desirable erodes respect for the fundamental principles of constitutional government and the rights of individuals. It becomes easier with time to justify ever greater intrusions into other civil rights in the name of attaining desirable social goals based on the same rationale. This erosion of rights is particularly insidious because regulatory intrusions are typically accomplished in piecemeal, cumulative fashion. It is only when individual intrusions are totaled that the magnitude of the erosion becomes apparent. By the time the full extent of the erosion is known, a reversal of the trend may be impossible.

The Constitution's property protections, particularly the takings clause, serve even more concrete purposes. The Constitution was created by persons who, despite their adherence to the principle that property rights are inviolate, recognized that there would be circumstances in which any government needs to acquire resources that are in private hands to carry out its legitimate functions. The Fifth Amendment's takings clause, which mandates compensation whenever the government takes private property for public use, is an acknowledgment of that need. At the same time, the clause serves as a brake on hasty or ill-considered actions, encouraging the government to act in a cost-effective manner. This and corollary functions comprise the clause's most valuable but least considered purposes. To more fully understand these functions, however, an explanation and examples are needed.

One precept on which all seem to agree is that resources are not infinite. Private ownership and control of property are preferable to state ownership and control, a view most recently validated by more than seventy years of experience in eastern Europe. Market mechanisms are demonstrably more efficient than centralized governmental decision making in ensuring that resources are properly allocated. One reason for this is that costs are associated with acquiring resources. Where sufficient information is available to allow individuals to do so, they will be more likely to correctly weigh costs and benefits in determining how resources will be used. Since individuals are in a much better position to know their particular needs, to weigh costs and benefits, and to respond to changes in their individual circumstances, they can act with a greater certainty of fulfilling those needs than government can. The net effect is to guarantee the most efficient use of resources overall. While government is generally less economically efficient in most instances, it too responds to costs.

One function of the takings clause is to keep resources in private hands where they will be more efficiently used unless government genuinely needs the resource. The clause encourages this outcome because government will more carefully consider its need for a particular resource if it knows it must pay to acquire that resource. Put differently, one is more careful spending one's own money than spending another's. It can be argued, of course, that government never spends its own money but instead spends taxpayers' money; therefore, it is not concerned with costs. There is some truth to this observation. However, to the extent that it is valid, the observation applies most to legislatures that have the power to acquire more money by raising taxes or, in the current jargon, by "establishing revenue enhancement mechanisms." On the other hand, regulatory bodies tend to view their budgets as their own checkbooks and are prone to be more careful if takings judgments cut into their operating budgets than they are when a general judgment fund pays. Payments from a general fund have no fiscal impact on the regulatory body and do not encourage responsible behavior.[16]

Even legislatures are not wholly free to ignore costs, however. Their members must respond to voters. Voters will tolerate a great deal, to be sure, but their patience is not endless. In fact, it is precisely because voters are attuned to cost issues that governmental bodies go to great lengths to suggest that a new regulation has no taxpayer costs. California voter pamphlets from the past several years consistently attempted to minimize the potential cost impact of voter initiatives on the ballot. Furthermore, the proposition that a regulation is costless is never true. At a minimum, such regulations *always* have administrative costs, which can be considerable and will directly affect taxpayers. Regulations may also have indirect costs that taxpayers would not tolerate if they were aware of those costs. For example, regulations invariably impose additional costs on the consumers of the goods or services regulated. Those costs may be sufficiently large to make the goods or services too expensive for any but the most well-to-do consumers.

If government decides it needs a resource and spends public funds to acquire it, use of the resource, once acquired, is more likely to be efficient. Further, if and when the resource is no longer needed for the purpose for which it was acquired, government will have more of an incentive to find another useful purpose for it. Government may, on the other hand, decide to sell the property back to the private sector. The government then recoups its monetary investment, which it may use for other public purposes, and the private property is restored to private use, allowing its efficient management. In either case, the useful life of the resource will be enhanced. This is of no small importance when considering the extent of governmental ownership of property in the United States. The federal government presently owns outright approximately one-third of all the real property in the United States. This figure does not include property in which it owns some easement, either directly or through regulation. This figure also does not give any clue to the amount of land in the hands of local, county, and state governments, entities that are by no means minor landholders.

A second, related function of the takings clause is to encourage government to more carefully design its regulatory programs to enhance the likelihood that they will achieve their objectives in a cost-effective manner. The logic is simple and unassailable. If a governmental agency understands that regulations may result in its having to compensate an owner whose resource it controls from its own budget, the agency will work harder to design a program more closely tailored to the objective it is trying to achieve to minimize potential costs and maximize program benefits. In so doing, the regulatory body will be less likely to act from political expedience or out of bureaucratic inertia and territorial motivation.[17]

At present, regulators and those who advocate more governmental regulation see regulations as essentially costless because the public does not spend money directly to acquire a resource controlled by regulation. The first result of this attitude is that the resource is undervalued. Therefore, not enough attention is paid to the question of whether the resource is best used for the proposed purpose. The second result is that this attitude generally deprives the public—who ultimately pays a price for an improperly evaluated regulation—of the information it needs to decide whether a regulation in question is desirable. By requiring compensation for public utilization of private resources, the cost of regulation is brought "on budget" where the public can decide for itself the relative costs and benefits of the regulation.[18]

For example, the Comprehensive Environmental Response, Compensation and Liability Act (CERCLA or Superfund) was enacted hastily after the Love Canal disaster to aid in cleanup of toxic wastes in the ground and water. CERCLA retroactively imposed liability on persons whose conduct was not only legal at the time it occurred but also completely reasonable. Worse, CERCLA imposed liability on people whose only connection with the waste was that they eventually came to own the land under which the waste was found.

The additional cancer risks posed by some contamination is frequently rated extremely low (1 in 50,000), yet the costs of cleanup are extremely high, with individual cleanups and their preceding studies sometimes costing well over $120 million. In one Superfund case in which I represented a client, the initial study and proposal for cleanup (the remedial investigation/feasibility study or RI/FS) cost $60 million. The RI/FS concluded that the cleanup itself would cost another $60 million. The common experience in Superfund cases is that cost estimates are invariably significantly lower than the ultimate costs. The Environmental Protection Agency (EPA) justifies Superfund on the basis that the polluters pay all and the public pays nothing. This is completely false reasoning. The public ultimately pays in higher prices or in limited supply. If voters were asked individually whether they would accept such a price for minimal benefit, the answer would most likely be "no."

Given the above, is the resource enhancing value of the takings clause real or only of marginal utility? Experience suggests that this function is of genuine value. Research and experience both demonstrate that the exercise of regulatory power unrestrained by economic considerations or constitutional mandate can have devastating effects on individuals and can have serious adverse effects on many problems considered important by society.

For example, studies considering various programs whose stated purposes were to remedy the housing crisis demonstrate that these programs not only failed to provide a remedy but actually exacerbated the problem.[19] Among the various types of regulations that have had an adverse impact on housing costs are general zoning and land use laws (including growth control ordinances), excessive building codes and standards, exclusionary zoning, environmental regulations, and rent control.[20]

Studies done to measure the impact of regulatory programs that were undertaken for other stated purposes also show an adverse impact on housing costs. Research on the effect of residential growth control regulations on housing prices in the south coast region of California, for instance, demonstrated that these measures alone contributed significantly to the increase in housing prices that occurred during the study period of 1974 and 1979.[21] Studies that evaluated the impact of California Coastal Commission activities on housing prices yielded similar results.[22] One study by Kneisel examined the impact of Coastal Commission regulatory activities on Los Angeles housing prices, adjusted for inflation, and demonstrated that the Coastal Commission's activities alone accounted for a housing cost increase of approximately 21 percent in the coastal zone. Nor did the commission's activities have an impact only on the zone it managed. Its actions also forced home prices up in the area directly bordering the zone by approximately 16 percent, while in the inland areas of Los Angeles, its activities precipitated a 7 percent housing cost increase.[23]

Regulation-imposed housing costs are not purely a California phenomenon. In his first term, President Reagan formed a commission to examine the housing problem. That commission reported that regulations had a major impact on the cost of housing, a significant factor in the housing crisis. The commission's report estimated that as much as 25 percent of home costs in some areas of the United States could be attributed to duplicative or sometimes just plain unnecessary regulation.[24] Among the imposed costs were those related to dedications and exactions, carrying costs, and taxes which accumulate during the time it took to process an application, plus its related costs. That estimate was probably low in light of contemporary and subsequent studies. Even were it accurate, the cost attributable to regulation is even higher today, particularly where the pressure for increased housing is highest. HUD Secretary Jack Kemp formed a special housing commission in 1991, which found that the impact of regulatory barriers to affordable housing grew more severe in the late 1980s. The Kemp commission estimated that 40 to 50 percent of the cost of a new home could be attributed to regulation in many regions.[25]

It is not hard to understand how regulations can adversely affect social goals. If the goal is providing adequate and affordable housing, environmental and land use regulations can result in taking suitable land off the housing market, thereby increasing the cost of remaining land. Similarly, conditions imposed on granting a development permit will invariably increase housing costs. These conditions frequently include requiring payment of a fee, or dedication of some of the owner's land for public use. While the cost of each individual exaction may be relatively small, a typical single condition might increase costs by $1500 to $2000 per unit, that cost will be only one of many imposed in the same process. The fee is not merely $1500 to $2000 per unit but that much per unit for one purpose, another amount per unit for another purpose, and still another amount for yet another purpose. If each fee is considered in isolation, a policymaker and certainly the public get a distorted view of the costs heaped on individuals seeking housing.

One of the most significant costs imposed by regulations is the cost of pursuing the regulatory process itself. Regardless of the extent of use of the land ultimately allowed, applying for that use is horrendously expensive. Those costs include application fees plus those for various consultants and attorneys whose services would not otherwise be required. The applicant will also incur extra taxes and carrying costs accruing from lengthy delays in the permitting process—delays as long as two or three years. During that time, of course, the property cannot be used for its intended purpose, even if the necessary permits are ultimately granted. These process costs will be built into the price of the home or of the goods or services provided if the development is commercial.

In many instances, the applicant may be required to complete an environmental review. These documents are extremely expensive to prepare. They require a complicated set of hearings and proceedings as well as the services of environmental consultants. At the same time, the complex laws and regulations imposing the environmental review process on applicants allow project opponents endless opportunities to delay those projects by technical challenges. Each challenge eats up resources at an enormous rate and increases the cost of doing business proportionately. The administrative agency's costs are passed to the applicant and, along with the applicant's other costs, are ultimately passed on to the consumer. Since homes and other structures are usually financed over a period of years, the actual additional costs are still higher because interest must be paid on regulatorily imposed costs. A prospective buyer who might be able to pay those additional costs if imposed as property taxes over a period of years cannot afford to pay a lump sum up front or to pay the interest on that additional cost over the period of a loan, which could be as long as fifteen or thirty years.

As a further example of how regulations can adversely affect stated social goals, regulations aimed at remedying environmental or other problems in practice often provide little or no benefit while costing enormous sums that could be used more effectively. Regulations of this type take a toll in economic competitiveness, increase the cost of goods and services, and impose other social costs without offering genuine solutions to the actual problems they purport to solve.[26] Meaningful enforcement of property rights would have the salutary effect of encouraging more careful consideration of such programs and would, at the very least, ensure that the public has a chance to make meaningful choices on public policy, an opportunity not now available because vital information is withheld.

Obviously, a book of this size cannot answer all questions or explore every aspect of the property rights debate in minute detail. This is the opening phrase in what I hope will be a long and fruitful discussion that will lead to a recognition that all rights, including economic and property rights, must be respected if any rights are to survive.

Mark Pollot

PART I

ORIGINS AND MEANINGS

1

PRINCIPLES AND RIGHTS

> *We hold these truths to be self-evident, that all men ... are endowed by their Creator with certain unalienable rights.*
> Thomas Jefferson[1]

There is a tension between the need for government to have sufficient authority to achieve its legitimate goals and the need to guard against invasion of liberties and the rights of individuals by that same government. This tension has become increasingly apparent in the United States as life becomes increasingly complex and segments of society look to government to solve perceived social problems.

Regrettably, the complexities of the modern world cause many people to strive for a return to a simpler time that never existed except in someone's imagination. Too few remember, or have experienced, the realities of times past in which to live past age sixty without disability was so uncommon as to be remarkable, when disease was rampant, and when epidemics that decimated human populations were frequent occurrences. The world of the past was, in real terms, a far more dangerous place than today's world. The wilderness was not a place to be looked upon fondly but was a place of dangers, hidden and obvious, that could deprive individuals or whole families of livelihood or life with startling suddenness. Life in civilization was barely less dangerous.

The perception of danger and the drive to eliminate all risk from life moves people to abandon the protection of rights and liberties as being secondary to the goal of protection against real and imagined dangers. Rather than seeking creative ways to address the problems of modern life while maintaining civil rights and liberties, instead of carefully tailoring solutions to problems, Americans have gradually abandoned the concept of individual rights. In the process we have accepted exception after exception to the protection of those rights against encroachment, and justification after justification for the erosion of those rights until neither liberty *nor* safety is secure. This tendency toward a flight from freedom has been noted by such eminent and diverse individuals as Erich Fromm, F.A. Hayek, and Alexis DeTocqueville.[2]

Combined with the tendency of individuals to join with other people in majorities that can rationalize extraordinary intrusions on the rights of others for each majority's own gain, the drive toward safety and security is perhaps the greatest modern source of the institutions and states of mind that lead ultimately to a loss of freedom and to the decline of a civilization. Together, the drives toward safety and security strangle initiative and experimentation, the concomitants of freedom that are necessary for effective problem solving. It is no coincidence that the greatest growth in government occurs in times of crisis—real, imagined, or manufactured. It is also no coincidence that additional powers granted to government and its agencies to deal with crises are never abandoned after the crisis of the moment has abated. A temporary law or agency is as illusory a concept as a temporary tax or toll.[3]

Of course, the drive toward safety and security is not the only force that leads us to abandon the fundamental concepts of liberty. The human tendency to resist change plays a major role in this process as well, a factor that becomes painfully obvious in the regulatory context, especially where regulation focuses on land use. The all-too-human tendencies toward greed, particularly the desire to get something for nothing, also play their part in the equation, as does the drive toward personal or group power.* Of course, sheer human nosiness, the tendency of people to be certain that they know what is best for others and to view it as their job to protect those others against their own poor judgment, plays a significant role in curtailing liberty. However, even when another factor motivates rights-destructive behavior, safety and security are invariably the rallying cry.

The greatest if not the sole protection against the tendency to sacrifice rights to expedience and security is an adherence to principles. Therefore, any discussion of rights, including property rights, must begin, as civil rights advocate Clint Bolick states, "with an understanding of principles and an historical perspective."[4]

---

* Some may argue that the drive for power is equally or more responsible for liberty-eroding institutions and laws. However, the drive for power is itself more properly understood as a manifestation of a desire in the power-seeker to increase security by exerting as much control over the external world and those in it as possible. The second is that those with a drive to power could not succeed if those who accept the power-seeker's control were not seeking the security that he promises. One need only examine Adolf Hitler's rise to power in post-World War I Germany for a modern example.

Civil rights and liberties are not creatures of the last third of the twentieth century but are at the root of our system of government. They have their birth in centuries of political thought and practical experience. To the extent that they have been preserved and their enjoyment enhanced until recent years, it has been because of the keen grasp of history among the Framers of the Constitution, a grasp of history that modern Americans generally lack.

For these reasons it is not appropriate to confine a discussion of rights, particularly property rights, to the specific provisions of the Bill of Rights. To make the discussion complete, we must consider the nature of rights generally, the historical context of the adoption of the Constitution and Bill of Rights, and the general principles they were intended to describe. Neither can we confine our discussion of rights of any stripe to a recitation of modern cases, many of which have drifted far from the principles for whose protection the Constitution was created.

The discussion that follows, therefore, explores the nature of property and property rights by considering them in their historical context and examining the early application of the Constitution to concrete factual circumstances. This context should help develop a complete understanding of what the Constitution was intended to accomplish with respect to protecting property rights. Curiously, while discussions of some constitutional provisions, such as the First Amendment's religion and speech clauses, almost invariably examine those clauses' historical antecedents and the philosophy on which they were based as clues to their scope and meaning, most discussions of property rights tend to focus on policy-based arguments, largely ignoring historical sources. There are, of course, sound public policy reasons for vigorously protecting property rights. However, it is not the province of courts to extend or reject the Constitution's provisions on the basis of judicial notions of sound public policy.

To develop a sense of how far the modern judicial treatment of property rights has deviated from that intended by the Framers, we must review the circumstances under which the Constitution and Bill of Rights were created and the sources on which their framers relied in drafting their provisions. Modern courts have virtually abandoned any pretense at applying the Fifth and Fourteenth Amendments' due process and equal protection clauses when property and economic liberties are at issue. Where claims are made that regulatory actions have taken property within the meaning of the just compensation clause, those same courts have taken the position that they have been unable to "discover" general principles to be applied to determine whether a given regulatory action—on its face or as applied to specific property—constitutes a compensable taking of property under the just compensation clause. This is not a defensible position.

Just as there are clearly protected areas of speech susceptible to definition by readily applied general principles, there are clearly protected areas of property rights susceptible to definition by principles of general applicability. These principles may be found in property rights cases as they may be in other civil rights cases, in the Constitution itself, and in the history and principles underlying the Constitution.

Stated differently, ad hoc analysis is no more necessary in regulatory takings cases than in any case involving other statutory, constitutional, or common law issues. To be sure, regardless of whether it involves regulatory conduct, takings law may become unclear at the fringes, but this is true of every area of law including other branches of constitutional law. A lack of clarity at the outer limits is inherent in any enterprise that depends on language for its effectiveness. A need to consider the facts of individual cases in the context of general principles is the norm in law. The refusal of modern courts to apply readily available principles is an abandonment by courts of their assigned role as guardians of constitutional rights. The next chapters will unearth the principles to be found in the Constitution and its underlying history. Later chapters will consider how those principles should apply when the government conduct at issue is regulatory.

2

THE CONSTITUTIONAL SCHEME TO PROTECT PROPERTY RIGHTS

> *[A]t times I have thought that the bills of rights in Constitutions were overworked—but these chaps remind me if I needed it ... that they embody principles that men have died for, and that it is well not to forget in our haste to secure our notion of general welfare.*
>
> Oliver Wendell Holmes[1]

CONSTITUTIONAL INTERPRETATION AND PROPERTY RIGHTS

The Constitutional Convention

On Monday, May 14, 1787, delegates to what was to become known as the Constitutional Convention gathered in Philadelphia for the first time, although the convention's proceedings did not begin in earnest for eleven more days. The original purpose of the convention was to effect a reformation of the Articles of Confederation, which were widely recognized even by their supporters as being dangerously defective. Some convention delegates, such as James Madison and Alexander Hamilton, however, were convinced that the Articles' defects were irremediable. They called for the creation of a strong national government, believing such to be necessary to protect the interests of both the states and their citizens. John Jay, in explaining why the convention went beyond the bounds set by Congress, argued that

> This intelligent people perceived and regretted these defects [in the Articles] ... they observed the dangers that immediately threatened

7

[union] and more remotely [liberty]; and being persuaded that ample security for both could only be found in a national government more wisely framed ... convened the late convention in Philadelphia.[2]

This group of convention delegates convinced others to broaden the convention's scope to include creation of an entirely different kind of government. The debate over the propriety of this deviation from the authorized purpose of the convention raged for the better part of the convention's proceedings, but the constitutionalists prevailed.[3]

The Constitution that emerged could not rightfully be called complete until two years after the convention when the Bill of Rights was written by Congress and ratified by the states. Several key states had imposed creation of a Bill of Rights as a condition for ratifying the proposed new Constitution.[4]

While the convention was public knowledge, its proceedings were secret. This secrecy was not prompted, as some have suggested, by the delegates' desire that future generations not be guided in interpreting the Constitution's provisions by the intent of those who wrote and adopted them* but by very practical and political considerations. The proponents of the Constitution were pragmatists and feared that arguments used in the debates during the convention would be used by its opponents during the ratification process. They were also worried that their arguments and actions during the convention would be used against them politically and that too much time would be wasted if state governments could recall their delegates for instructions during the convention process.

These fears moved Rufus King of Massachusetts to propose that the journals of the convention be destroyed or deposited in the custody of the convention president. King argued that "if [they] were suffered to be made public, a bad use would be made of those who would wish to prevent the adoption of the Constitution."[5] The response to this proposition by other delegates undermines the claims of those like Leonard Levy who contend that the Framers did not wish the Constitution to be interpreted according to their intent. James Wilson of Pennsylvania, for example, preferred to destroy the journals but moved that the second option, retention by the president, be selected specifically because "false suggestions may be propagated and it should not be made impossible to contradict them."[6]

---

* In a recent book, *Original Intent and the Framers' Constitution* (1988), Leonard Levy argues that the delegates planned that their intentions as to the meaning of the Constitution's provisions should not guide interpretation of those provisions (which is itself something of a paradoxical statement). He then goes on to propose that even if the delegates had *wanted* their intentions to govern, courts should ignore their intentions because the Framers' Constitution is not relevant to the modern world. Levy takes an extraordinarily large number of pages to explain his thesis and succeeds only in establishing the correctness of the delegates' belief that strong measures are needed to restrain the actions of the majority.

King's and Wilson's fears were not unrealistic. The need for frank and open debate in governmental decision making is well recognized today, as is the potential chilling effect of disclosure on predecisional debate. For this reason, privileges such as the "deliberative process" or "executive privilege" continue to be applied both by the courts in litigation discovery and by Congress in the Freedom of Information Act.[7] In considering what would ultimately become Exemption 5 to the act (the deliberative process or executive privilege), the Senate committee considering the matter remarked:

> It was argued [in comments on the bill] that efficiency of government would be greatly hampered if, with respect to legal and policy matters, all Government agencies were prematurely forced to "operate in a fishbowl." The committee is convinced of the merits of this general proposition."[8]

The Supreme Court, citing its past decisions in interpreting Exemption 5 reinforces the notion that some secrecy may be beneficial. "Human experience teaches that those who expect public dissemination of their remarks may well temper candor with a concern for appearances ... to the *detriment of the decisionmaking process*" (citations omitted).[9]

Congress applies the same principle to its own activities and often operates in closed meetings. No one would suggest that Congress does not wish to have its intentions in legislation recognized. The Framers were equally aware of the need for such secrecy and considered the ability of the executive to maintain it one of the virtues of a strong, single executive.[10]

The Constitutional Convention operated in much the same fashion as any legislature. Its members proceeded according to the rules of parliamentary procedure: appointing committees, taking votes, and engaging in floor and committee debates. The convention's product was a statute designed to delineate the powers of government and control its operations. The new Constitution, in short, was a typical legislative enactment resulting from classical legislative action despite its character as the supreme law of the land.

The Debate over Constitutional Interpretation

Over time, a peculiar debate emerged as to how the Constitution is to be interpreted. This now perennial debate is not about what the Constitution means *per se*; that debate is inherent when the application of any document is at issue, whether it be a simple bumper sticker, a philosophical treatise, or a complex contract or statute. Rather, the peculiarity of this debate (which fills volumes of books and innumerable law reviews and journals) is the proposition—advanced over and over by those who would cut the ties between history, principles, and the conduct of society—that we should not determine the meaning of the Constitution's provisions by referring to the intentions and expectations of those who drafted and ratified it. This approach is akin to suggesting to a court that it need not consider the intent of Congress in passing a statute and is reminiscent of Humpty Dumpty's declaration: "'When I use a word,' Humpty Dumpty said in a rather scornful tone, 'It means just what I choose it to mean—neither more nor less.'"[11]

The idea that the most fundamental law of a nation, intended to ensure against infringement on liberty, was created without a fixed reference point from which its meanings could be ascertained is flawed from its inception. Such an idea is without any serious analogue in any other debate over the meaning of written words.[12] The claim that the Constitution is an endlessly elastic document to be reinterpreted at will is a proposition calculated to free both the electorate and an activist judiciary from the constraints of the Constitution—precisely what a written constitution is designed to prevent. This flawed theory may be employed as easily in the suppression of civil rights as in their creation.

Discerning the original meaning of the words of the Constitution and Bill of Rights assigned to them by the people who created and ratified them may be a difficult task. That a duty may be hard to perform is not an excuse for abandoning it, however. A failure to treat the Constitution as *law* with definite and discernable purposes and with stable meanings and themes will have devastating consequences. Refusing to treat the Constitution as endlessly elastic and capable of endless reinterpretation does not make it a static document, unable to meet changing times, however. There is, after all, an amendment process, which was deliberately made difficult to provide protection from too rapid change and fluctuations in the face of popular passions. The constitutional and ratification debates as well make clear that the amendment process was intended to force deliberation over thorny problems.[13] Equally important, the themes stated in the Constitution are broad enough to ensure its continuing relevance without making it so elastic in meaning as to destroy its essential nature.

A discussion of constitutional interpretation is not an idle exercise when considering the issue of property rights. A significant portion of the debate over property rights, as with other civil rights, concerns itself with the issue of what those rights are and the extent to which the Constitution provides specific protection for those rights. Note, however, that this is a separate question from that of the origin of property rights, a question with much deeper philosophical and political implications.

The Constitution and the Bill of Rights contain numerous provisions relating to the protection of rights. Other provisions have been added over the years, including the Civil War amendments, particularly the Fourteenth Amendment. At a minimum, the Constitution's provisions establish a baseline number and level of rights which individuals are entitled to expect the courts to protect. Former federal appeals court judge Robert Bork and others believe that these rights are the only ones to which individuals may lay claim and that all else is subject to the will of the majority.[14]

If Judge Bork is correct, rights derive their existence and, hence, legitimacy wholly from a social compact that may be altered through the political process at the will of some number of people specified in the governing document. In his view, the Constitution provides a positive grant of liberty, revocable at any time, and individuals are entitled to no more. If, on the other hand, rights exist independent of governing documents (without regard to and, in some cases, in spite of human social enactments), then the Constitution is no more than an implicit recognition of some rights without prejudice to the existence of other rights. It is a grant of limited authority to government in which people give up a small measure of those rights to secure the protection of a greater measure.

This latter view, as will become obvious, was clearly the view of the Framers and ratifiers. This can be seen by closely examining not only the convention records, the ratification debates, the history of the Bill of Rights, and even the Civil War amendments but also the contemporary literature of the day.

We may argue about whether we have rights other than those specified in the Constitution. But it is clear that the people who drafted that document believed that fundamental liberties, which included the right to own and use one's own property and to acquire additional property, exist independent of any governing document. To the extent that the Constitution *does* specify rights to be protected, regardless of their origin, an understanding of the provisions of the Constitution relative to property is necessary to determine the minimum protection an individual is entitled to expect.

PROPERTY RIGHTS AND THE ORIGIN OF THE CONSTITUTION

That those responsible for the Constitution intended that the rights of people in their property be given full protection against invasion is beyond serious dispute.[15] Even were we without direct evidence of the intentions and beliefs of the people who created the Constitution and Bill of Rights, those documents contain their own confirmation of the seriousness with which those rights were regarded.

More than twenty provisions of the Constitution directly or indirectly concern themselves with the protection of property and economic rights.

Article I, Section 10, for example, prohibits states from impairing the obligation of contracts. Article III, Section 3, prohibits Congress from declaring forfeiture in an attainder of treason. Article VI guaranteed that the new government would honor the debts and contractual obligations of the government assumed under the Articles. The Third Amendment prohibits nonconsensual housing of soldiers in private homes in peacetime and restricts the wartime use of private homes for military housing. The Fourth Amendment protects homes, papers, and effects against unreasonable search and seizure, as much a protection of property as privacy. The Fifth Amendment provides that no person shall "be deprived of ... property, without due process of law" and further provides that "private property [shall not] be taken for public use, without just compensation."

The Fourteenth Amendment, adopted after the Civil War, carries the property rights theme forward. The Fourteenth Amendment incorporates the due process language of the Fifth Amendment in Section 1, and Section 4 prohibits any questioning of the legitimacy of the public debts and obligations of the United States incurred in prosecuting the Civil War. In fact, the Fourteenth Amendment, which was the constitutional embodiment of the Civil Rights Act of 1866, was specifically designed to ensure that the same economic rights enjoyed by the white population were not denied to the newly freed slaves, including the right to enter into and enforce contracts and the like.[16]

Those constitutional provisions that at least indirectly concern themselves with property and economic rights include the commerce clause of Article I, Section 10 (particularly the so-called negative commerce clause); the uniformity clauses of Article I, Section 8; the *ex post facto* and bill of attainder clauses of Article I;* Sections 9 and 10; the equal protection and privileges and immunities clauses of the Fourteenth Amendment; and the jury guarantees of the Sixth and Seventh Amendments. (The precursor to the jury provisions may be found in the bill of rights provisions proposed by the Virginia ratifying convention, discussed below. Its eleventh paragraph provided that "in controversies respecting property, and in suits between man and man, the ancient trial by jury is one of the greatest securities to the rights of the people, and to remain sacred and inviolable."[17])

---

* Some have argued that the *ex post facto* clauses of Article I were intended to protect solely against retroactive criminal laws. That was certainly the position of the U.S. Supreme Court in *Calder v. Bull*, 3 U.S. (3 Dall.) 386 (1798). However, Madison's notes of the Constitutional Convention place this view in serious doubt. When the clauses were proposed, James Wilson objected on grounds similar to those raised about the inclusion of a bill of rights. *Notes* at 510-511. Only later did John Dickenson of Delaware raise the question as to whether more was needed to protect against retroactive civil laws. He was concerned that Blackstone's assertion that the prohibition on *ex post facto* laws applied only to criminal laws could be used to impose retroactive civil laws. (Dickenson) *Notes* at 547.

The Ninth Amendment protects other unenumerated rights that may include other rights related to property.[18]

The Ninth Amendment is of particular importance to this discussion because the notions of "substantive due process" and "law of the land" play a significant role in the debate over property rights and economic liberty. The Ninth Amendment contains principles derived from these notions important to the protection of economic liberties and property rights. In this, I differ from Judge Bork, who has dismissed the Ninth Amendment, comparing it to an "ink blot."

The history of the Ninth Amendment shows that it was included to satisfy those who opposed including a bill of rights in the Constitution on the grounds that a bill would inevitably fail to include some right and would, by implication, deny the existence of such rights. The existence of the Ninth Amendment, in fact, renders unnecessary theories involving substantive due process (to the extent that the term includes recognition of rights not named in the Constitution as opposed to the degree of protection to be given to rights) or "penumbras" emanating from existing constitutional provisions.

To be pure about this discussion, however, I believe that the Ninth Amendment is, in the final analysis, a codification of a portion of the term "law of the land" that would otherwise be embodied in the due process clause. Bork's real objection, like that of many others, appears to be that to follow the plain meaning of the Ninth Amendment would leave courts standardless, free to follow whatever whim they choose, creating rights that even the Framers would not have recognized, and defeating the will of the legislature and the people in the process.

As in other cases, where objection to following original meaning has rested on the ground that we cannot know what was in the Framers' minds, we have plenty of evidence as to what rights were believed to exist at the time of the framing of the Constitution and to apply the principles found in constitutional era sources to concrete situations faced in the present. To argue that the plain language of the Ninth Amendment is not to be taken as written (particularly given the wealth of information available concerning the purpose for including the amendment) is to accept the notion that we may ignore the Constitution whenever adhering to it would be uncomfortable or inconvenient.

Having discussed the specific provisions of the Constitution, we should recognize that we do not need to rely solely on the bare words of the Constitution's provisions to understand either the fact or the depth of the former colonists' concern for protecting property rights. The records of the Constitutional Convention (of which Madison's *Notes* are the most authoritative and complete), the Federalist and Antifederalist Papers, and other contemporary sources, such as the sources that the Framers themselves relied upon, provide more than adequate documentation both in fact and depth. These sources included, for example, the works of Aristotle, Cicero, Sidney, and Locke.[19] These multiple sources make it possible to gauge the meaning of the bare words in a manner that permits their application in concrete situations.

Statements in the Constitutional Convention and the ratification debates reveal that the Framers and their contemporaries believed the protection of property rights to be one of the primary purposes, if not the sole justification, for government. Gouverneur Morris of Pennsylvania, deemed by many to be one of the principal architects of the Constitution (along with Madison and Jay),[20] expressed the commonly held fear that democratic government would violate liberty and property.

> What is [the senate's] object? to check the precipitation, changeableness, and excesses of the first branch [the house of representatives]. Every man of observation has seen in the democratic branches of the State department excess against personal liberty, private property, and personal safety.[21]

While, Gouverneur Morris pointed out, life and liberty were often said to be of more value than property, protection of property was the major impetus for organized society.

> An accurate view of the matter would nevertheless prove that property was the main object of Society. The savage State was more favorable to liberty than the Civilized and sufficiently so to life. It was preferred by all men who had not acquired a taste for property; it was only renounced for the sake of property which would only be secured by the restraints of regular government.[22]

Others, such as Rufus King, Pierce Butler, Charles Pinckney, and James Madison,[23] while not necessarily agreeing with Gouverneur Morris's solution to protecting property rights (Gouverneur Morris made this remark while advocating considering property in addition to population when apportioning legislative seats), expressed similar sentiments as to the purpose of government. This same recognition of the purpose of government was reflected in the Federalist and Antifederalist papers.*

---

* It should be noted that reliance on the *Federalist Papers* have been criticized on a number of grounds, including the claim first that they were targeted at a specific audience, the citizens of New York, and second that the papers represented the views of only three men, Hamilton, Madison, and Jay.

The first objection makes no sense. It presumes (a) that no one else would read the papers and (b) that the papers' authors did not believe or had no reason to believe that others would read them. This claim attributes a naivete to Madison, Jay, and Hamilton that is not plausible. Such papers were

It was in large part the failure of the Articles of Confederation to fulfill the property-protective purpose which led to adoption of the Constitution after all. In fact, in the first of the Federalist Papers, a series of articles written for and published by New York newspapers to sell the proposed Constitution, Alexander Hamilton described the task of the papers to be: "to discuss the following interesting particulars ... The additional security which [the Constitution's] adoption will afford to the preservation of [the republican species of government], to liberty, and to property."[24]

By the time of the convention, states had (more than once) passed special legislation deliberately interfering with existing private contracts to benefit one party over another. These laws abolished debts and undermined interstate commerce and credit institutions, inciting public outrage and reinforcing the delegates' distrust of legislatures. Examining the origins and history of the contracts clause of Article I, Section 10, Professor Benjamin Wright described these state laws in this way:

> Most of these laws took the form of providing for the issuance of paper currency, with the addition of the requirement that this currency be accepted as legal tender in the payment of private debts. In addition there were "stay laws" (laws staying or postponing the payment of debts beyond the time fixed in contracts), installment laws (acts providing that debts could be paid in several installments over a period of months or even years rather than in a single sum as stipulated in the agreement), and commodity payment laws (statutes permitting payment to be made in certain enumerated commodities at a proportion, usually three-fourths or four-fifths, of their appraised value). Naturally the creditors preferred to receive payment at the stipulated time, and in money rather than in land, cattle, tobacco, slaves, flour, hemp, or whatever the state in question saw fit to make legal tender. We have the contemporaneous statement of Madison to support the conclusion that "the evils issuing from these sources" contributed heavily toward

frequently reprinted in the former colonies. For example, "Centinel" Numbers 1 to 18 were printed in the Philadelphia *Independent Gazetteer* and Philadelphia *Freeman's Journal* between October 5, 1787, and April 9, 1788, by Samuel Bryan. Some were reprinted particularly widely. So too were the *Letters from the Federal Farmer*. All three authors of the Federalist Papers had to be aware of this tendency for reprinting and wide circulation. It strains credulity to believe that they would have written anything in the Federalist Papers that they believed would offend other states whose votes were needed to ratify the Constitution, although New York was certainly critical. Further, the defense of the Constitution offered in the papers reflected the arguments raised in the convention itself. This fact not only authenticates the *Notes* but also invalidates Leonard Levy's theory that the secrecy of the convention demonstrates that the framers did not intend us to be guided by their intent.

The second objection is equally specious. While Madison, Hamilton, and Jay did indeed write the papers, a detailed comparison of both the papers and the convention records shows that the arguments offered by the papers closely parallel those offered in support of the Constitution in convention. Ultimately, of course, the Constitution was ratified by those to whom the papers were directly addressed and to whom they were available, although only upon the condition that a Bill of Rights be added.

preparing the public mind for a general reform. The Fathers were undoubtedly opposed to the continuance of state legislation of this kind.[25]

Commercial discriminations between states threatened the solidarity of the newly formed confederation as well as the states' economic prosperity. Some of the delegates argued persuasively that such discriminations laid the former colonies open to exploitation by foreign countries. Hamilton, for instance, argued that:

> In a state so insignificant [as that wrought by the Articles] our commerce would be a prey to the wanton intermeddlings of all nations at war with each other, who, having nothing to fear from us, would with little scruple or remorse supply their wants by depredations on our property as often as it fell in their way.[26]

The interference by states with the accepted principles of property rights and economic liberties precipitated the charge that a new governing document was necessary. The threat to property rights from such conduct was seen as so serious that it resulted not only in the ruination or serious injury of creditors, in the destruction of confidence in ordinary business transactions, and in a weakening of general commerce[27] but it literally threatened civil war.

> Laws in violation of private contracts, as they amount to aggressions on the rights of those States whose citizens are injured by them, may be considered as another probable source of hostility. We are not authorized to expect that a more liberal or more equitable spirit would preside over the legislations of the individual States hereafter, if unrestrained by any additional checks, than we have heretofore seen in too many instances disgracing their several codes. We have observed the disposition to retaliation excited in Connecticut, in consequence of the enormities by the legislature of Rhode Island; and we reasonably infer that, in similar cases under other circumstances, a war, not of *parchment*, but of the sword, would chastise such atrocious breaches of moral obligation and social justice.[28]

Such "atrocious breaches of moral obligation and social justice,"[29] it was argued, resulted in an "accumulation of guilt" that necessitated the "voluntary sacrifice on the altar of justice"[30] of the Articles of Confederation that had allowed what was deemed to be "a universal prostration of morals."

These observations, and numerous others like them made in convention and elsewhere, flatly refute Justice Randall Shepard's claim that the former colonists found legislatures to be particularly trustworthy. Such limited trust as was reposed in them was shattered by their conduct in interfering with property rights. This constant clamor against legislatures and the view that legislatures were particularly potent instruments of tyranny also answers the question of whether the Framers would find acceptable the deference that modern courts extend towards legislatures when issues of rights are involved. They would not. Even less would they find acceptable the deference extended by courts toward administrative agencies that combine the powers of the legislative, executive, and judicial departments with none of the safeguards applicable to the legislature, a combination of which the Framers were justly afraid.[31]

The Structure of Government and the Protection of Rights

The delegates to the Constitutional Convention did not struggle over whether property and other rights and economic liberties should be protected, but only over how such protection was to be achieved. "The issue," said Roger Sherman of Connecticut, "is not what rights naturally belong to men; but how they may be most equally & effectually guarded in society,"[32] a sentiment shared by other delegates. Having just completed a war against a government that had failed to protect liberties, the delegates had taken the lessons of history and their own experience to heart. Their experience had demonstrated the tendency of men to form interested majorities that would, without conscience or by rationalization, oppress the liberties of others. Early in the convention's proceedings, Madison put this issue squarely before the delegates:

> In all cases where a majority are united by a common interest or passion, the rights of the minority are in danger. What motives are to restrain them? A prudent regard to the maxim that honesty is the best policy is found by experience to be as little regarded by bodies of men as by individuals. Respect for character is always diminished in proportion to the number among whom the blame or praise is to be divided. Conscience, the only remaining tie, is known to be inadequate in individuals. In large numbers, little is to be expected of it.[33]

The principal cause of this tendency to combine and oppress was, ironically, the same reason that government was deemed necessary in the first place—property. Madison noted:

> [T]he most common and durable source of factions has been the verious [sic] and unequal distribution of property. Those who hold and those who are without property have ever formed distinct interests in society. Those who are creditors, and those who are debtors, fall under a like discrimination. A landed interest, a manufacturing interest, a mercantile interest, a moneyed interest, with many lesser interests,

grow up of necessity in civilized nations, and divide them into different classes, actuated by different sentiments and views.[34]

In Madison's view, the solution to the problem of factions was not to remove the cause of factions, such as private property. To do so, he noted, would defeat the ultimate purpose of government, which was to preserve liberty and property. The ultimate solution, he maintained, was to ensure that no faction attained a majority.

> [A] pure democracy ... can admit of no cure for the mischiefs of faction. A common passion or interest will, in almost every case, be felt by the majority of the whole; a communication and concert results from the form of government itself; and there is nothing to check the inducements to sacrifice the weaker party or an obnoxious individual. Hence it is that such democracies have ever been spectacles of turbulence and contention; have ever been found incompatible with personal security or the rights of property.[35]

Madison and those who supported his views saw that the division of power among various branches would operate in much the same manner as a quarantine operates to prevent the spread of a disease. As visualized by Madison:

> A rage for ... an abolition of debts, for an equal division of property, or for any other improper or wicked project, will be less apt to pervade the whole body of the Union than a particular member of it, in the same proportion as such a malady is more likely to taint a particular county or district than a state.[36]

Any form of cure other than division of power was strewn with potential pitfalls. To remove the causes of faction, the exercise of liberty and the existence of private property were properly viewed as worse than the disease. Madison continued:

> As long as the reason of man continues fallible, and he is at liberty to exercise it, different opinions will be formed. As long as the connection subsists between his reason and his self-love, his opinions and his passions will have a reciprocal influence on each other; and the former will be objects to which the latter will attach themselves. The diversity in the faculties of man, from which the rights of property originate, is not less an insuperable obstacle to a uniformity of interests. The protection of these faculties is the first object of government. From the protection of different and unequal faculties of acquiring property, the possession of different degrees and kinds of property immediately results; and from the influence of these on the sentiments and views of

the respective proprietors ensues a division of the society into different interests and parties.[37]

In fact, Hamilton argued, the unequal division of property was itself a by-product of liberty and one that could not be erased unless one first curtailed liberty. Hamilton told the delegates that "[i]t was certainly true that nothing like an equality of property existed: that inequality would exist as long as liberty existed, and that it would unavoidably result from that very liberty itself."[38]

Thus, the delegates focused first on ensuring that the powers given to the new government would be limited and second on devising structural barriers against the accumulation of power and the banding together of majorities to oppress the rights of minorities. One could accurately say, however, that the first protective mechanism used by the Framers was the simple expedient of not giving rights away in the Constitution.[39] The structural protections were erected in an attempt to keep the government from taking for itself what was not given.

Being supremely distrustful of legislatures, noting their scandalous actions with respect to property rights, and considering them to have the highest potential for tyrannical action, a number of delegates proposed that the government be constructed so as to diffuse power among the different branches while retaining sufficient strength to deal with incursions on liberties by the states. Madison, in speaking of legislative tyranny, made a statement that has special significance in an era in which Congress consistently enacts legislation not binding on it, such as the Civil Rights Act of 1964, the Occupational Health and Safety Act, and others:

> If this spirit [that nourishes freedom] shall ever be so far debased as to tolerate a law not obligatory on the legislature, as well as on the people, the people will be prepared to accept everything but liberty.[40]

The structural solution was urged by its proponents not only as the most effective protection against violation of rights, but as the only remedy.

> What has been the source of those unjust laws complained of among ourselves? Has it not been the real or supposed interest of the major number? Debtors have defrauded their creditors. The landed interest has borne hard on the mercantile interest. The Holders of one species of property have thrown a disproportion of taxes on the holders of another species. The lesson we are to draw from the whole is that where a majority are united by a common sentiment, and have an opportunity, the rights of the minor party become insecure. In a Republican Government the Majority if united have always an opportunity. The only remedy is to enlarge the sphere, and thereby divide the community into

so great a number of interests and parties, that in the first place a majority will not be likely at the same moment to have a common interest separate from that of the whole or of the minority; and in the second place, that in case they should have such an interest they may not be apt to unite in the pursuit of it.[41]

Others, of course, disagreed, believing that more was required. However, Madison's statement ought not be read to suggest that he believed that the courts did not have the power to strike down actions violative of rights. Madison felt that structure alone could ensure that other parts of government had sufficient vigor to protect rights and to make their violation less likely to occur through combinations of interested minorities. Indeed, the power of courts to protect individuals required their structural separation from companion branches.

Even among those who agreed with a structural solution, however, the precise mechanisms by which the government could be molded to protect property rights were matters of contention. Hamilton, criticizing both the New Jersey Plan and the Virginia Plan, observed that if one gives "all the power to the many, they will oppress the few. Give power to the few, they will oppress the many. Both, therefore, ought to have power, that each may defend itself against the other. To the want of this check we owe our paper money, installment laws &c."[42] Continuing, he expressed considerable fear over the potential tyranny of democratic majorities.

The house of Lords is a most noble institution. Having nothing to hope for by a change, and a sufficient interest by means of their property, in being faithful to the national interest, they form a permanent barrier against every pernicious innovation, whether attempted on the part of the Crown or of the Commons. ... Gentlemen differ in their opinions concerning the necessary checks from the different estimates they form of the human passions. They suppose seven years a sufficient period to give the senate an adequate firmness, from not duly considering the amazing violence & turbulence of the democratic spirit. When a great object of government is pursued, which seizes the popular passions, they spread like wildfire and become irresistible.[43]

At the end of the convention, it fell to Madison to explain the overall plan for protecting rights through structural means. In Federalist Paper No. 51, Madison explained the theory and practice of the separation of powers doctrine and the structural provisions for the protection of liberty and property:

To what expedient, then, shall we finally resort, for maintaining in practice the necessary partition of power among the several departments as laid down in the Constitution? The only answer that can be given is that as all these exterior provisions are found to be inadequate the defect must be supplied, by so contriving the interior structure of the government as that its several; constituent parts may, by their mutual relations, be the means of keeping each other in their proper places.[44]

This structural approach was, he explained, "essential to the preservation of liberty."[45]

It was Hamilton, however, who most strongly urged that the proposed Constitution be adopted on the grounds that its combination of strength and structural protections would best serve to protect property and economic liberties.

The additional securities to republican government, to liberty, and to property, to be derived from the adoption of the plan under consideration, consist chiefly in the restraints which the preservation of the Union will impose on local factions and insurrections, and on the ambition of powerful individuals in single States who might acquire credit and influence enough from leaders and favorites to become the despots of the people ... and in the precautions against the repetition of those practices on the part of the State governments which have undermined the foundation of property and credit.[46]

The greatest threat to liberty and property in the eyes of most of the convention delegates was the legislature. Their understanding of history and their experience with state legislatures brought this point home.[47]

Experience had proved a tendency in our governments to throw all power into the Legislative vortex. The Executives of the States are in general little more than Cyphers, the legislatures omnipotent. If no effectual check be devised for restraining the instability & encroachments of the latter, a revolution of some kind or other would be inevitable.[48]

Both the executive and the judiciary needed protection against the legislature, which Madison conceived of as the greatest threat to liberty and property. In commenting on a motion brought to add language to the Constitution regarding the veto or revision of the laws passed by Congress, Madison argued that the only objection to giving a portion of that power to the executive or judiciary could be that such a power would give too much strength to either. But,

[h]e did not think there was the least ground for this apprehension. It was much more to be apprehended that notwithstanding this co-operation of the two departments, the Legislature would still be an over-match for them. Experience in all the States had evinced a powerful

tendency in the Legislature to absorb all power into its vortex. This was the real source of danger to the American Constitutions; & suggested the necessity of giving every defensive authority to the other departments that was consistent with republican principles.[49]

Others agreed with this sentiment. Nathaniel Ghorum of Massachusetts pointed to the Rhode Island legislature as a case in point.

Rh. Island is a full illustration of the insensibility to character, produced by a participation by numbers, in dishonorable measures, and of the length to which a wicked body may carry wickedness & cabal.[50]

The observation that legislatures were the primary threat to liberty is wholly consistent with the theme played over and over during the convention and in the postconvention written and spoken debates that men were to be trusted even less in groups than individually, a fact that makes modern judicial deference to legislatures somewhat puzzling. Nor is this distrust born solely of a fear of those who would engage in a tyranny for selfish or evil reasons. The protections of the Constitution were designed to guard equally against the well-intentioned. Hamilton observed that "the people commonly *intend* the PUBLIC GOOD. This often applies to their very errors. But their good sense would despise the adulator who should pretend that they always *reason right* about the *means* of promoting it."[51]

In further describing his distrust of groups, Hamilton stated: "Has it been found that bodies of men act with more rectitude or greater disinterestedness than individuals? The contrary of this has been inferred by all accurate observers of the conduct of mankind; and the inference is founded upon obvious reason."[52] Years later, that astute observer of the American culture, Alexis DeTocqueville, echoed Hamilton's distrust of groups.

A majority taken collectively is only an individual, whose opinions, and frequently whose interests, are opposed to another individual, who is styled a minority. If it may be admitted that a man possessing absolute power may misuse that power by wronging his adversaries, why should not a majority be liable to the same approach? Men do not change their characters by uniting with each other; nor does their patience in the presence of obstacles increase with their strength. For my own part, I cannot believe it; the power to do everything, which I should refuse to one of my equals, I will never grant to any number of them.[53]

The Framers' observation that protection is needed as much against the acts of the well-meaning as against those less well-motivated has a special relevance today and shows an uncanny degree of prescience on their part, or perhaps just indicates that the Framers were excellent rule-of-thumb psychologists. Most incursions on property rights today are justified by calls to some public good. This relevance is accentuated when coupled with another observation made during the period of constitutional formation in considering the impact of the modern environmental movement on property rights.

> It is natural for men, who wish to hasten the adoption of a measure, to tell us, now is the crisis—now is the critical moment which must be seized, or all will be lost: and to shut the door against free enquiry, whenever conscious the thing presented has defects in it, which time and investigation will probably discover. This has been the custom of tyrants and their dependents in all ages. If it is true ... that the people of the country cannot change their condition for the worse, I presume it still behooves them to deliberately change it for the better.[54]

We cannot overestimate the importance of the distrust of legislatures by the Framers and their contemporaries. For many in the Convention, fear for the rights of property was the order of the day whenever the legislature was in session. Gouverneur Morris, for example, "concurred in thinking the public liberty in greater danger from Legislative usurpations than from any other source." Morris observed that:

> It has been said that the Legislature ought to be relied on as the proper Guardians of liberty. The answer was short and conclusive. Either bad laws will be pushed or not. On the latter supposition no check will be wanted. On the former a strong check will be necessary. And this is the proper supposition. Emissions of paper money, largesses to the people—a remission of debts and similar measures, will at some times be popular, and will be pushed for that reason. At other times such measures will coincide with the interests of the Legislature themselves, & that will be a reason not less cogent for pushing them. It may be thought that the people will not be deluded and misled for the latter case. But experience teaches another lesson.[55]

We see echoes of this distrust today in the proposals that have multiplied in recent years for limiting the terms of state and federal legislators. This fervent distrust of legislatures led the Framers of the Constitution to propose a strong executive and a strong judiciary as critical counterbalances even over a Bill of Rights. For example, in defending the concept of a strong executive, Hamilton argued that a strong executive "is essential to the ... protection of property against those irregular and highhanded combinations which sometimes interrupt the ordinary course of justice."[56]

The Framers designed the Constitution's structural provisions to make actions contrary to rights more difficult to undertake, although such actions were clearly void, the government not having the authority to undertake them. A Bill of Rights, on the other hand, was viewed as being no more than a parchment protection, easily breached, as the experience with state legislative usurpations of property rights had shown.

The Bill of Rights and the Protection of Rights

Others both within the convention and during the ratification debates were less convinced that the Constitution's structural provisions would be sufficient to protect rights against incursions. Proposals were made to include a Bill of Rights[57] but the majority of delegates rejected those proposals for two principal reasons. First and foremost was the belief of the Framers that rights are natural, inherent, and inalienable. Therefore, governments could neither grant such rights nor take them away. Since, in the Framers' view, rights were beyond the power of governments to bestow or deny, to include a Bill of Rights, at a minimum, was redundant and at a maximum would open the United States to ridicule.[58]

The second reason for rejecting a Bill of Rights was most delegates' fear that the enumeration of rights would lead to future arguments limiting rights and liberty. In short, they were afraid they might leave something out that would lead to claims that the rights enumerated were the sole rights. People might use the bill to curtail liberties and rights instead of to protect them.[59]

After the convention and during the ratification debates, opponents of the Constitution, who were moved by the same concern over liberties and economic and property rights as its proponents, differed as to the proper remedy. They pressed either for a return to the original goal of amending the Articles of Confederation, fearful that a strong central government would more likely remove rights than protect them, or for the inclusion of a Bill of Rights in the proposed Constitution.

In "Letter from the Federal Farmer, No. II," published October 9, 1787, one advocate for a Bill of Rights argued that the inclusion of a Bill of Rights was critical to the acceptability of the Constitution because

> [t]here are certain unalienable and fundamental rights, which in form-
> ing the social compact, ought to be explicitly ascertained and fixed—a
> free and enlightened people, in forming this compact, will not resign
> all their rights to those who govern, and they will fix limits to their
> legislators and rulers, which will soon be plainly seen by those who
> are governed, as well as those who know they cannot be passed
> unperceived by the former, without giving a general alarm.[60]

To a certain extent, this call for a Bill of Rights that would "explicit[ly] ascertain and fix" rights was precisely the kind of thing feared by Hamilton and others who felt that such a bill could only be imperfect. This fear led to the inclusion of the Ninth Amendment. However, still others were no more convinced by the argument, which was advanced to justify the lack of a Bill of Rights, that government was given no power not expressly stated and that, therefore, no enumeration of rights retained was necessary. While agreeing that the government had no power not expressly granted to it, John DeWitt was nevertheless adamant that a bill should be included simply because he distrusted governments.

> That the want of a Bill of Rights to accompany this proposed System, is a solid objection to it, provided there is nothing exceptionable in the System itself, I do not assert.
> If, however, there is at any time, a propriety in having one, it would not have been amiss here. A people, entering into society, surrender such a part of their natural rights, as shall be necessary for the existence of that society. They are so precious in themselves, that they would never be parted with, did not the preservation of the remainder require it. They are entrusted in the hands of those, who are very willing to receive them, who are naturally fond of exercising them, and whose passions are always striving to make a bad use of them. They are conveyed by a written compact, expressing those which are given up, and the mode in which those reserved shall be secured. Language is so easy of explanation, and so difficult is it by words to convey exact ideas, that the party governed cannot be too explicit. The line cannot be drawn with too much precision and accuracy. The necessity of this accuracy and this precision encreases in proportion to the greatness of the sacrifice and the numbers who make it.
> That a Constitution for the United States does not require a Bill of Rights, when it is considered, that a Constitution for an individual State would, I cannot conceive. ... The insatiable thirst for unconditional controul over our fellow creatures, and the facility of sounds to convey essentially different ideas, produced the first Bill of Rights ever prefixed to a Frame of government. The people, although fully sensible that they reserved every tittle of power they did not expressly grant away, yet afraid that the words they made use of, to express those rights so granted might convey more than they originally intended, they chose at the same moment to express in different language, those rights that the language did not include, and which they never designed to part with, endeavoring thereby to prevent any cause for future altercation and the intrusion into society of that doctrine of tacit implication which has been the favorite theme of every tyrant from the origin of all governments to the present day.[61]

The ratifying conventions also called for a Bill of Rights. The State of Virginia proposed an addition to the proposed Constitution. On June 27, 1788, in its ratifying convention, Virginia included the following provisions regarding property rights that incorporated the general understanding of rights as inalienable without regard to the existence or lack of a social compact. The proposal, significant both because of its characterization of the nature of rights and because of some of the rights it chose to enumerate, asked

> [t]hat there be a declaration or bill of rights, asserting, and securing from encroachment, the essential and unalienable rights of the people, in some such manner as the following—
> 1st. That there are certain natural rights, of which men, when they form a social compact, cannot deprive or divest their posterity: among which are the enjoyment of life and liberty, with the means of acquiring, possessing, and protecting property, and pursuing and obtaining happiness and safety.
>
> * * * * * * *
>
> 9th. That no freeman ought to be taken, imprisoned, or disseized of his freehold, liberties, privileges, or franchises, or outlawed or exiled, or in any manner destroyed or deprived of his life, liberty, or property, but by the law of the land.
>
> * * * * * * *
>
> 11th. That, in controversies respecting property, and in suits between man and man, the ancient trial by jury is one of the greatest securities to the rights of the people, and to remain sacred and inviolable.
>
> * * * * * * *
>
> 12th. That every freeman ought to find a certain remedy, by recourse to the laws, for all injuries and wrongs he may receive in his person, property, or character. He ought to obtain right and justice freely, without sale, completely and without denial, promptly and without delay; and that all establishments or regulations contravening these rights are oppressive and unjust.
>
> * * * * * * *
>
> 13th. That no soldier in time of peace ought to be quartered in any house without the consent of the owner, and in time of war in such manner only as the law directs.[62]

Ultimately, the insistence on including a Bill of Rights as additional protection gained sufficient strength that the preparation and adoption of a Bill of Rights was promised to ensure ratification of the Constitution. Several states, including Massachusetts, Virginia, New Hampshire, South Carolina, and New York, ratified the Constitution only on the condition that Congress's first significant act would be the adoption of a bill of rights to be presented to the states for ratification. The bill adopted and ratified in 1789 included the property specific provisions already listed plus the Ninth Amendment. This addition was designed to secure from encroachment all other liberties and rights not enumerated, specifically to address the fears expressed by Hamilton and DeWitt that the inclusion of a bill would be dangerous and would deny rights by implication.

The Judiciary's Role in Protecting Property Rights

A reservation of rights, regardless of the manner in which those rights are reserved, is essentially meaningless without some mechanism to enforce that reservation. The protection of rights, whether economic and property rights, rights of expression, or rights of any other species, can be said to depend on a number of factors. Among these factors are the willingness of the general public to respect the rights of others and the willingness of legislatures and regulatory agencies to be sensitive to those rights when designing or implementing legislation intended to address issues of public concern. Each of these factors requires an education, since no one—legislator, regulator, or member of the general public—can respect that of which he or she is ignorant. However, an education is not the universal panacea it is often touted to be. It is a necessary but not sufficient condition. Rights will not be respected by any person without, among other things, an ability and willingness to accept occurrences or outcomes that may on occasion conflict with what that individual would personally find desirable. No amount of education can provide this respect.

In an ideal world, perhaps these factors would be enough. Ultimately, however, as the Constitution's draftsmen recognized, other mechanisms are necessary to protect rights. They chose the judiciary, a fact of which courts were aware from the beginning and which guided their actions without question for more than one hundred years.

> In such cases there is no safety for the citizen except in the protection of the judicial tribunals, for rights which have been invaded by officers of the government, professing to act in its name. There remains to him but the alternative of resistance, which may amount to a crime.[63]

There is no question that the courts have the *power* to accomplish this task, and for the most part their determinations are voluntarily accepted by the public. But whether they have the power to act as a guardian of rights is a different question from that of whether they have the authority to do so. The difference between power and authority is at the heart of constitutional government, and the extent of the judiciary's authority to act as a guardian of rights is constantly debated.

The Constitution was devised in large part to protect rights against governmental encroachment. The convention delegates attempted to restrain the raw exercise of governmental power, especially legislative power, to proper objects and means primarily by diffusing power. By doing so, they hoped to prevent its accumulation in any one branch of government in a manner that would permit that branch to exercise its power in excess of its authority. That authority was limited not only by express provisions of the Constitution but by the notion that some rights are inalienable and forever beyond the authority of any government to abridge.

The Constitution (as originally proposed and ratified before adoption of the Bill of Rights) was designed to protect liberty through two mechanisms: (1) the structural design, intended to make it difficult, if not impossible, for any branch of government to gather the raw power necessary to usurp rights, and (2) the enumerated powers doctrine, which was cited by Hamilton in the Federalist Papers as the reason no Bill of Rights was necessary and as the reason an enumeration of rights would be dangerous. (Not naming a right would imply a grant of power to invade that right.)[64]

The enumerated powers doctrine is the thesis that the federal government can exercise only such powers as are expressly granted to it in the Constitution and those "necessary and proper" to the execution of the enumerated powers—no others. The antifederalists, as well as members of the convention, feared that the "necessary and proper clause" would ultimately be used to defeat the enumerated powers doctrine.[65] Despite assurances that this would not happen, since a misconstrual of the grant of authority of the necessary and proper clause would require a failure of the executive and judiciary departments,[66] the worst fears of the antifederalists were realized when this clause and the commerce clause were ultimately interpreted so broadly as to render the enumerated powers doctrine completely ineffective, at least in limiting the objects of federal legislation. However, this fact should not make us conclude that the courts have no power to protect rights against invasion by resort to the enumerated powers doctrine. These clauses specify only subjects on which legislation may be made and do not give an authority to invade rights in the process.

The Framers and ratifiers intended that the judicial branch would provide an additional brake on the raw exercise of legislative and executive power, as well as a device for enforcing the powers of the federal government deemed necessary to make the Constitution a more effective device for maintaining the union than were the Articles of Confederation.

In an effort to persuade New York and others to ratify the new Constitution, Hamilton explained the protective role of the judiciary under the proposed constitution and emphasized the need for maintaining independence in the judiciary to enable it to fulfill its assigned role. To him and his colleagues, "[t]he complete independence of the courts of justice is peculiarly essential in a limited Constitution."[67] He further explained that a limited Constitution was one which contains certain specified exceptions to the legislative authority; such, for instance, as that it shall pass no bills of attainder, no *ex post facto* laws, and the like. The limitations of this kind can be preserved in no other way than through the medium of the courts of justice, whose duty it must be to declare all acts contrary to the manifest *tenor* of the Constitution void. Without this, all the reservations of particular rights or privileges would amount to nothing.

* * * * *

There is no position which depends on clearer principles than that every act of a delegated authority, contrary to the tenor of the commission under which it is exercised, is void. No legislative act, therefore, contrary to the Constitution, can be valid. To deny this is to affirm ... that men acting by virtue of powers may do not only what their powers do not authorize, but what they forbid.[68]

The use by Hamilton of the term "limited Constitution" as he defined it may engender some confusion when compared to the enumerated powers doctrine, discussed earlier. The enumerated powers doctrine stands for the proposition that the federal government has no power not expressly given, whereas, the term "limited Constitution," as defined by Hamilton, suggests a constitution of broad power except where specifically limited. However, these two terms are harmonized by viewing the limitations stated by Hamilton as limitations on the expressly granted powers. In other words, Congress has the power to legislate only as to the enumerated objects and even as to those objects, the power to legislate is circumscribed. This is made clear in Hamilton's statement that to deny the principle that acts contrary to the Constitution are void "is to affirm ... that men acting by virtue of powers may do not only what their powers do not authorize, but what they forbid."[69]

The courts, Hamilton asserted, "were designed to be an intermediate body between the people and the legislature in order, among other things, to keep the latter within the limits assigned to their authority"[70] and as a "bulwark of a limited Constitution against legislative encroachments."[71] Where the judiciary acts to enforce the Constitution, he pointed out, its decisions were to be guided not only by the letter of the Constitution but also by its tenor or spirit.[72] This was true despite the fact, as Hamilton noted, that "there is not a syllable in the plan under consideration which *directly* empowers the national courts to construe the laws according to the spirit of the Constitution, or which gives them any greater latitude in this respect than may be claimed by the courts of every State." This was a doctrine "not deducible from any circumstance peculiar to the plan of convention, but from the general theory of a limited Constitution."[73]

However, Hamilton also noted that an independent judiciary is not only necessary to protect against constitutional violations but also to provide a remedy to violations of individual rights. His view was consistent with the common law traditions of courts, natural rights theory, the Framers' belief that groups of men act with no greater rectitude—and often a great deal less—than individuals, and the Framers' and ratifiers' understanding that the rights of individuals need protection against combinations of interested majorities and hasty or ill-considered actions.

> This independence of the judges is equally necessary to guard the Constitution and the rights of individuals from the effects of those ill humors which the arts of designing men, or the influence of particular conjunctures, sometimes disseminate among the people themselves, and which, though they speedily give place to better information, and more deliberate reflection, have a tendency, in the meantime, to occasion dangerous innovations in the government, and serious oppressions in the minor party in the community.[74]

And, Hamilton continued,

> it is not with a view to infractions of the Constitution only that the independence of the judges may be an essential safeguard against the effects of occasional ill humors in the society. These sometimes extend no farther than to the injury of the private rights of particular classes of citizens, by unjust and partial laws. Here also the firmness of the judicial magistracy is of vast importance in mitigating the severity and confining the operation of such laws. It not only serves to moderate the immediate mischiefs of those which may have been passed but it operates as a check upon the legislative body in passing them; who, perceiving that obstacles to the success of an iniquitous intention are to be expected from the scruples of the courts, are in a manner compelled, by the very motives of the injustice they meditate, to qualify their attempts.[75]

Modern courts tend to confuse the issue of protection against encroachments on individual rights with that of judging the wisdom of a measure, at least when the right or liberty at issue is an economic or property right. Whether a measure is wise is a question of public policy; that is, whether the measure will, on balance, benefit or harm the public or is effective in achieving its stated purpose. The question of protecting individual rights, on the other hand, is an issue of whether the measure will unnecessarily or overbroadly impair individual rights or liberties regardless of whether the measure is good or bad for the public or is effective or ineffective.

Those same modern courts have no trouble understanding this distinction, however, when the right or liberty involved is one they believe to be worthy of protection. When the right or liberty at issue is one that is considered by modern courts to be fundamental, such as those embodied in the expression or free exercise clauses of the First Amendment, the courts require that the governmental interest involved be compelling, that the means chosen to achieve that end be closely tailored, and that the interference with the right be no more than necessary to achieve that end.

Like the First Amendment rights, property rights are explicitly recognized in the Constitution, but courts do not maintain the distinction when property is at issue. The irony of this state of affairs is that, if *any* hierarchy of rights is to be found at all in the history of the framing of the Constitution and Bill of Rights, it is that individuals' property rights are considered most fundamental because their protection is a necessary precondition to enjoying all other rights.

This is not to say that courts have, or were intended to have, the authority to void *any* legislative act with which a particular member of the judiciary—or even the judiciary as a whole—disagrees on the pretext of enforcing or protecting some right. Limitations on judicial power are recognized in the Constitution, which provides means for restraining the unauthorized exercise of judicial power, for example, through the application of impeachment powers. Exploring all the dimensions of the issue of the limits of judicial authority to discover and protect "new" rights is beyond the scope of this book. It is unnecessary to do so with respect to property rights because those rights are expressly recognized in the Constitution. Thus, the general power of the judiciary to enforce the Constitution protects those rights by authorizing courts to enforce the Constitution in accordance with original understanding. In thinking about the general question of the judiciary's authority to enforce rights not specifically listed, however, one would do well to consider the Ninth Amendment.[76]

It was clear to the Framers that the need for "inflexible and uniform adherence to the rights of the Constitution, *and* of individuals,"[77] required that the judiciary be constituted in a manner ensuring its independence from both legislature and executive. The judiciary should therefore have no part in making laws on which it might be required to pass judgment. For this reason, the Framers decided that Congress could not diminish the salaries of sitting judges; that judges would be appointed for life, subject to impeachment for improper conduct; and that their appointment would not be at the sole discretion of either the legislature or the executive. They would be nominated by one and confirmed by the other. Convention delegates also rejected proposals for including members of the judiciary, such as the Chief Justice of the Supreme Court, on a "council of revision of the laws" or any other advisory post.[78] In short, there was no thought that the judiciary should defer to the legislature or the executive when issues of rights were involved.

3

THE ORIGINS AND MEANINGS OF THE DUE PROCESS AND JUST COMPENSATION CLAUSES

> *Yesterday the active area in this field [constitutional analysis] was concerned with "property." Today it is "civil liberties." Tomorrow it may again be "property." Who can say that in a society with a mixed economy like ours, these two areas are sharply separated, and that certain freedoms in relation to property may not again be deemed, as they were in the past, aspects of individual freedom.*
>
> Felix Frankfurter[1]

> *Property does not have rights. People have rights.... A fundamental interdependence exists between the personal right to liberty and the personal right in property. Neither could have meaning without the other.*
>
> Potter Stewart[2]

The most significant of the more than twenty property rights and economic liberty-related provisions of the Constitution and Bill of Rights are the due process and just compensation clauses. While other provisions protect narrow classes of property against specific types of invasion, these two clauses provide broad coverage intended to protect individuals' rights in all species of property against invasion. Neither clause contains any qualifying terms as to type of property or property interest to be protected.

Although there is significant debate as to the substantive content of the due process clause, it is clear that it at a minimum specifies the manner in which government must conduct itself when it seeks to interfere with life, liberty, or property. The just compensation clause specifies the remedy to be given when government "takes" property and limits the exercise of government's power to do so to takings for public use.

While this book focuses on the just compensation clause, it must inevitably discuss the role of the due process clause in property protection because of the intersection of these two clauses in practical terms. First, the evolution of due process clause enforcement has clouded the takings issue. Modern courts, as will be seen, have confused the issue of due process—at least in its minimum meaning of following correct legal form that is related to whether the government can "do it at all" or do it in the manner in which it did—with the issue of whether the government must pay when it otherwise acts correctly. This confusion is responsible for sapping the vigor of property rights protection under the just compensation clause. Second, an examination of the constitutional, early judicial, and modern judicial treatment of the due process clause illustrates the increase in hostility to those rights by the judiciary over time. Third, an examination of the origins of the due process clause exposes some of the property rights principles that underlie the just compensation clause.

The principles governing both clauses can be found in the development of natural rights philosophy as expounded by John Locke and Vattel and echoed later by Sir William Blackstone, and as seen in English common law tradition.* An examination of these sources is, therefore, essential to an understanding of the meaning and scope intended to be given to these two clauses.

The first clear articulation that an individual right to property transcends the powers of a sovereign can be found in the Magna Carta, the precursor to the due process clauses and the just compensation clause of the Fifth and Fourteenth Amendments. Chapter 39 of the Magna Carta, accepted at swordpoint by King John at Runnymeade in 1215, provided that no freeman "shall be arrested, or detained in prison, or deprived of his freehold, or outlawed, or banished, or in any way molested ... unless by the lawful judgment of his peers and by the law of the land." Chapter 28 provided that "[n]o constable or other bailiff of ours shall take corn or other provisions from anyone without immediately tendering money therefore, unless he can have postponement thereof by permission of the seller." This latter provision of the Magna Carta not only demonstrates an early recognition of the power of eminent domain and the obligation to provide compensation

---

* If John Locke was the greatest articulator of the philosophy of natural rights, particularly property and other economic rights, then Sir William Blackstone, born in 1723, provided the historical and legal basis for the British and American view of the absolute rights of property. Blackstone's *Commentaries* on English law provided a comprehensive legal framework not only for the framing and ratification of the Constitution, but also for courts in the newly formed country.

for its exercise but also illustrates that, even as early as 1215, the concern with property rights extended beyond real property into other areas in direct refutation of the theory advanced by Justice Randall Shepard, discussed below, which contends that the just compensation clause was intended to apply only to physical invasions of real property.

The Magna Carta's pronouncements, though they ring of the language that later found its way into the Constitution, which was intended to apply to all people, were not intended to be so all-encompassing when the great charter's provisions were forced upon King John. Extension of the rights to property, life, and liberty beyond the peerage occurred only over time. More than one hundred years passed before the rights of the Magna Carta were expressly extended, by statute of Parliament, to all British subjects. ("No man of what state or condition he be, shall be put out of his lands or tenements nor taken, nor disinherited, nor put to death, without he be brought to answer by due process of law.")[3] These rights, and other rights like them, were further entrenched in written law in, for example, the Petition of Right of 1628, the Religious Toleration Act, and the English Bill of Rights of 1689.[4]

The inclusion of these rights in written law of a less than constitutional stature did not necessarily open them to abrogation at the whim of Parliament, however. British courts felt quite capable of invalidating those acts of Parliament that they believed to be contrary to natural law and reason. Natural law took precedence over man-made law. Any law contrary to natural law was, according to the tenets of natural law, void *ab initio*.[5] Unlike modern courts, however, early British courts invalidating a legislative enactment confined themselves largely to telling Parliament what it could not do rather than what it must do.

This fact answers the frequently levied criticism that a court is usurping legislative functions and substituting its judgment for the legislature's when it invalidates a statute. This is an issue that seems to bother Robert Bork, former appeals court judge. A court's constitutional duty is to invalidate unconstitutional actions, however efficient they may be. It is *not* the province of court to determine what the government must do instead of the invalid action.

By the late 1780s the philosophy of natural rights was clearly entrenched in America, which adhered to Blackstone's admonition that "[n]o human laws are of any validity, if contrary to [natural law], and such of them as are valid derive all their force and all their authority, mediately and immediately, from this original."[6] Among the rights inhering to individuals in natural law were the "absolute rights of property" considered "inherent in every Englishman."[7] These rights included the "free use, enjoyment, and disposal of all his acquisitions without any control or diminution, save only by the laws of the land."[8] These absolute rights were not entirely absolute, however. The rights of property did not permit property to be used in a manner injurious to the rights of others, for example.

> For preserving Property the law hath these rules, 1st, No man is to deprive another of his Property, or disturb him in enjoying it. Secondly, Every person is bound to take due care of his own Property, so the neglect thereof may not injure his neighbor. Thirdly, all persons must so use their right, that they do not, in the manner of doing it, damage their neighbor's Property."[9]

The last two limitations are the basis of the so-called nuisance exception to the just compensation clause discussed below, although what could be considered injurious was more narrowly defined than at present. There is no evidence that these last two limitations necessarily provided government with the authority to directly regulate property use by fiat, however. At most, we can be sure that these rules allowed injured property owners to bring an action in court to protect their property against actual harm.

The absolute rights of property were bounded in at least two specific ways. The first was that an individual's private property could be affected by the government if done so according to "the law of the land." The second is found in the ancient power of eminent domain, which permits the sovereign to obtain property it needs for legitimate governmental functions.

The acceptance of natural rights as a restraint on government before the Constitution is plainly seen in the written acts of both state and national governments. The Continental Congress, in a series of declarations, objected vehemently to British intrusions on property rights, particularly through its taxing power. In 1774, the Congress reminded England "[t]hat the inhabitants of the English colonies in North-America ... are entitled to life, liberty, and property ..."[10], and in the Second Declaration of the Continental Congress (1775), it indignantly proclaimed that "[i]n our own native land, in defense of the freedom that is our birthright, and which we ever enjoyed till the late violation of it ... for the protection of our property, acquired solely by the honest industry of our fore-fathers and ourselves, against violence actually offered, we have taken up arms."[11]

Congress's sentiments were later echoed, much more strongly, in the Declaration of Independence,[*] the records of the convention, the Federalist and Antifederalist papers, and the Bill of Rights.

Interestingly, in the year of the convention and before framing and

---

[*] Although Jefferson substituted the broader phrase of "life, liberty and the pursuit of happiness" for "life, liberty, and property" in the Declaration, it is clear from the evidence available that the rights of property were an integral part of the Declaration's principles.

ratifying the Bill of Rights, the Continental Congress established a govern-ing document for newly acquired territories north and west of the Ohio River, which provided, in part, that

> No man shall be deprived of his liberty or property, but by the judgment of his peers, or the law of the land, and should the public exigencies make it necessary, for the common preservation, to take any person's property, or to demand his particular services, full compensation shall be made for the same. And in the just preservation of rights and property, it is understood and declared, that no law ought ever to be made or have force in the said territory, that shall, in any manner whatever, interfere with or affect private contracts, or engagements, *bona fide*, and without fraud previously formed.[12]

This declaration of rights for the new territories not only bears a strong resemblance to provisions of the Constitution and Bill of Rights eventually adopted but also finds its counterparts in various state constitutional pro-visions and in the Bill of Rights proposed by Virginia during the conven-tion. These documents establish that the idea of natural rights had already been incorporated into American political philosophy in a practical fashion before framing and ratifying the Constitution. They contain the limitations ascribed to proper government by Locke, Blackstone, and others. They also show that pre-constitutional American government included the concepts of an inherent right to due process and compensation.

The scope of the right to property was equally broad, including more than real property. As stated by James Madison, the term "property"

> ... in its particular application, means "that dominion which one man claims and exercises over the external things of the world, in exclusion of every other individual." In its larger and juster meaning, it embraces everything to which a man may attach a value and have a right; and which leaves to every one else the like advantage. In the former sense, a man's land, or merchandise, or money, is called his property. In the latter sense, a man has a property in his opinions and the free commu-nication of them. He has a property of peculiar value in his religious opinions, and in the profession and practice dictated by them. He has a property very dear to him in the safety and liberty of his person. He has an equal property in the free use of his faculties, and free choice of the objects on which to employ them. In a word, as a man is said to have a right to his property, he may equally be said to have a property in his rights.[13]

Madison's view was consistent with the positions taken in the Federalist Papers and by the Constitutional Convention that the rights of property spring from the faculties of man and are an essential concomitant and inevitable by-product of liberty.[14] They are also consistent with the views on the breadth of property beyond real property believed to be within the absolute rights of property recognized by Blackstone, Jacob, and other chroniclers of British and American law. Madison, in asserting that property "is that sole and exclusive dominion which one man claims and exercises over the external things of the world, in total exclusion of the right of any other individual in the universe" was quoting Blackstone. Jacob, another constant source of reference for American lawyers, defined property as:

> ... the highest right that a man can have to anything; being used for that right which one hath to lands or tenements, goods or chattels, which no way depend on another man's curtesy [sic] ...[15]

Put differently, those who created the Constitution's property protective provisions saw property as being a complex of rights and relationships rather than a physical or symbolic object. However much modern courts may have eroded property protections generally, in this regard the courts have retained the broad view of property to which the Framers unquestionably subscribed. However, there are disturbing indications that some members of the modern judiciary are willing to abandon even the broad conception of property.

Some of these indications are found in a recent law review article by Randall Shepard, who is Chief Justice of the Indiana Supreme Court and former chairman and present trustee of the board of advisers for the National Trust for Historic Preservation.[16] In that startling article he argued that the just compensation clause was intended to apply only to physical occupations of real property. He wrote that the protection of any other property right is solely the province of the due process clause and that protection is limited to merely ensuring the barest minimum of procedure.

Among other arguments made by Shepard are the claims (1) that the former colonists found legislatures to be trustworthy repositories of rights, and (2) that Madison's original proposed language regarding takings "restrained only the acquisition of property."

The first claim—to be charitable—is an inaccurate and superficial observation at best. As discussed above, reliable evidence points to the conclusion that the Framers and their contemporaries considered legislatures to be the greatest potential source of tyranny. The excesses of state legislatures against all manner of property led directly to abandonment of the Articles of Confederation and to framing the Constitution, a fact early recognized by the U.S. Supreme Court.

> Whatever respect might have been felt for the state sovereignties, it is not to be disguised that the framers of the constitution viewed, with

some apprehension, the violent acts which might grow out of the feelings of the moment; and that the people of the United States, in adopting the instrument, have manifested a determination to shield themselves and their property from the effects of those sudden and strong passions to which men are exposed. The restrictions on the legislative power of the states are obviously founded in this sentiment; and the constitution contains what may be deemed a bill of rights for the people of each state.[17]

As to the second claim, Madison's language makes no distinction between species of property and property rights. Shepard ignores the vast evidence demonstrating that Madison and his peers gave property the broadest possible interpretation and that the term "relinquish," in light of historical evidence and Madison's writings, is meant in the broadest sense of allowing the invasion of any one or number of the rights that Madison viewed as property.

Shepard's arguments and viewpoints are completely irreconcilable with the specific and well-documented perspective of the Framers and their philosophical forebears. They saw the protection of property rights as *the* principal purpose of government, and their concern was that property rights be given the broadest protection against invasion. Shepard also thoroughly misinterprets even the evidence he does cite. He utterly fails to explain why the term "property" should be given one meaning in the due process clause, which he apparently believes applies to all other types of property and species of invasion, and another in the just compensation clause, which immediately follows the due process clause in the same amendment. No such qualification appears in the language of the amendment itself.

As we have already seen, every species of property was subject to the power of eminent domain and to the remedy of "indemnification." Personal services could be demanded as could personal property. In each case, compensation was considered to be required by principles of natural law. Of course, compensation must be available or the rights of property would be hollow indeed.[18] To even suggest that the Framers and ratifiers would be so myopic as to require compensation if the legislature's usurpation of an individual's property rights was overt seizure but not if it acted covertly to achieve the same objective by regulation (simply labeling its action as something else) verges on the preposterous.

THE DUE PROCESS CLAUSE AND ORIGINAL MEANING

The proviso that the exercise of property rights is subject to the law of the land consistently gives rise to controversy and debate whenever the due process clauses are at issue. Cases following the Civil War reinterpreted the meaning of due process to require little more than that the government follow specific formalities in contrast to constitutional and pre-Civil War era cases, in which the requirement of due process clause of the Fifth Amendment was given substantial meaning.*

The changed view of the due process clause holds that due process is satisfied if legal formalities are observed, that is, that due process means no more than "the process that is due." However, as will be seen, the phrase "due process" has its origins in the phrase "law of the land," a phrase equated with natural law. Because the law of the land included unwritten law involving immutable principles not subject even to the will of a properly constituted legislature, neither British courts nor early American courts considered every enactment of Parliament or any legislature to be a "law of the land." Those courts routinely invalidated legislative enactments because they were contrary to the law of the land, meaning natural law. Thus, while it is correct that pre-Civil War courts did not often specifically state that they were applying the due process clause of the Fifth Amendment to invalidate federal actions, as we shall see, their rejection of duly enacted legislation because it conflicted with natural law was consistent with the due process clause and its history. Court invalidation of regulation, therefore, was not a new product of later "substantive due process era" courts, as is frequently charged.

British cases known to the Framers, such as *Dr. Bonham's Case*,[19] which was decided in 1610, both illustrate this point and shed some light on the original meaning of due process and law of the land. Numerous constitutional and post-constitutional era American cases, such as *Calder v. Bull, Vanhorne's Lessee v. Dorrance, Leep v. St. Louis, I. M. & S. Ry. Co., Godcharles & Co. v. Wigeman*, and *In re: Jacobs*,[20] also illuminate our understanding of those phrases. These cases demonstrate that not every act of a legislature, even when enacted using proper legislative procedure, is to be deemed a law of the land for due process purposes. Were this not true, courts would have no authority to reject a statute enacted according to formal procedures in the absence of a specific provision in a constitutional document, something both British and constitutional-era American courts clearly believed they had the authority to do.**

---

* The modern weakening of the due process clause is particularly apparent where the governmental body is the legislature or an administrative agency.

**However, even these cases do not mean that the due process clauses, which are universally recognized as having had the "law of the land" language of the Magna Carta as their origin, should be used as the basis for discerning unenumerated rights. That authority, to the extent necessary, is found in the Ninth Amendment and is, I believe, bounded by the rights and general principles that existed at common law, in its broader sense, at the time of the framing of the Constitution and Bill of Rights. It is proper to view the due process clause of the Fifth Amendment and the Ninth Amendment in their entirety in

Indeed, Blackstone, on whom the former colonists relied, held the protection of rights to be so much the proper end of society that the people were entitled first to seek judicial relief, then to petition king and Parliament and, as a last resort, to use armed force when rights were threatened.[21] Blackstone embraced the natural law philosophy and the Lockean concept of the limited powers of government, which held that government's authority "can never be supposed to extend further than the peace, safety, and public good of the people."[22] Blackstone explained this concept at length, stating that civil liberty

> is no other than natural liberty so restrained by human laws (and no farther) as is necessary and expedient for the general advantage of the public. Hence, we may collect that the law, which restrains a man from doing mischief to his fellow citizens, though it diminishes the natural, increases the civil liberty of mankind; but every wanton and causeless restraint of the will of the subject, whether practiced by a monarch, a nobility, or a popular assembly, is a degree of tyranny. Nay, that even laws themselves, whether made with or without our consent, if they regulate and constrain our conduct in matters of mere indifference without good end in view, are laws destructive of liberty ... that constitution or frame of government, that system of laws, is alone calculated to maintain civil liberty, which leaves the subject entire master of his own conduct, except in those points wherein the public good requires some direction or restraint.[23]

The limits on governmental authority can not be avoided by resorting to the notion that individuals surrendered that right in the social contract, thereby giving government the unlimited power to redefine rights over time. Even Locke—who argued that an individual could consent to having a part or all of his property taken and that such consent could be given individually or on his behalf through elected representatives—did not endorse such a concept. He contended that there are limits to consent through elected representatives.

> It cannot be supposed that [individuals] should intend, had they a power to do so, to give to any one, or more, an absolute arbitrary power

combination as containing all of the fundamentals of the law of the land concept as it existed in the latter half of the eighteenth century.

The "substantive" aspects of the due process clauses are more accurately viewed as a requirement that existing rights and liberties be infringed upon only in circumstances of significant need, and then only to the extent truly necessary to achieve those significant goals. While the law of the land contained within it the power to invalidate laws inconsistent with rights, regardless of whether those rights were enumerated, that principle was embodied in the Ninth Amendment. However, the satisfaction of the due process requirement is a separate question from whether the exercise of the government's power gives rise to an obligation to pay.

over their persons and estates, and put a force into the magistrate's hand to execute his unlimited will arbitrarily on them. This were to put themselves into a worse condition than the state of nature, wherein they had a liberty to defend their rights against the injuries of others, and were upon equal terms of force to maintain it, whether invaded by a single man or many in combination.[24]

The due process clauses must extend to more than the question of whether specific formalities were used, or their protections would be worthless.[25] Certainly, adherence to formalities by Parliament had not prevented the American colonists from believing that their rights had been violated by either Parliament or King George. That belief resulted in the American Revolution. Equally certainly, when the new Constitution was created, the former colonists relied on more than formalities for protection. They insisted on structural and judicial mechanisms for the protection of rights. Courts considering governmental actions that affected the property and other economic rights of individuals routinely held that such violations were void, putting the government to the test of justifying its actions as being truly to protect the public against significant harm. If this were not done, and unlimited deference to legislative or administrative action were given, rights could be violated merely by engaging in a labeling game.

To a certain extent, modern courts accept the notion that they are obliged to ignore governmentally affixed labels when protecting constitutional or statutory rights that they find acceptable. When such rights are at issue, modern courts will require the government to justify its actions under strict standards and will not accept the government's characterization of its actions. However, when the civil rights at issue are economic or property rights, judicial deference to the legislature or agency is the rule.[26]

THE RIGHTS OF PROPERTY, POWER OF
EMINENT DOMAIN, AND JUST COMPENSATION

Despite the colonists' strong adherence to the notion of the inviolability of property rights, it was clear that they also understood the need for government to acquire rights in private property for legitimate governmental ends. This need was served by the government's power of eminent domain which is the power to "take" property. Importantly, that power was understood to be available to acquire all species of property, including the services of individuals. The extension of the power of eminent domain to even the services of individuals is consistent with the idea expressed by Madison and his contemporaries that the "faculties of man," which are used in providing services, are themselves a property. The place eminent domain occupies among the powers of government was succinctly described by Van Bynkershoek.

> Now this eminent authority extends to the person and the goods of the subject, and all would readily acknowledge that if it were destroyed, no state could survive ... That the sovereign has this authority, no man of sense questions.[27]

The ability to acquire the services of people through the power of eminent domain was expressly carried forth into Northwest Ordinance, cited above ("should the public exigencies make it necessary, for the common preservation, to take any person's property, or to demand his particular services, full compensation shall be made for the same").

The power of eminent domain was not unlimited, however, and it was not seen as abrogating absolute rights. The absolute rights of property were to be maintained by paying compensation for the interference.[28] To fail to pay was a violation of natural law because, "so great ... is the regard of the law for private property, that it will not authorize the least violation of it; not even for the general good of the whole community."[29]

The remedy for such an intrusion on private property, however driven by governmental necessity, was "a full indemnification and equivalent for the injury thereby sustained" except in the case of forfeiture for crimes such as felonies.[30] This is, Blackstone opined, only one example "in which the law of the land has postponed even public necessity to the sacred and inviolate rights of private property."[31] In the exercise of the eminent domain power, "the public is now considered as an individual, treating with an individual for an exchange. All that the legislature does [that is unique as compared to an individual] is to oblige the owner to alienate his possessions for a reasonable price."[32]

Other early legal writers also recognized the obligation to pay. Samuel Pufendorf wrote that "[t]he third right is Eminent Domain, which consists in this, that when public necessity demands it, the goods of any subject which are urgently needed at the time, may be seized and used for public purposes, although they may be more valuable than the allotted share which he is supposed to give for the welfare of the republic. On this account, the excess value should ... be refunded to the citizen in question."[33] Another scholar, Grotius, professed that the power of eminent domain gave government the right "to use and even alienate and destroy property." Government was also, in such instances, "bound to make good the loss to those who lose their property."[34]

In both these observations, clearly more than physical occupation of real property is subject to the compensation requirement. Certainly, the term "goods," used by Pufendorf, is broader than real property by common definition. And real property, while it may be alienated and used, cannot be destroyed. In none of these examples did the authorities use the terms "land" or "real property." They always spoke in the broader terms of property, including various forms of property such as goods and chattels. Grotius's statement that the right of eminent domain permitted use as well as alienation also suggests that something less than deprivation of title was recognized as being sufficient to be a taking.

Early official writings, including Chapter 28 of the Magna Carta, recognized both the power of eminent domain and the obligation to pay. British statutes specified objects for exercise of the eminent domain power and appointed officials to carry out those objects.[35] Although such statutes failed to expressly provide for compensation, it was, nevertheless, generally paid.[36] Subsequent acts of Parliament more or less routinely recognized the obligation to pay and provided procedures for compensation.[37]

Both the existence of the power of eminent domain and the obligation to pay were confirmed in revolutionary, constitutional, and postconstitutional era courts. At least as early as 1795, American courts recognized the importance of the power of eminent domain to governmental functioning.

> The despotic power, as it is aptly called by some writers, of taking private property, when state necessity requires it, exists in every government ... government could not subsist without it.[38]

It does not follow from this, however, that the need for the power of eminent domain dispenses with the need to compensate owners when the power is exercised.

Nothing in any state constitution at the time or in the federal Constitution expressly granted the power of eminent domain, unless one considers the clause of Article I, Section 8 of the Constitution (which provides that Congress has the exclusive power of legislation "over all Places purchased by the Consent of the Legislature of the State in which the Same shall be, for the erection of Forts, Magazines, Arsenals, Dock-Yards, and other needful Buildings") to be a modified extension of the power of eminent domain. Nevertheless, that power was exercised without question as it existed in common law. Similarly, while few states had constitutional provisions expressly requiring just compensation, the requirement that the sovereign pay just compensation for property taken and the limitation on the power to take, restricting the sovereign's exercise of that power to the taking of property for a public use, were nevertheless recognized as common law and were applied notwithstanding the lack of express constitutional provisions.[39] By 1800, only three states—Vermont (which was not one of the original ratifiers of the Constitution or, for that matter, one of the original thirteen colonies), Massachusetts, and Pennsylvania—had express constitutional provisions requiring compensation. However, states had other property protective provisions in their constitutions. The Delaware Declaration of Rights and Fundamental Rules, for example, incorporated the Blackstonian view of representation, declaring that

> every Member of Society hath a Right to be protected in the Enjoyment of Life, Liberty, and Property; and therefore is bound to contribute his Proportion towards the Expense of that Protection ... but no part of a Man's Property can justly be taken, or applied to public Uses without his own Consent or that of his legal Representatives.[40]

By 1820 nearly all existing states had supplemented this judicially recognized right by adding either a constitutional provision or enacting a statute securing the right to compensation.

It is not surprising, then, that once a Bill of Rights was accepted as necessary, a provision recognizing both the existence and limitations on the power of eminent domain found its way into the bill. It was simply included in the original Bill of Rights submitted to Congress by James Madison in June 1789, and it was passed without substantial change and without significant debate.*

The consistency of the eminent domain provision in the bill, together with the general concern for protecting property rights (as expressed in the constitutional convention and ratification debates) and the lack of controversy over the takings clause's inclusion in the Bill of Rights, establish that the Framers and ratifiers saw nothing innovative about its inclusion.

However, a few persons were concerned that *other* provisions of the new Constitution, such as the contracts clause or the prohibition of *ex post facto* laws, if given their intended and natural scope, could be viewed as eliminating the power of eminent domain. This may seem odd given that there was an express provision placing limits on the exercise of the eminent domain power, which would have been unnecessary if the power itself did not exist. Nevertheless, U.S. Supreme Court Justice Iredell, dissenting in *Calder v. Bull*, expressed his view of the importance of eminent domain to government,

> The policy, the reasons and humanity of the prohibition, do not, I repeat, extend to civil cases, to cases that merely affect the private property of citizens. Some of the most necessary and important acts of

---

* The seventh provision of the original bill submitted by Madison, included, among other clauses, language directing that "[n]o person shall be ... obliged to relinquish his property, where it may be necessary for public use, without a just compensation." *Annals of Congress*, 1st Cong., 1st Sess., cols. 433–436.

legislation are, on the contrary, founded upon the principle, that private rights must yield to public exigencies. Highways are run through private grounds; fortifications, lighthouses, and other public edifices, are necessarily sometimes built upon the soil owned by individuals.[41]

This statement is reminiscent of modern court opinions justifying intrusions into property rights in the name of public necessity or expedience. However, Justice Iredell did not reject the notion of compensation for the exercise of the power of eminent domain, but went on to say that "[i]n such and similar cases, if the owners should refuse voluntarily to accommodate the public, they must be constrained, so far as the public necessities require; *and justice is done, by allowing them a reasonable equivalent.*"[42]

As Bernard Siegan of the University of San Diego Law School points out, Justice Iredell raised this issue as an objection to an application of the *ex post facto* clause to civil matters. The objection was based on Iredell's belief that civil application would abrogate the power of eminent domain. Siegan also, correctly, points out that Justice Iredell was incorrect in this assessment.[43] The significance of Justice Iredell's statement for purposes of this discussion, however, is his recognition—commonly understood as correct by his contemporaries—that the *manner* in which accommodation of private property rights and public needs is achieved is through exercise of eminent domain and payment for property, thus avoiding an *ex post facto* action. This is an important point. Modern courts abrogating property rights do so based on a claim that they must perform a balancing calculation between private rights and public needs. They neglect to note that the balancing was done by those who constructed the Bill of Rights and that the just compensation clause reflects that balance.

THE FOURTEENTH AMENDMENT
AND THE CONTINUING PROTECTION OF
ECONOMIC LIBERTIES AND PROPERTY RIGHTS

The theme of property rights as essential liberties was carried through into the post-Civil War era in undiluted fashion through the Fourteenth Amendment. Ratified in 1868, the Fourteenth Amendment was one of a trilogy of amendments that followed the Civil War. The Thirteenth Amendment abolished slavery and involuntary servitude, and the Fifteenth protected the right to vote. Section 1 of the Fourteenth Amendment defines "citizen of the United States" and then provides that

[n]o State shall make or enforce any law which shall abridge the privileges and immunities of citizens of the United States; nor shall any State deprive any person of life, liberty, or property, without due

process of law; nor deny to any person within its jurisdiction equal protection of the laws.

These three clauses—the privileges and immunities clause, the due process clause, and the equal protection clause—have become the most important provisions in the Constitution in the sense that they have been held to incorporate most, but not all, provisions of the Bill of Rights for the purposes of applying their protections to state conduct. The incorporation doctrine is correct in general. However, I see no reason to believe that the incorporation doctrine was intended to leave some provisions of the Bill of Rights out of its purview.

Before its ratification, courts routinely held that the Constitution's protections did not apply to states except where—as in the contracts clause of Article I, Section 10—the Constitution expressly so stated. Nothing in the Fourteenth Amendment or its history, however, suggests that the Fourteenth Amendment was intended to change the meaning of the first ten amendments, which, as we have seen, were born of a distrust of legislatures and a well-defined concern that property rights be preserved. Quite the contrary, the Fourteenth Amendment was based on an understanding of the nature and scope of rights, with a goal of protecting such rights virtually identical to those of the Framers and ratifiers of the Constitution and Bill of Rights discussed above. The rights presumed to be protected by the federal Constitution against intrusions by the federal government were now to be protected against state intrusions through the power of the federal government.

Section 1 of the Fourteenth Amendment was drafted by John Bingham, a member of the House of Representatives from Ohio, and was essentially a means of achieving goals set forth in the Civil Rights Act of 1866, which was drafted by Republican Senator Lyman Trumbull as a specific remedy against state aggression on property rights. In its substantive provisions it provided that

> all persons born in the United States ... are hereby declared to be citizens of the United States, and such citizens ... shall have the same right in every State and Territory to make and enforce contracts, to sue, to be sued, be parties and give evidence, to inherit, purchase, lease, sell, hold, and convey real and personal property, and to be entitled to full and equal benefit of all laws and proceedings for the security of person and property as is enjoyed by white citizens, and shall be subject to like punishment, pains and penalties and to none other."

Although enacted as a result of the Civil War, it was intended to apply to both blacks and whites, and was particularly intended to guarantee to all born in the United States "the same *civil rights*, the right to the fruit of their own labor, the right to make contracts, the rights to buy and sell, and enjoy liberty and happiness."[44] Its principal focus, like that of the Constitution and Bill of Rights, was on property and economic rights. The authorities on which Trumbell and, later, Representative Bingham, relied most heavily were Blackstone and Kent, both of whom were advocates of natural law and the absolute rights of property. Bingham, particularly, expressed his perspective on the meaning of due process and the law of the land. His view, ratified by his colleagues, is essential to an understanding of the scope to be given to provisions of the Fourteenth Amendment, which he wrote. His public pronouncements, familiar to his colleagues who supported and passed the amendment, reflect the general attitude towards property rights and economic liberties still prevailing in the United States when the amendment passed and was ratified. Bingham was not impressed with the notion of deference to legislatures. On the contrary, he remarked that

> [n]atural or inherent rights, which belong to all men *irrespective of all conventional regulation*, are by this constitution guaranteed by the broad and comprehensive word "person," as contradistinguished by the limited term citizen—as in the fifth article of amendments, guarding those sacred rights that are as universal and indestructible as the human race, that "no person shall be deprived of life, liberty, or property but by due process of law, nor shall private property be taken without just compensation."[45]

Bingham repeatedly returned to the rights of *all* individuals in property. He characterized the origins of property in the same manner as the Framers had approximately eighty years earlier.

> [T]he absolute equality of all, and the equal protection of each, are principles of our Constitution. ... It protects not only life and liberty, but also property, the product of labor. It contemplates that no man shall be wrongfully deprived of the fruit of his toil any more than of his life.[46]

Bingham clearly included within his bill the requirement of just compensation for abridgments of property rights as an aspect of the Fourteenth Amendment, asserting that no one would "be bold enough to deny that all persons are equally entitled to the enjoyment of the rights of life and liberty and property, and that no one should be deprived ... of his property, against his consent and without due compensation."[47] Congress's understanding of rights was strengthened by judicial decisions that clearly stated the numerous economic and property rights that were each person's birthright.[48] The language used, over and over again, by sponsors and authors of the Civil Rights Act, and the Fourteenth Amendment intended to embody the act's principles, are remarkably similar to that used during the Constitutional Convention and the ratification debates.

Subsequent events show that Section 1 was specifically intended to extend the protections of the Bill of Rights (in their original meanings) to the states. That Section 1 had protection of property as a primary purpose is further supported by subsequent events. The Civil Rights Act of 1871 was the statutory successor to the Civil Rights Act of 1866[49] and was designed to implement Section 1 of the Fourteenth Amendment. The 1871 act was enacted in part as a response to results of an investigation by a select Senate committee that had been formed to determine, among other things, "whether persons and property are secure."[50]

Representative Shellabarger, chairman of the House committee that drafted the 1871 act, described its purpose as the protection of "the enjoyment of life and liberty, with the right to acquire and possess property of every kind, and to pursue and obtain happiness and safety,"[51] quoting *Corfield v. Coryell.*[52]

Urging Congress to adopt the legislation, President Ulysses S. Grant specifically included the rights of property as an important focus of any such legislation.

> A condition of affairs now exists in some States of the Union rendering life and property insecure. ... I urgently recommend such legislation as in the judgment of Congress shall effectually secure life, liberty, and property and the enforcement of law in all parts of the United States.[53]

So did numerous Senators and Representatives.[54]

Ironically, it was not long after the enactment of the 1871 act that federal courts began to undermine the protection of economic liberties and property rights, beginning with *The Slaughter-House Cases.*[55] It is perhaps appropriate here to note the possibility that the seeds for the demise of the protection of property rights were sewn by the infamous *Dred Scott* decision which—as much as any single act—precipitated the Civil War. *Dred Scott* was decided on due process, law of the land grounds, ostensibly to protect a property right: the ownership of a slave. However, if any validity exists to the natural law concept, it is that human beings cannot be property to be owned by other human beings. Thus, *Dred Scott* is a fine example of how a law made by humans—according to whatever procedures they choose to adopt—may, nevertheless, not be law. Had the *Dred Scott* Court applied the due process, natural law theory appropriately, it would have held that humans cannot be property. It did not. In failing to do so, it weakened the due process clause and property rights protections when they were most needed.

4

EARLY JUDICIAL PROTECTION OF PROPERTY RIGHTS

Until 1872, the courts fulfilled their assigned role as guardians of individual rights in property with admirable, if not complete, consistency. Even though the 1872 Supreme Court decision in the *Slaughter-House Cases*[1] was the beginning of the end of this consistent protection, the judiciary's nearly complete abdication of its responsibilities in this area did not take place until much later. As a result, significant protections continued to be given to property rights and economic liberties well into the 1930s, the so-called substantive due process era.

Nevertheless, the *Slaughter-House Cases* cut the heart out of the constitutional scheme for protection of rights and laid the foundation for the gradual development of a jurisprudence that insisted on tiering rights according to some undefined scale into fundamental rights (deserving strict protection) and nonfundamental rights (entitled to only the barest minimum protections). This development was without any basis in constitutional or judicial history.

Of the early cases that considered limitations on the legislature's power to deprive property owners of their rights in property, few were decided in the context of the just compensation clause of the Fifth Amendment.*

Most of these early cases were decided under either the due process clause, general principles of natural law, or—generally and appropriately, since the due process clause was grounded in principles of natural law— both. Of those cases considering the just compensation clause, the bulk considered the clause only indirectly, most often treating it as an aspect of

---

* These phrases, "just compensation clause" and "takings clause," are synonymous and will be used interchangeably.

due process. None did so when the actor was a state, as opposed to the federal government because the just compensation clause was not considered applicable to the states before adoption of the Fourteenth Amendment.[2] We must explore early cases involving due process if we are to understand the evolution of courts' treatment of property rights generally, the development of judicial treatment of the just compensation clause specifically, and the deviation from the intent and purposes of both due process and takings clauses.

Virtually all the significant early cases decided within the first hundred years following ratification of the Constitution and Bill of Rights extended significant protection to property rights and explored the relationship between governmental powers and individual rights. Among the most significant of the myriad cases considered by state and federal courts are: *Fletcher v. Peck,*[3] *United States v. Lee,*[4] *Corfield v. Coryell,*[5] *Baltimore v. Pittsburgh & C. R. R.,*[6] *Hepburn v. Griswold,*[7] *Bloomer v. McQuewan,*[8] *Knox v. Lee,*[9] *Bartemeyer v. Iowa,*[10] *Wynhamer v. People,*[11] *Ogden v. Saunders,*[12] *Allgeyer v. Louisiana,*[13] *Trustees of Dartmouth College v. Woodward,*[14] *Bank of Columbia v. Oakley,*[15] *Bowman v. Middleton,*[16] *Trustees of the University of North Carolina v. Foy,*[17] *Dash v. VanKleeck,*[18] *Vanhorne's Lessee v. Dorrence,*[19] *Wilkinson v. Leland,*[20] *Calder v. Bull,*[21] *Terrett v. Taylor,*[22] *Loan Ass'n v. Topeka,*[23] *Chicago, Burlington & Quincy RR Co. v. Chicago,*[24] *Fallbrook Irrigation District v. Bradley,*[25] and *Missouri Pacific Ry. Co. v. Nebraska.*[26]

All but one of these cases, *Ogden* (and, of course, the 1872 decision in *The Slaughter-House Cases*), resulted in decisions supporting the property owner's rights against governmental invasion. Even in *Ogden*, Chief Justice John Marshall's dissenting opinion was both consonant with the other decisions listed (as were the multiple dissenting opinions in *The Slaughter-House Cases*) and more influential in subsequent cases than the majority's opinion. All these cases, with the exception of *Ogden* and *The Slaughter-House Cases*, have several features in common.

GOVERNMENT WAS INTENDED TO PROTECT PROPERTY RIGHTS

First, the courts in these cases, in line with the thoughts expressed during the debates in the Constitution and the ratification period, saw the principal purpose of government as the protection of rights, particularly property rights. Their decisions were consistent with the principles of natural law espoused by Locke, Blackstone, and others on whom the Framers relied. These decisions also carried through on the Framers' and ratifiers' distrust of legislatures. In one of the earliest postratification cases to consider an invasion of property rights, for example, Justice Samuel

Chase relied on principles of natural justice to strike down a Connecticut statute. He held that

> I cannot subscribe to the omnipotence of a state legislature, or that it is absolute and without control; although its authority should not be expressly restrained by the constitution or fundamental law of the state. The people of the United States erected their constitutions or forms of government, to establish justice, to promote the general welfare, to secure the blessings of liberty, and to protect their persons and property from violence.... An act of the legislature (for I cannot call it a law), contrary to the great first principles of the social compact, cannot be considered a righ[t]ful exercise of legislative authority.
>
> * * * * * * *
>
> A law that punished a citizen for an innocent action ... a law that destroys or impairs the lawful private contracts of citizens; a law that makes a man a judge in his own cause; or a law that takes property from A. and gives it to B.; it is against all reason and justice, for a people to intrust [sic] a legislature with such powers; and therefore, it cannot be presumed that they have done it. The genius, the nature and the spirit of our state governments, amount to a prohibition of such acts of legislation; and the general principles of law and reason forbid them.[27]

The Court further expounded on the nature and limitations of legislative power:

> The purposes for which men enter into society will determine the nature and terms of the social compact; and as they are the foundation of the legislative power, they will decide what are the proper objects of it. The nature, and ends of legislative power will limit the exercise of it.... There are acts which the federal, or state legislature cannot do, without exceeding their authority. There are certain vital principles in our free republican governments, which will determine and overrule an apparent and flagrant abuse of legislative power.[28]

Chief Justice John Marshall, in a subsequent opinion considering the meaning of the term "law of the land" (which, as we have seen, was embodied in the due process clause of the Fifth Amendment) contained in the Pennsylvania Constitution, recognized, in language reminiscent of that discussed in preceding chapters, that

> the right of acquiring and possessing property, and having it protected, is one of the natural, inherent, and inalienable rights of man.... No man could become a member of a community, in which he could not enjoy the fruits of his honest labour and industry.[29]

While, he said, "[e]very person ought to contribute his proportion for public purposes and public exigencies," Marshall also noted that

> no one can be called upon to surrender or sacrifice his whole property, real or personal, for the good of the community, without receiving a recompense in value. This would be laying a burden on the individual, which ought to be sustained by the society at large.... [T]he parliament, with all their boasted omnipotence, never committed such an outrage on private property; and if they had, it would have served only to display the dangerous nature of unlimited authority; it would have been an exercise of power and not of right. Such an act would be a monster in legislation and shock all mankind. The legislature, therefore, had no authority to make an act divesting one citizen of his freehold, and vesting it in another, without a just compensation. It is inconsistent with the principles of reason, justice and moral rectitude; it is incompatible with the comfort, peace and happiness of mankind; it is contrary to the principles of social alliance in every free government; it is contrary to both the letter and spirit of the constitution [of the State of Pennsylvania].[30]*

As in the debates of the constitutional convention, the legislature's usurpation of property rights was cast in moralistic tones by these early courts.[31]

In a later case in which the meaning of the phrase "law of the land" was at issue, this time in the Maryland Constitution, Supreme Court Justice Johnson traced its derivation to the Magna Carta and understood it to limit the scope of governmental authority.[32] Numerous state decisions held likewise.[33] While these courts generally agreed that they were not free to inquire into the *motives* of legislators in enacting statutes,[34] this limitation on judicial inquiry into the propriety of legislative acts did not prevent inquiry into the *effects* of legislative acts on rights nor did it prohibit the courts from applying limits to legislatures regardless of legislators' motives, even where those motives were pure. Chief Justice John Marshall's opinion in *Fletcher v. Peck* made it clear that he believed that legislative motives were not a ground on which legislation can be invalidated. In considering the validity of a Georgia statute which had declared void an

---

* This language is superficially akin to that found in modern takings decisions that state that the fundamental issue in any takings case is whether "fairness and justice" require that the public at large bear the cost of a governmental measure rather than the individual property owner. In modern cases, however, as we will see, fairness and justice seem almost invariably to favor the government despite the fact that great benefits are generally bestowed on the public. The public would have to pay only fractions of a penny for benefits obtained, while the property owner often must bear a loss of thousands, hundreds of thousands, and sometimes millions of dollars. There is generally no satisfactory explanation, if any explanation is given, as to why this should be so. The use of this language by modern courts demonstrates how courts may use the same words but alter their meaning.

earlier enactment on the ground that the earlier enactment had been improperly induced,* Marshall, as a general observation, rejected the notion that a law could be declared void because of the legislature's motives, a position taken by many modern courts.

> It may well be doubted how far the validity of a law depends upon the motives of its framers, and how far the particular inducements, operating on members of the supreme sovereign power of a state, to the formation of a contract by that power, are examinable in a court of justice.[35]

Not only was the premise doubtful to Marshall, its execution was itself fraught with difficulties.

> If the principle be conceded, that an act of the supreme sovereign power might be declared null by a court, in consequence of the means which procured it, still would there be much difficulty in saying to what extent those means must be applied to produce this effect. Must it be direct corruption, or would interest or undue influence of any kind be sufficient? Must the vitiating cause operate on a majority, or on what number of the members? Would the act be null, whatever might be the wish of the nation, or would its obligation or nullity depend upon the public sentiment?[36]

There is a problem with Marshall's reasoning here. The difficulty in applying a principle is not enough by itself to justify refusing to undertake the exercise. Where a government body is obligated to fulfill a role, it has no license to refuse to do so on the claim that carrying out that duty is too difficult. This point aside, however, we should understand that what Justice Marshall doubted was whether a law could be voided on the basis of the *motives* of the legislators and not the purpose of the legislation. There is a considerable difference between the two, and there should be no bar to a court going behind statements or declarations of purpose or surface appearances to determine the actual *purpose* of legislation as opposed to what motivated the legislature to attain that purpose. Courts, including modern courts, consistently and properly probe the deeper purposes of legislation when the issue is one they are deeply concerned about, for example, in cases of racial discrimination.

---

* The later statute declared that all deeds to land transferred from the state under the earlier act, and all contracts relating to that land, were void and of no effect.

LEGISLATURES HAVE LIMITED POWERS

Second, these early courts unhesitatingly declared that there are limits on legislative power grounded both in the Constitution and on general principles of law, including the relationship of individual to government. When faced by a claim by the State of Georgia that it could, by legislative enactment, void a prior legislative transfer of property on the grounds that the previous legislature was improperly influenced, Chief Justice John Marshall declared that it was improper for the legislature to act as judge in its own cause. The legislature must instead submit to the judgment of the courts, "which are established for the security of property and to decide on human rights."[37]

> The validity of this rescinding power, then, might well be doubted, were Georgia [not a part of the United States, but it is] and in that union has a constitution the supremacy of which all acknowledge, and which imposes limits to the legislatures of the several states, which none claim a right to pass. The constitution of the United States declares that no state shall pass any bill of attainder, *ex post facto law*, or law impairing the obligation of contracts.[38]

Not only did the Constitution require such a result, Marshall said, but other general principles operated to restrain the actions of state and federal legislatures. Those principles were embodied in the Constitution and arose from the very nature of the relationship of government to individuals (that is, natural law).

> It may well be doubted whether the nature of society and of government does not prescribe some limits to the legislative power; and, if any be prescribed, where they are to be found, if the property of an individual, fairly and honestly acquired, may be seized without compensation.
>
> * * * * * * *
>
> [T]he state of Georgia was restrained, *either by general principles* which are common to our free institutions, or by the particular provisions of the constitution of the United States, from passing a law whereby the estate of the plaintiff in the premises so purchased could be constitutionally and legally impaired and rendered null and void.[39]

This view was shared by Justice Johnson who, in a concurring and dissenting opinion, stated:

> I do not hesitate to declare that a state does not possess the power of revoking its own grants. But I do it on general principle, on the reason and nature of things; a principle which will impose laws even on the deity.[40]

Like so many others, Johnson insisted that more than constitutional restrictions were necessary to protect liberty. The courts needed to constantly refer to "first principles."[41] Those first principles, he emphasized, had nothing to do with any specific constitutional provision but were based on general tenets and on a major theme of the Constitution. These principles were embodied in the Constitution generally and were explicated in "the letters of Publius [Hamilton and Madison], which are well-known to be entitled to the highest respect, [and which state] that the object of the convention was to afford a general protection to individual rights against the acts of the state legislatures." This did not mean, however, that government was entirely restrained from obtaining such property rights as it needed. Justice Johnson expressed his concern that the Constitution not be interpreted in a manner that

> would operate to restrict the states in the exercise of that right which every community must exercise, of possessing itself of the property of the individual, when necessary for public uses; a right which a magnanimous and just government will never exercise without amply indemnifying the individual, and which perhaps amounts to nothing more than a power to oblige him to sell and convey, when the public necessities require it.[42]

Certainly, when the Constitution's provisions were expressly applicable such that resort to general principles were unnecessary, the early courts were not inclined to allow the government to avoid a finding of unconstitutionality by an overly restrictive reading of the Constitution's specific provisions. They were unwilling to elevate form over substance. In *Fletcher v. Peck*, for example, Chief Justice Marshall observed that

> [t]he legislature is ... prohibited from passing a law by which a man's estate, or any part of it, shall be seized for a crime which was not declared, by some previous law. ... Why, then, should violence be done to the natural meaning of words for the purpose of leaving to the legislature the power of seizing, for public use, the estate of an individual in the form of a law annulling the title by which he holds that estate? The court can perceive no sufficient grounds for making this distinction. This rescinding act would have the effect of an *ex post facto* law. It forfeits the entire estate of Fletcher for a crime not committed by himself, but by those from whom he purchased. This cannot be effected in the form of an *ex post facto* law, or a bill of attainder; why, then, is it allowable in the form of a law annulling the original grant?[43]

Nor were these assertions made only by federal courts. In *Dash v. VanKleeck*,[44] Chancellor Kent of New York observed that there is no distinction in principle, nor any recognized in practice, between a law punishing a person criminally, for a past innocent act, or punishing him civilly by devesting [sic] him of a lawfully acquired right. The distinction consists only in the degree of the oppression, and history teaches us that the government which can deliberately violate the one right, soon ceases to regard the other.*

Similarly, in *Corfield v. Coryell*,[45] on which the drafters and supporters of the Fourteenth Amendment relied, the court interpreted the meaning of privileges and immunities clause of Article IV, Section 2. In doing so, it recognized the rights of individuals in their property to be among the most fundamental of rights:

We feel no hesitation in confining [the clause] to those privileges and immunities which are, in their nature, fundamental; which belong, of right, to the citizens of all free governments.... What these fundamental principles are, it would be perhaps more tedious than difficult to enumerate.** They may, however, be all comprehended under the following general heads; Protection by the government; the enjoyment of life and liberty, with the right to acquire and possess property of every kind ... to take, hold, and dispose of property, either real or personal; and an exemption from higher taxes or impositions than are paid by the other citizens of the state. ... These, and many others which might be mentioned, are, strictly speaking, privileges and immunities.[46]

The U.S. Supreme Court consistently reinforced this view of a court's proper role as a protector of rights and of the limitations on legislative actions. In *Wilkinson v. Leland*, the Court refused to accept the notion that the legislature had free reign over property rights.

That government can scarcely be deemed free, where the rights of property are left solely dependent upon the will of a legislative body, without any restraint. The fundamental maxims of a free government seem to require, that the rights of personal liberty and private property

---

* These observations by Justice Marshall and Chancellor Kent take on added meaning today in an era in which the government relies heavily on "civil penalties" as a means of avoiding the procedural guarantees that attend criminal prosecutions. Civil penalties are frequently used in regulatory schemes and other so-called "strict liability" offenses (in which no criminal intent or knowledge of criminal wrongdoing is necessary), as well as in forfeiture proceedings. The irony of this latter is that individuals who are found not guilty of a crime can, nevertheless, be punished because their property was used in or was the "fruit of" a crime that they were found not to have committed. In modern courts, form is often elevated over substance.

**This statement suggests that Judge Washington, author of the majority opinion, believed that more was involved than those rights enumerated in the Bill of Rights. Otherwise, he could have listed privileges and immunities by the simple expedient of referring to the bill.

should be held sacred. At least no court of justice in this country would be warranted in assuming, that the power to violate and disregard them; a power so repugnant to the common principles of justice and civil liberty, lurked under any general grant of legislative authority, or ought not be implied from any general expressions of the will of the people. The people ought not to be presumed to part with rights so vital to their security and well being.[47]

This view is completely consistent with the attempts of those who wrote and ratified the Constitution to protect the minority against invasions of individual rights by majorities.

COURTS SHOULD ENFORCE RIGHTS

Third, these courts believed a primary role of the judiciary was to enforce rights, including property rights, against unnecessary governmental encroachment, as expressed by Hamilton. In their view, even were the legislatures not required to submit their acts to the courts, legislatures would be obliged, when acting as courts, to follow the rules binding courts in reaching their determinations. This interpretation suggests that due process requires much more than the rather loose fact-finding procedures used in ordinary legislative proceedings. If this is correct—and I believe it is—to the extent that *any* deference is due a legislative body, none can be given to statutes adopted by initiative or referendum, such as those enacted in states such as California, because absolutely no procedural safeguards are present, not even the political processes that operate in organized legislatures.

This view was expressed in detail by the Court in *Fletcher v. Peck*.

If the legislature of Georgia was not bound to submit its pretensions to those tribunals *which are established for the security of property, and to decide on human rights*, if it might claim to itself the power of judging in its own case, yet there are certain great principles of justice, whose authority is universally acknowledged, that ought not to be entirely disregarded. If the legislature be its own judge in its own case, it would seem equitable that its decision should be regulated by those rules which would have regulated the decision of a judicial tribunal. The question was, in its nature, a question of title, and the tribunal which decided it was either acting in the character of a court or a justice, and performing a duty usually assigned to a court, or it was exerting a mere act of power in which it was controlled only by its own will.[48]

Certainly, these early courts were not to be restrained in fulfilling their guardianship role by an unwarranted deference to a coequal branch of government, unlike modern courts. The Court in *United States v. Lee* rejected the very notion of judicial deference to coordinate branches of government.

> Under our system, the *people*, who are [in Britain] called *subjects*, are the sovereign. Their rights, whether collective or individual, are not bound to give way to a sentiment of loyalty to the person of a monarch. The citizen here knows no person, however near to those in power, or however powerful himself, to whom he need yield the rights which the law secures to him when it is well administered. When he, in one of the courts of competent jurisdiction, has established his right to property, there is no reason why deference to any person, natural or artificial, not even the United States, should prevent him from using the means the law gives him for the protection and enforcement of that right.[49]*

Neither, these early courts noted, should the judiciary be deterred in its role by what has become the standard defense of government to any assertion of individual rights: Essential operations of government would become "impossible" if such rights were respected. This issue was also raised, and answered decisively, in *Lee*.

> The fact that the property which is the subject of this controversy is devoted to public uses, is strongly urged as a reason why those who are so using it under the authority of the United States shall not be sued for its possession even by one who proves a clear title to that possession. In this connection many cases of imaginary evils have been suggested, if the contrary doctrine should prevail. Among these are a supposed seizure of vessels of war, and invasions of forts and arsenals of the United States. Hypothetical cases of great evils may be suggested by a particularly fruitful imagination in regard to almost every law upon which depend the rights of the individuals or the government, and if the existence of laws is to depend upon their capacity to withstand such criticism, the whole fabric of the law must fall.[50]

Ultimately, said the *Lee* Court, property rights are coequal with the rights to life and liberty.[51] Claims that the government will fall if such rights are

---

* This case involved an attempt by the United States to obtain property in a tax sale. The United States was not directly sued. Its agent, who held the land for a national cemetery, was sued instead. The federal government entered the case at the Supreme Court level arguing that it "cannot lawfully be sued without its consent in any case, and that no action can be maintained against any individual without such consent, where the judgment must depend on the right of the United States to property held by such persons as officers and agents for the government" *Id.* at 204.

There could be no judgment against the United States (or granting a right to the plaintiffs), the Solicitor General argued, "because the [named defendants] hold the property as officers and agents of the United States and it is appropriated to lawful public uses." *Id.* The Court disagreed with the notion that agents of the United States could not be sued and compelled to turn property over.

protected are fallacious, and courts are essential to protect rights against governmental claims that effective functioning of government requires uncompensated takings.

> In such cases there is no safety for the citizen except in the protection of the judicial tribunals, for rights which have been invaded by officers of the government, professing to act in its name. There remains to him but the alternative of resistance, which may amount to a crime.[52]

In fact, these courts held, to deny a remedy because property is seized for some public use or good would be to

> sanction a tyranny which has no existence in the monarchies of Europe, nor in any other government which has a just claim to well-regulated liberty and the protection of personal rights. ... The evils supposed to grow out of the possible interference with the exercise of the powers of the government essential to some of its most important operations, will be seen to be small indeed compared to this evil, and much diminished, if they do not wholly disappear, upon a recurrence to a few considerations.[53]

According to these courts, the opportunity for an individual to prevail against a claim that governmental efficiency requires a person to yield his or her rights becomes even more strongly guaranteed when the right is expressly recognized in the Constitution itself. Thus, when the *Lee* Court was confronted with the argument that no remedy was available to the plaintiff because the federal government had appropriated the property for public use, the Court held that not only was the argument that government efficiency would be crippled not to be credited, but the very fact that property was being devoted to public use absolutely *required* the attention of the judiciary. The fact that the public use is a proper one has no relevance to the right to a remedy:

> The objection is also inconsistent with the principle involved in the last two clauses of Article 5 of the amendments to the Constitution of the United States, whose language is "That no person ... shall be deprived of life, liberty, or property without due process of law, nor shall private property be taken for public use without just compensation."

> Conceding that the property in controversy in this case is devoted to a proper public use, and that this has been done by those having authority to establish a cemetery and a fort, ... [it was] the private property of the plaintiff, and was taken without any due process of law and without just compensation. Undoubtedly those provisions of the Constitution are of that character which it is intended the courts shall enforce, when cases invoking their operation and effect are brought before them.[54]

These early decisions are admirable in their reasoning, consistency, and adherence to the principles under which the Constitution was framed. They stand in stark contrast to those of modern courts that, at least when economic liberties and property rights are concerned, appear at a minimum to have abandoned their proper constitutional role and at a maximum to have reversed that role, casting themselves as protectors of the "rights" of the government or the public to undertake whatever action they choose, regardless of the extent to which that action impairs the rights of individuals in their property. The language of these modern decisions should be contrasted with that of the early decisions.

For example, modern courts have asserted that the government has a "substantial power to ... redistribute the benefits and burdens of economic life."[55] This assertion would have very much surprised the people who drafted and ratified the Constitution. They had determined to scrap the Articles of Confederation and to adopt the Constitution in large part precisely *because* of such tinkering by state legislatures. The Framers of the Bill of Rights, who feared that the Constitution would not be a sufficient bulwark against just such a claim by the federal government, would have been equally disturbed.

Similarly, for more than one hundred years courts recognized that both states and the federal government were barred from legislatively altering the terms of existing contracts and were not deterred in so holding by claims of an unjustified trust in, or deference to, state legislatures. The Court in *Fletcher v. Peck* observed that

> [w]hatever respect might have been felt for the state sovereignties, it is not to be disguised that the framers of the constitution viewed, with some apprehension, the violent acts which might grow out of the feelings of the moment; and that the people of the United States, in adopting the instrument, have manifested a determination to shield themselves and their property from the effects of those sudden and strong passions to which men are exposed. The restrictions on the legislative power of the states are obviously founded in this sentiment; and the constitution contains what may be deemed a bill of rights for the people of each state."[56]

As we have seen, the Framers of the Constitution deemed legislative actions readjusting contractual rights and obligations to be "atrocious breaches of moral obligations and social justice" and a sign of a "universal prostration of morals." Constitutional era and postratification courts recognized that the prohibition on such actions by the states by virtue of the contracts clause was equally applicable to the federal government by virtue of the Fifth Amendment. For this reason, the Court in *Hepburn v. Gris-*

wold,[57] a case that involved a congressional enactment authorizing the issuance of paper notes to finance the war and that mandated that such money be accepted in payment of existing debts, held that requiring the payee to take paper money instead offended due process and the remainder of the Fifth Amendment's property clauses. That is to say, the Fifth Amendment's guarantees applied to the federal government with regard to contracts in the same manner that the contracts clause applied to the states. Justice Samuel Chase, writing for the *Hepburn* Court, noted that the due process clause and other Fifth Amendment provisions operate "directly in limitation and restraint of the legislative powers conferred by the Constitution." He stated:

> The only question is, whether an act which compels all those who hold contracts for the payment of gold and silver money to accept payment in an inferior value deprives such persons of property without due process of law.

> It is quite clear; that whatever may be the operation of the [Legal Tender Act], due process of law makes no part of it. Does it deprive any person of property? A very large proportion of the property of civilized men exists in the form of contracts. These contracts almost invariably stipulate for the payment of money. And we have already seen that contracts in the United States prior to the Act under consideration, for the payment of money, were contracts to pay the sums specified in gold and silver coin. And it is beyond doubt that the holders of these contracts were and are as fully entitled to the protection of this constitutional provision as the holders of any other description of property.[58]

It is not surprising that the *Hepburn* Court should understand the Fifth Amendment's provisions to protect contracts against federal intrusion as the contracts clause protected them against state intrusion. Not only did the Court have judicial precedent and well-established principles of natural justice (as espoused by Locke, Blackstone, Kent, and others) to rely on, as well as substantial evidence as to the Framers' intent, it defies reason to suggest that those responsible for the Constitution would have found such conduct shameful when carried out by state legislatures but acceptable if Congress were the actor.

Nevertheless, modern courts have refused to respect the constitutional injunction prohibiting such interference and have equally declined to abide by the long-standing precedent set by these courts. Thus, in the 1986 case of *Connolly v. Pension Benefit Guaranty Corporation*, the U.S. Supreme Court felt perfectly free to hold that it was quite permissible under the Constitution for the government to impose liabilities or duties on some individuals and to grant rights to others that they were previously not entitled to "even though the effect of the legislation in question was to impose a new duty or liability based on past acts"[59] even if such regulations may have unduly harsh effects on individuals.[60]

These latter-day courts are undeterred by the fact that the past acts were perfectly legal when undertaken. The employer and employees had entered unquestionably valid contracts that specifically limited the employer's liability. Undeniably vested and long-standing property interests have been held to be subject to destruction by government without compensation despite the fact that such actions violate every precept upon which the Constitution rests. These violations were upheld on an assertion that would have astounded those who framed and ratified the Constitution, that "there must be progress, and if in its march private interests are in the way they must yield to the good of the community."[61]

This statement utterly ignores the fact that the Constitution provides a manner in which private interests can be acquired to fuel progress. If the statement is taken to its logical extreme, it can be used to justify the abrogation of every right since, by their nature, the existence of rights is an impediment to progress, however those in power define progress, in the sense that adhering to those rights increases the cost of progress. Some extreme modern courts have virtually inverted the relationship between government and the individual as the Framers understood it to be: The Framers understood that government exists to protect individuals against intrusions on their personal rights.

These same courts have grossly misperceived the ancient limitation on the recognized right of an individual to use his or her own property in any manner he or she chooses by creating a concept of "public rights" in private property, a concept that would have been abhorrent to the Framers.

Under this concept, resources that clearly would have been understood by the Framers and by the constitutional and postratification era courts to belong entirely to the individual are viewed as actually belonging to the public with the private property owner merely being their custodian. Thus, for example, the Wisconsin Supreme Court in *Just v. Marinette County*[62] declared that the state could prevent the Justs from using their property to build a residence for themselves because the Justs had no right to deprive the public of its "right" to have the Justs' property preserved in the state in which nature had created it. In so holding, in a footnote the court cited (with approval) the motto of the Jackson County Zoning and Sanitation Department: "the land belongs to the people ... a little of it to those dead ... some to those living ... but most of it belongs to those yet to be born."[63] This whole concept is alien to the tenets on which the Constitution is founded with respect to property rights. The sole limitation on property rights, other than the power of eminent domain, was that an individual cannot make a use of his property that affirmatively harms the *property rights of other individuals*. It contains no room for the notion of public "rights."

These same modern courts have issued decisions that directly oppose more than a century's worth of precedent grounded in the words and history of the Constitution. They ignore Justice Miller's ringing declaration in *United States v. Lee* (that "there is no reason why deference to any person, natural or artificial, not even the United States, should prevent [an individual] from using the means the law gives him for the protection and enforcement of [his property] right"[64]) when they declare that legislative determinations are entitled to a virtually complete deference because the legislature is a "superior branch of government" over whose enactments the court holds no authority so long as the legislation is rationally related to some legitimate governmental purpose. In those cases in which this standard is applied, the government always wins.

This abandonment by the judiciary of its role as a guardian of individual rights can be traced to the *Slaughter-House Cases*.[65] The *Slaughter-House* Court, by a slim five to four majority, upheld an act of the Louisiana legislature that granted to a state-created corporation, a twenty-five-year monopoly power over the livestock and slaughter-house trade throughout an 1150 square mile area. The Court argued that its refusal to vindicate the rights clearly intended to be protected by the Fourteenth Amendment was necessary. In the view of the majority, any contrary interpretation would "radically change the whole theory of the relations of the State and Federal governments to each other and of both these governments to the people."[66] The majority's view of the judiciary's role rejected long-standing constitutional law grounded in the words of the documents and their history and principles, which had established that the courts were to serve the purpose of vindicating individual rights against intrusions by the federal government.

The *Slaughter-House* majority also literally ignored the clearly expressed intent of the creators and ratifiers of the Civil War amendments, which was to extend the guardianship role of the federal courts to violations of rights by state government in areas other than contract. Just as the Constitution itself was to change the relationship between the states and the federal government that existed under the Articles of Confederation, the Civil War amendments were intended to further change that relationship. This is not to say that the Civil War amendments abolished all notions of federalism, but their framers had clearly intended to change the relationship of state and federal government because of what it had found in its postwar investigations. As previously discussed, the amendment's sponsors, numerous congressmen, and President Ulysses S. Grant, found that neither liberty nor property was safe, particularly from state legislators.

In short, Justice Miller gutted the core of the amendment and thoroughly misunderstood the constitutional understanding of the relationship of government to individual. The majority's claim that the judiciary was not constituted to be "a perpetual censor upon all legislation of the States, on the civil rights of their own citizens, with authority to nullify such as it did not approve as consistent with those rights, as they existed at the time of adoption of [the Fourteenth Amendment]"[67] was an odd statement. This was *precisely* what the judiciary was constituted to do.

One should not conclude from this brief comparison of early and modern cases, however, that modern courts wholly agree with the notion that they should refrain from acting as a significant restraint on legislative and administrative action and as a protector of individual rights and liberties. Courts do this on a daily basis and frequently consider the closeness of the fit between asserted public goals and the means chosen by the legislature or agency to accomplish those goals. In doing so, they apply a rule requiring the governmental interest at issue to be significant or compelling and the action taken to achieve that goal to be the least restrictive alternative for its achievement. While such a rule arguably requires courts to substitute their judgment for that of the legislature, they nevertheless do this whenever they deem the right at issue to be "fundamental." I say arguably because the question at issue in a constitutional case is not whether the legislature has properly judged the rationality of a measure or even whether it is acting in the public interest but whether the rights of an individual or individuals have been violated in the process. It is unquestionably the role of the judiciary in our society to determine the meaning and constitutionality of laws. That task, especially the determination of constitutionality, has never been the province of the legislature. The courts, therefore, have usurped nothing, a fact they recognize when they invalidate laws impinging on rights they deem fundamental. Their errors emerge (1) when they give meaningful protection to only some rights by deeming those rights to be fundamental while refusing to protect the rights they decide are not fundamental;* and (2) when, on deciding that a legislative measure is unconstitutional, they direct the government as to what it must do instead rather than merely invalidating the offending act. This is not to say that those actually harmed by an unconstitutional act are not entitled to a meaningful remedy for such injuries they sustained as a result of the unconstitutional conduct.

---

* No constitutional or historical basis exists for drawing such a distinction; the application of the label of "fundamental" to a right or liberty reflect the particular political or social philosophy and values of the majority of the controlling members of the judiciary more than an understanding of constitutional principles and origins.

PART II

REGULATIONS AND THE EVOLUTION OF THE JUST COMPENSATION CLAUSE

5

THE TAKINGS CLAUSE
AND REGULATORY CONDUCT

The remainder of this book, which deals with property rights and the evolution of judicial treatment of those rights, takes place in the context of the takings (or just compensation) clause. I will focus on application of the clause to regulations of property, so-called regulatory takings. The reason for this focus is the major role regulations have come to play in modern American society following ratification of the Fourteenth Amendment and entry of the federal government into direct regulation of private property.

Regulatory expansion is generally based on claims that the proposed regulations are necessary to promote some public good or to respond to some crisis or emergency and that something must be done *now* if a solution is not to come too late. At just such times, public passions—against which the Framers attempted to construct a barrier—are at their highest.[1] And it is at just such times that a constitution proves its worth. As observed by Supreme Court Justice Sutherland in a scathing and utterly correct dissenting opinion in *Home Building and Loan Ass'n v. Blaisdell*, "[i]f the provisions of the Constitution be not upheld when they pinch as well as when they comfort, they may as well be abandoned."[2]

The fact that property regulations may have been or may be motivated by a genuine concern for public benefit is irrelevant to Justice Sutherland's observation. The Constitution is based as much on a concern about well-motivated governmental action as it is on a concern about governmental actions motivated by selfishness or other improper desire.[3]

Given that courts have abandoned their protective role as to property rights under the due process clause, the actions of courts in interpreting and enforcing the just compensation clause will indicate the ultimate protection individuals may anticipate. Fortunately, relatively recent Supreme Court lower court decisions issued since 1987 indicate a revivification of the takings clause.

THE TAKINGS CLAUSE IN
THE NONREGULATORY CONTEXT

Even for a considerable time after the ratification of the Fourteenth Amendment, most takings cases were decided in the context of a more classical application of the takings clause; they involved direct condemnation actions in which the government initiated court proceedings to acquire title to real property for some governmental purpose. While I will not discuss development of eminent domain law in this classical setting in detail, I will discuss some of these cases from time to time because they will aid our understanding of regulatory takings cases and will demonstrate the general principles that can be derived from such cases. They also demonstrate how regulatory takings cases diverge from the principles underlying the takings clause. One thing will become clear in the process: general principles can be gleaned from nonregulatory takings cases and applied in regulatory takings cases. These principles may be found in physical occupancy and invasion and in title acquisition cases. Such cases cannot, in any rational fashion, be distinguished from cases involving regulatory conduct.

The difficulty comes not from a lack of guiding principles but from the social and political perspectives of judges and from the policy concerns they have but deny they have. As I will show, courts frequently make decisions based not on principles of jurisprudence and constitutional precepts but on public policy grounds, particularly when faced with questions of property or economic rights. While courts deny having the power to base decisions on public policy grounds and insist that policy determinations are the sole province of the legislature, the courts consistently exercise their power in derogation of constitutional principles and the clear policies expressed by the Framers. Thus, courts will often reject the clear and express meaning of a statute or a constitutional provision, arguing that the legislature or Framers "could not really have meant that," because, in the court's view, such would be poor public policy.

Endless examples of this judicial behavior abound both in statutory law and in constitutional law, even outside the arena of property or economic rights. Title VII of the Civil Rights Act of 1964, for example, declared in part that it shall be an unlawful employment practice for an employer ... to limit, segregate, or classify his employees or applicants for employment in any way which deprives or tends to deprive any individual of employment opportunities or otherwise adversely affects his status as an employee, because of such individual's race, color, religion, sex, or national origin.[4]

In fact, another section of the same act specifically stated that

[n]othing contained in this title shall be interpreted to require any employer ... subject to this title to grant any preferential treatment to any individual or to any group because of the race, color, religion, or sex, or national origin of such individual or group on account of an imbalance which may exist [between the number or percentage of members of that group in the employer's workforce or training program and that] in any community, state, section, or other area.[5]

When confronted endlessly with the question of whether the statute could be used to create affirmative action programs or to discriminate in favor of one group or another, the act's sponsors and supporters declared incessantly and in various ways that the goal of the bill was complete racial, religious, and sexual neutrality in hiring decisions. The statute could not be used to achieve numerical balance in employment as "[t]he Bill would do no more than prevent ... employers from discriminating against or in favor of workers because of their race, religion, or national origin."[6]

Nevertheless, when the issue of reverse discrimination under the act came before the Supreme Court in *United Steelworkers v. Weber*,[7] the Court majority held that the statute authorized reverse discrimination as opposed to requiring utter racial, religious, and sexual neutrality in hiring, promotion, and the like—despite the acknowledged literal language of the statute and overwhelming legislative history to the contrary. As Justice Warren Burger recognized in his dissent, the majority refused to accept the clear language and central legislative history of the statute. The majority essentially amended the statute to achieve goals that Justice Burger agreed he would "be inclined to vote for were [he] a member of Congress" but which appeared nowhere in the statute. The majority did so, Burger recognized, because of its own view of policy.[8]

The property arena abounds with similar examples. In *Home Building and Loan Ass'n v. Blaisdell*, for instance, we have seen a court ignore the express command of the Constitution barring the passage by any state of laws impairing the obligations of existing contracts. The *Blaisdell* Court was faced with a situation in which the state of Minnesota deferred foreclosures on mortgages to prevent defaulting property owners from having their property sold in a foreclosure sale. This statute, at least in preconstitutional times, would have been considered one of a class of laws called "stay laws." The *Blaisdell* majority took an intellectually and historically insupportable position with respect to the contracts clause and argued that a public emergency existed that permitted Minnesota to pass this law to give debtors relief from the express terms of their mortgages. (The court did not seem concerned that a primary reason why many people were unable to meet their mortgage payments was because they had no access to their money because the banks had been closed—by the government.)

The dissent pointed out first that the contracts clause was included in the Constitution specifically because of such debtor relief laws, which were enacted when the economic situation in individual states was no less a "public emergency" than that existing in *Blaisdell* and, second, that among the laws disapproved of by the convention delegates were stay laws. Despite those facts, the majority declared that the express language in the Constitution which provided that "*no* state shall ... pass *any* ... law impairing the obligation of contracts" did not really mean what it seemed to say. Instead, the majority, ignoring an unambiguous history as to what kinds of actions prompted the Framers to include the clause in the Constitution, and previous Supreme Court decisions, asserted that the clause really meant that all states may pass some laws impairing the obligation of contracts.

INVERSE CONDEMNATION AND THE TAKINGS CLAUSE

The tendency of courts to refuse to extend the underlying principles of the takings clause to nontraditional cases became manifest only after the federal courts began to consider the takings clause in earnest after ratification of the Fourteenth Amendment. The trickle of takings cases that had made their way into the federal courts became a flood. In short order, these courts were confronted with a somewhat different class of cases. This is the class to which regulatory takings cases belong, the so-called inverse condemnation cases. Such cases are called "inverse" because the property owner rather than the government initiates the court action. Inverse condemnation cases invariably involve some governmental conduct, or the result of some governmental conduct, which is argued to be so intrusive on the rights of a private property holder that they amount to a taking of that property.

Inverse Condemnation by Physical Invasion and Occupancy: *Pumpelly*-type Cases

One group in this class of takings cases is that in which some physical invasion or occupancy of property occurred of a somewhat different kind than the traditional overt acquisition of a specific interest, such as fee title or an easement for a road, airport, or park. An early example of this class of inverse condemnation cases is found in *Pumpelly v. Green Bay Co.*[9] The *Pumpelly* Court awarded compensation to a private property owner whose property was flooded by construction of a dam when water backed up further than was predicted by the dam's engineers. In finding that a taking had occurred, the Court rejected the state government's claim that the damages to the owner's interests were mere "consequential" injuries for which compensation could not be required. The Court refused to allow the government to avoid its responsibility by the simple expedient of labeling its action or by stopping one step short of formalizing its action. It observed that it would be a strange thing indeed if the government could avoid liability by simply refraining from taking title and engaging in a labeling game.

> It would be a very curious and unsatisfactory result if in construing [the takings clause] ... it shall be held that if the government refrains from the absolute conversion of real property to the uses of the public it can destroy its value entirely, can inflict irreparable and permanent injury to any extent, can, in effect, subject it to total destruction without making any compensation, because, in the narrowest sense of the word, it is not *taken* for the public use.[10]

Pumpelly illustrates a fundamental truth, usually ignored in regulatory takings cases, that the effect of the governmental action should be decisive in determining whether a taking has occurred. The label applied by the government to its action and the mechanism employed by the government to achieve its goal are irrelevant to the analysis of whether a taking has occurred.

Inverse Condemnation without Physical Invasion and Occupancy: *Causby*-type Cases

The next group of inverse condemnation cases is typified by the 1946 case of *United States v. Causby*,[11] a case one step removed from the physical occupancy cases illustrated by *Pumpelly*. In *Causby*, the Supreme Court required the government to pay just compensation to the owner of a chicken ranch when the noise and disturbance caused by air traffic at an adjacent military airport rendered the property unsuitable for use as a chicken ranch. The Court awarded compensation despite the fact that it believed that no physical invasion of the property had occurred. Of course, one could quibble—as lawyers and social activists are wont to do—over whether the noise and lights of planes flying over constituted a physical impact. Whatever a physical sciences major would conclude, the Court did not find physical invasion to be a necessary component for compensation.

The *Causby* decision is important for several reasons, some of which I will return to later. First, like the *Pumpelly* Court, the *Causby* Court rejected a claim by the government that the impact on the property owner was a "mere" consequential injury for which no compensation could be had. Second, the case took place during a national emergency,[12] giving the court an opportunity to create some "national necessity exemption," an opportunity it did not take. Third, the Court specifically found that the overflights had not destroyed all value in the ranch but merely rendered it unsuitable for chicken ranching.[13] Compensation was, nevertheless, awarded. Fourth, the conduct amounted to only a temporary taking, and a taking of less than a fee interest.[14] Thus, while the Court held that there was only a limitation of use and a mere diminution in the value of the land, and that the property could be used for other purposes, compensation was required.[15] This is in contrast to regulatory takings decisions that have permitted regulations to so drastically change use that more than 90 percent of the value of property was lost without requiring the payment of compensation.

Fifth, the Court held that the amount of compensation due was not due only for the value of the existing use but also for uses to which the land could be readily converted.[16] Sixth, the Court rejected the notion that the legislature or regulatory agency could, simply by an otherwise proper legislative fiat declaring a necessary public servitude, avoid the constitutional obligation to pay if its action results in "an intrusion so immediate and direct as to *subtract* from the owner's full enjoyment of the property and to limit his exploitation of it."[17]

Inverse Condemnation by Regulation: *Pennsylvania Coal v. Mahon*

It was not until 1922, however, that the Supreme Court appropriately confronted a third group of inverse condemnation cases, the regulatory cases. In this group, the question is whether government regulations themselves can result in a compensable taking of property even though the government neither physically occupied property, permanently or temporarily (or permitted others to occupy property), nor took title to property. The answer, in an opinion written by Justice Oliver Wendell Holmes in *Pennsylvania Coal Company v. Mahon*,[18] was that regulations could indeed constitute a compensable taking.

This holding should not have been unanticipated. It was correct as a matter of logic and common sense and in light of the historical evidence as to the meaning of, and principles underlying, the Fifth Amendment. This is so simply because the *Mahon* decision recognizes an obvious fact, a fact that Supreme Court Justice Brennan, not a major champion of property rights, even recognized at least once:

> Police power regulations such as zoning ordinances and other land-use restrictions can destroy the use and enjoyment of property in order to promote the public good just as effectively as formal condemnation or physical invasion of property. From the property owner's point of view, it may matter little whether his land is condemned or flooded, or whether it is restricted by regulation to use in its natural state,* if the effect in both cases is to deprive him of all beneficial use of it. From the government's point of view, the benefits flowing to the public from preservation of open space through regulation may be equally great as from creating a wildlife refuge through formal condemnation or increasing electricity production through a dam project that floods private property. ... It is only logical, then, that government action other than acquisition of title, occupancy, or physical invasion can be a "taking," and therefore a *de facto* exercise of the power of eminent domain, where the effects completely deprive the owner of all or most of his interest in the property.[19]

Nor, Justice Brennan stated, could government avoid liability by claiming that it did not mean to take property.

> Appellees implicitly posit the distinction that the government *intends* to take property through condemnation or physical invasion whereas it does not through police power regulations. [Cite omitted.] But "the Constitution measures a taking of property not by what a State says, or by what it intends, but by what it *does*." [Cites omitted.][20]

In a footnote, Justice Brennan noted with approval that the Court of Appeals in the case had recognized that "the city's objective was to have the property remain unused, undisturbed and in its natural state so open space and scenic vistas may be preserved. In this sense the property is being 'used' by the public."[21]

The only real flaw in Justice Brennan's analysis is his apparent insistence that regulations can give rise to a compensable taking only if all or nearly all use is destroyed by the regulations. For reasons that will soon become clear, this qualification cannot be sustained. Justice Brennan's fundamental

---

* This appears to be a direct recognition by Justice Brennan that the right of individuals to use their property encompasses more than the limited right to use of the property in its "natural state" held by some courts to be the extent of the individual's right to use property. The Supreme Court's decision in *Nollan v. California Coastal Commission* makes a more explicit statement on this issue.

premise is sound, however. That premise is that regulations can be used to accomplish the same purpose either as the physical invasion or occupancy of property or as the formal acquisition of title to property. Thus, regulation should be susceptible to application of the same principles underlying more traditional takings cases.

Mahon bears some detailed discussion because it was the first case in which the principle was acknowledged that regulations could, in fact, cause a taking of property and because *Mahon* perfectly illustrates many of the issues raised by regulatory takings cases. It raises, for example, (1) issues of the extent of the police power and the meaning or existence of the so-called nuisance exception; (2) questions as to the definition of property and as to what property must be affected and to what extent before a taking may be found; (3) the question of whether and to what degree property rights are subject to a limitation based on the raw power (or even the authority) of the government to regulate *in the future* (a critical issue); (4) the meaning of terms "use" and "public use"; (5) the degree of judicial scrutiny to be given to legislative assertions of purpose and the means selected to achieve those purposes; and (6) the degree to which the courts may compel the government to tailor means to ends.

The contrast between the majority and dissenting opinions also illustrates perfectly the division between two wholly opposed philosophies of government and the relationship between government and the public and individuals. In this regard, the majority opinion consciously or unconsciously posits that government's authority to use a range of means to meet public desires (and even needs) is sharply circumscribed. The dissenting opinion advocates a view of virtually unlimited governmental authority in which the public may acquire whatever interests it chooses in private property with virtually no judicial scrutiny. It is precisely this battle that has consumed the regulatory takings debate.

The *Mahon* Court was faced with a challenge to a Pennsylvania statute, the Kohler Act, that forbade mining anthracite coal in a manner that resulted in surface subsidence—with some exceptions.*[22] One of the interesting features of the act was its limitation to mining anthracite coal and not bituminous coal, which is a softer coal, a fact pointed to by the coal owners in their brief as evidence that the Pennsylvania legislature had some purpose other than the stated one in mind when it enacted the Kohler Act.**

---

* The specific provisions of the Kohler Act are set forth in the notes.

**One might ask, tongue-in-cheek of course, why the majority in the 1987 *Keystone Bituminous Coal Association v. DeBenedictus* case (a case which will be discussed in detail below) did not cite the fact that the Antisubsidence Act (an act virtually identical in purpose and effect as the Kohler Act) covered bituminous coal as a reason for distinguishing the two cases and finding no taking in the latter case.

In the *Mahon* case, a couple who owned a home underlain by a coal deposit sued under a provision of the Kohler Act to prevent further mining that would cause subsidence. The problem for the Mahons was that Pennsylvania law recognized three separate estates or interests in real property, each of which could be owned and sold separately. These were (1) the right to use the surface, the surface estate; (2) the ownership of the subjacent minerals, the mineral estate; and (3) the right to have the surface supported by the subjacent strata, the support or "third" estate.[23]

The Mahons had, before enactment of the Kohler Act, purchased only the surface estate and had, at the same time, expressly waived any claim to damages resulting from subsidence in the sales contract.[24] The benefit of this arrangement to the Mahons was that they could purchase the property for a significantly lower price. By so doing, they explicitly took the risk that mining operations might cause subsidence. The Mahons were not alone in purchasing only the surface estate. Other private individuals and, apparently, the state and some local governments had also entered into such contracts.

When the coal company decided to commence mining, raising the specter that the risk they had assumed might actually materialize, the Mahons decided that the bargain they had struck was no longer worth it. They brought an action against the coal company under the Kohler Act to prevent further mining. The coal company defended against the action by alleging that the act violated both the due process clause of the Constitution (because it took property without just compensation) and the contracts clause.

The Mahons and the State of Pennsylvania argued, among other things, that the Kohler Act was merely a police power regulation, enacted for the public health, safety, and welfare. Hence, they claimed, the act was immune from a takings challenge. They further argued that the Court had to defer to the legislature's declaration of purpose, that the Court could not find a constitutional infirmity unless the act was patently unreasonable, and that the owners of coal mines know that their activities are subject to regulations. Hence, the owners had no right to compensation when the rules change.

> All property within the State is held, and all contracts are entered into subject to the future exercise of the police power of the State. Every such agreement was entered into by the parties with full knowledge that whenever the existence of such contracts and the exercise of the license reserved should threaten the life, health, or safety of the people, the Commonwealth in its sovereign power might interpose and restrict the use of those contract rights to such extent as might be necessary in the public interest. Owners of coal lands, who saw highways being laid out and improved; railroads and trolley lines built; sewers and gas

mains laid; light, telephone, and power wires stretched overhead; depots, stores, theaters, hotels, and dwellings constructed; and who, perhaps as many of the coal companies did, laid out the surface in building lots dedicating streets and alleys to public use, selling the lots for the purpose of having dwellings erected thereon—such owners were bound to know that whenever the time should come when the exercise of the license which they had reserved would threaten the welfare of the communities upon the surface, the police power of the State might be interposed to restrict their rights.[25]

That this argument was seriously advanced is chilling. If the Court accepted the argument, the contracts and takings clauses would disappear from the Constitution simply because individuals can always expect future governmental rulemaking. These two clauses and many others, however, were designed to ensure that certain rules would not be made unless the owners of the properties affected would be paid for that which was destroyed by the new rules.

Justice Oliver Wendell Holmes, speaking for the majority, rejected the state's and the Mahons' arguments completely. In so doing, he established the general principle that regulations, however valid otherwise, may nevertheless result in a taking of property for which compensation must be paid. It was not, he said, an issue of whether government must pay whenever a law is changed. After all, he suggested, "[g]overnment hardly could go on if to some extent values incident to property could not be diminished without paying for every such change in the general law."[26] Nevertheless, there was some limit to what he had privately described earlier as "the petty larceny of the police power."[27] Rejecting the notion that the fact that one could anticipate that regulations could change prevented takings from being found, Holmes added,

> As long recognized, some values are enjoyed under an implied limitation and must yield to the police power. But obviously the implied limitation must have its limits, *or the contract and due process clauses are gone.*[28]

The *Mahon* Court was not swayed in its determination by arguments that it must defer to the legislature's judgment. Instead, while acknowledging that "the greatest weight is given to the judgment of the legislature," the majority asserted that "it always is open to interested parties to contend that the legislature has gone beyond its constitutional power."[29] The right of interested parties to challenge the constitutionality of the legislature's action left the Court free to engage in a searching analysis as to the statute's purpose. It also felt free to consider whether other means existed to accomplish its avowed purpose in order to determine whether a taking occurred.

To do so, Holmes inquired into the statute's stated purpose, its operative provisions, the extent to which other means could be used to achieve its avowed purposes, and the rights it sought to abridge in the process. He concluded that the statute gave rise to a taking.

> The extent of the public interest is shown by the statute to be limited, since the statute ordinarily does not apply to land when the surface is owned by the owner of the coal. Furthermore, it is not justified as a protection of personal safety. That could be provided for by notice. Indeed the very foundation of this bill is that the defendant gave timely notice of its intent to mine under the house. On the other hand the extent of the taking is great. It purports to abolish what is recognized in Pennsylvania as an estate in land — a very valuable estate — and what is declared by the Court below to be a contract hitherto binding the plaintiffs. If we were called upon to deal with the plaintiffs' position alone, we should think it clear that the statute does not disclose a public interest sufficient to warrant so extensive a destruction of the defendant's constitutionally protected rights.[30]

Further, the Court did not quarrel with the defendants' assertion that the legislature acted in good faith when it determined that an emergency existed and that the steps taken were necessary to meet that emergency. The Court assumed that the legislature was sincere. The assumed existence of the legislature's good faith did not save the act from being a taking, however.

> We assume, of course, that the statute was passed upon the conviction that an exigency existed that would warrant it, and we assume that an exigency exists that would warrant the exercise of eminent domain. But the question at bottom is upon whom the loss of the changes desired should fall. So far as private persons or communities have seen fit to take the risk of acquiring only surface rights, we cannot see that the fact that their risk has become a danger warrants the giving to them greater rights than they bought.[31]

This observation illustrates the difference between judicial considerations of purpose and effect and judicial inquiries into motives.

Similarly, the Court felt free to exercise its independent judgment of whether the act served a public purpose or was truly the abatement of a public nuisance. Stated differently, the Court clearly did not feel bound by an implicit or explicit legislative declaration of purpose. The statute was, the Court found, designed in part to protect the homes of private parties who, like the Mahons, had purchased only one of the three estates. Hence, the Court found, the statute had no legitimate *public* purpose; the risk of subsidence to their homes did not amount to a public nuisance even though a number of private houses, or even public property, were involved.

> This is the case of a single private house. No doubt there is a public interest even in this, as there is in every purchase and sale and in all that happens within the commonwealth. Some existing rights may be modified even in such a case. ... But usually in ordinary private affairs the public interest does not warrant much of this kind of interference. A source of damage to such a house is not a public nuisance even if similar damage is inflicted on others in different places. The damage is not common or public.[32]

Even where the complaining party might be the public, however, such as when public buildings or roads are involved, and where it could legitimately be argued that a public interest is involved, the Court recognized two fundamental truths. First, it recognized the fact that regulations can be the equivalent of acquisition or destruction.

> It is our opinion that the act cannot be sustained as an exercise of the police power, so far as it affects the mining of coal under streets or cities in places where the right to mine such coal has been reserved. As said in a Pennsylvania case, "For practical purposes, the right to coal consists in the right to mine it." ... What makes the right to mine coal valuable is that it can be exercised with profit. To make it commercially impracticable to mine *certain* coal has very nearly the same effect for constitutional purposes as appropriating or destroying it. This we think that we are warranted in assuming that the statute does.[33]

Second, the Court recognized that strong public desires do not support a violation of constitutional protections and that the Fifth Amendment's provisions existed precisely to allow government to acquire resources it desires.

> The rights of the public in a street purchased or laid out by eminent domain are those that it has paid for. If in any case its representatives have been so short-sighted as to acquire only surface rights without the right of support, we see no more authority for supplying the latter without compensation than there was for taking the right of way in the first place and refusing to pay for it because the public wanted it very much. The protection of private property in the Fifth Amendment presupposes that it is wanted for public use, but provides that it shall not be taken for such use without compensation. A similar assumption is made in the decisions upon the Fourteenth Amendment.[34]

This observation is an implicit recognition of the difference between a public *interest* and a public *right*.

In what is perhaps one of the case's most famous and important passages, Justice Holmes warned against the tendency of individuals and governments to stretch exceptions until they swallowed the principles to which they were exceptions, a tendency that has been fully realized today.

When th[e] seemingly absolute protection [of the Fifth and Fourteenth Amendments] is found to be qualified by the police power, the natural tendency of human nature is to extend the qualification more and more until at last private property disappears. But that cannot be accomplished in this way under the Constitution of the United States.

* * * * * * *

The general rule at least is, that while property may be regulated to a certain extent, if regulation goes too far it will be recognized as a taking. It may be doubted how far exceptional cases, like the blowing up of a house to stop a conflagration, go — and if they go beyond the general rule, whether they do not stand as much upon tradition as upon principle. ... In general it is not plain that a man's misfortunes or necessities will justify his shifting the damages to his neighbor's shoulders.[35]*

Holmes's next words seem almost prophetic in light of subsequent developments. He was undoubtedly stirred by witnessing the trend in property and economic liberties, a trend caused in part by the positions he had taken in other cases.

We are in danger of forgetting that a strong public desire to improve the public condition is not enough to warrant achieving the desire by a shorter cut than the constitutional way of paying for the change. As we already have said, this is a question of degree — and therefore cannot be disposed of by general propositions. But we regard this as going beyond any of the cases decided by this Court. The late decisions upon laws dealing with the congestion of Washington and New York, caused by the war, dealt with laws intended to meet a temporary emergency and providing for compensation determined to be reasonable by an impartial board. They went to the verge of the law but fell far short of the present act.[36]

Certain aspects of *Mahon* ought to be noted for future reference and bear restatement here. First, although the majority stated that whether a taking has occurred is in some respects a matter of the degree of the interference, it found that the Kohler Act worked a taking regardless of the fact that the

---

* Like Holmes, I have strong doubts about the propriety of the proposition that one person or small number of people can be required to render great sacrifices, such as having their property totally destroyed—physically, legally, or economically—without recompense in the name of protecting or serving the greater number. It defies any concept of justice to suggest that one person or a small number of people can or should be required to bear the entire burden of saving all of the community's homes and businesses when the cost to that person is so great and the corresponding *pro rata* cost to each member of the community would be, by comparison, so small. It is a concept that is certainly at odds with our public self-image of a "compassionate society." The impropriety of destroying one person's property to benefit community without reimbursement is particularly evident where the danger to the community was not caused by the individual.

coal company had been able to profitably mine coal and was only prohibited from mining so much coal that the surface subsided.

> What makes the right to mine coal valuable is that it can be exercised with profit. To make it commercially impracticable to mine *certain* coal has very nearly the same effect for constitutional purposes as appropriating or destroying it. This we think that we are warranted in assuming that the statute does.[37]

Justice Brandeis dissented from the Court's judgment and argued for a balancing test that had been rejected by the majority. He claimed that the Court should compare what was taken with what was left and not find a compensable taking if the owner had remaining value.

> It is said that one fact for consideration in determining whether the limits of the police power have been exceeded is the extent of the resulting diminution in value; and that here the restriction destroys existing rights of property and contract. But values are relative. If we are to consider the value of the coal kept in place by the restriction, we should compare it with the value of all other parts of the land. That is, with the value not of the coal alone, but with the value of the whole property. The rights of an owner as against the public are not increased by dividing the interests in his property into surface and subsoil. The sum of the rights in the parts can not be greater than the rights in the whole. ... And why should a sale of underground rights bar the State's power? For aught that appears the value of the coal kept in place by the restriction may be negligible as compared with the value of the whole property, or even as compared with that part of it which is represented by the coal remaining in place and which may be extracted despite the statute.[38]

Brandeis's observation that "[t]he sum of the rights in the parts can not be greater than the rights in the whole" is true, but utterly irrelevant to any issue other than what compensation is due. It certainly has no relevance as to whether a taking has occurred in the first instance. It is akin to arguing that the government has taken nothing if it takes $999 of an individual's $1,000 bank balance because the remaining dollar still has value. These two approaches to determining whether a regulatory taking has occurred, that proposed by Brandeis (that no taking occurs if any property of value is left to its owner) and that applied by the *Mahon* majority (that a taking of any part of a person's property requires compensation, regardless of the amount left to the owner) have both been constantly and inconsistently applied in regulatory takings cases from *Mahon* to the present.

The second aspect of the *Mahon* decision to note is that the majority did not give significant deference to the legislature's determination as to the purpose or effect of the Kohler Act. Instead, it carefully examined the asserted purposes of the statute, compared them to the act's effects, and pointed out what steps the legislature could have taken to accomplish the act's stated goals without unduly burdening property rights. Justice Brandeis, on the other hand, would have upheld the regulation with virtually no scrutiny on the grounds that the coal company had not demonstrated that the act was completely irrational. In modern courts, Brandeis's test is impossible to meet in practical terms.

The third aspect to note is that the majority did not accept the argument that there can be no violation of the contracts clause or the due process and takings clauses because all contracts and property rights are absolutely subject to government's power to regulate in the future. Justice Brandeis, on the other hand, accepted this proposition without hesitation.

The fourth aspect, related to the majority's and dissent's positions on judicial deference, is their discussion of the so-called nuisance exception and the meaning of the term "use." While accepting that the legislature acted in good faith in deciding that an "exigency existed that would warrant" the restrictions of the Kohler Act, the majority determined for itself whether, in fact, a nuisance existed. The majority insisted that, to avoid the compensation obligation, the nuisance must be truly a *public* nuisance. Justice Brandeis would have left that determination to the legislature and would have allowed complete destruction of the economic value of property in the process.

These themes are constantly debated in regulatory takings cases. As I will show in the next chapter, the way these issues are resolved in individual cases varies widely with the individual circumstances of the cases, and not necessarily because the varying circumstances require the application of different principles *per se*. The inconsistency with which courts treat regulatory takings cases makes an analysis of these cases difficult.

6

REGULATORY TAKINGS AND CONSTITUTIONAL PRINCIPLES

> *We solemnly weigh the valuation of property and all the*
> *tests and decide pro or con—but really it is determining a*
> *line between grabber and grabbee that turns on the feeling*
> *of the community.*
>
> Oliver Wendell Holmes[1]

Any hunt for consistency among regulatory taking cases would be in vain. Such cases have more often been decided upon the Court's majority view of what constitutes sound public policy in any given instance rather than in an attempt to adhere to a consistent set of principles. That this is true becomes especially evident when dissents of Supreme Court Justices and lower court judges are examined whenever regulatory conduct is held to be a taking. It is also evident when virtually identical situations lead to wildly different results because of absurd factual distinctions.

For this reason, it is more useful to examine examples of diverse judicial responses to the various elements of takings and the major issues that arise when courts try to resolve regulatory takings claims. It is also more useful to examine the pressures, public and private, that tend to pull regulatory takings decisions in one direction or another. Among the issues worth discussing are (1) the definition and nature of property; (2) the extent to which rights in property may be interfered with before the interference rises to the level of a taking; (3) the meaning of public use; (4) what constitutes just compensation; (5) the extent to which private property rights must give way to public needs, including various concepts such as public nuisance and police power; (6) the existence of temporary regulatory takings; (7) the role of procedure in takings cases, and (8) the various judicial devices that enable courts to avoid dealing with regulatory cases in difficult circumstances. These judicial devices are of particular interest because not only do they permit courts to avoid difficult questions but they also permit regulatory bodies to interfere with property rights without serious risk. Before I proceed to a detailed discussion of these issues, however, a brief overview of the typical regulatory takings claim is in order.

THE NATURE OF REGULATORY TAKINGS

Regulatory takings cases have their genesis in a claim that some regulatory scheme—either on its face or as applied to a particular property—is so invasive of property owners' rights to acquire, enjoy, use, or dispose of their property that it has, in effect, taken either the entire property or an interest in that property. Typical cases involve impositions of local or other land use controls such as zoning; historical preservation ordinances; state, local, or federal price control schemes, such as rent control ordinances; or any one or more or a number of "environmental"* laws or regulations.

The regulatory scheme at issue will often require a property owner to obtain some type of permit or other government permission to use or market a property. Sometimes the scheme will flatly prohibit some action with respect to property, such as prohibiting the sale of eagle feathers or any object containing eagle feathers—even if the feathers were legally obtained before their sale was banned.[2] Conditions may be placed on granting the permit or on other governmental authorization to proceed.

To obtain the authorization, the property owner or applicant frequently must participate in a lengthy administrative process that usually involves public hearings, preparation of studies, and reams of paperwork. The owner must often, if not invariably, obtain an attorney's services to help the owner make sense of the regulatory scheme and to be certain that all formalities have been observed. Other consultants, such as environmental specialists, architects, and engineers, are also almost always involved. Processing the application can sometimes take years. It seldom, if ever, takes less than several months. In 1982, the President's Commission on Housing determined that the average time to process applications for housing permits in the United States was seven and one-half months.[3] This was probably an underestimate. The commission did not appear to account for time required to prepare the application for filing. Preapplication activities involve more than filling out forms, which may take only a few hours. Those activities generally involve preparing studies, drawing plans, and conducting numer-

---

* The word "environmental" is in quotes because, as will be seen, much of so-called environmental law and regulation is disguised land use law.

ous meetings with various governmental agencies and departments, including the following: planning department staffs; a planning director; planning commissioners; city councilmen or county supervisors; federal, state and local wildlife officials; the United States Army Corps of Engineers (if wetlands are involved—and they often are); and a host of local citizens' groups and organizations. Such preapplication dealings are often necessary to give applicants an opportunity to structure their applications in a manner that will give them a fighting chance. Even then, where virtually everyone agrees to the value and environmental sensitivity of a project design, one neighbor's opinion, however well- or ill-informed, may spark a political issue in public hearings. The political atmosphere may derail or kill that project. If we assume the President's Commission Report accurately estimated permit processing time in 1982, that figure is unlikely to be accurate today. Sure enough, the 1991 Kemp commission on housing regulation pointed to these recent trends as major factors in lengthening the time required for the review process.[4]

If an application for a permit or other authorization is rejected or subjected to conditions that the owner finds unacceptable, the owner's only choices are to begin the entire process again, challenge the action in court or—as often happens because the owner does not have the resources to do otherwise—abandon the project.

The Three-Pronged *Penn Central* Test

When faced with a claim that a regulatory scheme has resulted in a taking of property, modern courts generally apply a three-pronged "test." This test was first fully developed in the Supreme Court's decision in *Penn Central Transportation Co. v. New York City.*[5] This 1978 case involved New York City's landmark preservation ordinance. The *Penn Central* test appears to involve a coherent approach to regulatory takings analysis that should, if properly used, result in regulatory takings decisions of some consistency, if not ones that are constitutionally correct.

The *Penn Central* test requires that courts faced with a claim of regulatory taking consider primarily three factors: (1) the nature of the government action, (2) the economic impact of the regulation, and (3) the effect of the regulation on "reasonable investment-backed expectations."[6]* The coherence of the test is illusory. We can roughly divide cases decided after *Penn Central* into those in which (1) the "nature of the governmental action" is a physical invasion or occupancy of property and (2) those in

---

* I say "primarily three factors" since the Supreme Court has suggested that there may be other factors to consider but has never said what those might be.

which the action is characterized as not involving physical invasion or occupancy. Even this division is often arbitrary. Sometimes, as we will see, particularly in California, courts use this artificial distinction to avoid applying a property rights-favorable rule devised by the United States Supreme Court. No decision to date has given any of these factors meaningful content. Neither does the test lead to results consistent with the principles embodied in the takings clause.

Theoretically, under modern decisions, when the nature of the government's action is a physical invasion or occupancy of property, a *per se* taking has occurred regardless of the degree of intrusion. Courts do not engage in any balancing of public interests against private burdens or of value remaining against value taken.[7]

When the governmental action is not a physical invasion or occupancy, courts have deemed themselves free to engage in a balancing inquiry between their view of the intrusion's importance to the public and the burden the regulation places on individuals' property rights. As most commonly stated, in cases other than those involving physical invasion or occupancy, a taking is found if the governmental action either (1) fails to substantially advance a legitimate governmental purpose or (2) fails to leave property owners with economically viable use of their property.[8]

The terms "legitimate governmental purpose" and "substantially advance" are not to be taken literally in this context, however, although this view may change after the landmark decisions of the Supreme Court's 1987 term. Judicial deference to legislative and administrative declarations of governmental purpose, along with abandonment of meaningful judicial scrutiny in cases involving property or economic rights, means that virtually anything the legislature cares to label as a public purpose will be accepted as legitimate by courts. Judicial insistence on applying the so-called rational basis test to determine whether a given governmental action "substantially advances" that purpose renders that term meaningless as a restriction on governmental actions.

In actual practice, even the division of cases into physical occupancy and non-occupancy cases is illusory since the *per se* rule has not been consistently applied. Courts faced with cases involving physical intrusions of property hedge their bets by holding that mere physical *invasions* of property require courts to consider such factors as (1) the degree of the invasion and (2) the extent of the economic impact on the owner in determining whether a taking has occurred. Physical *occupancy* does not require or permit such balancing. The line between an invasion and an occupancy appears to be in the eye of the beholder.

In short, the three-factor *Penn Central* test simply gives an appearance of principled decision making. In actuality, it invites manipulation of outcome according to a court's policy preferences. The manipulation is easily accomplished by the simple expedient of attaching the right label to the government's action. The *Penn Central* Court's minority (led by now Chief Justice Rehnquist, then Chief Justice Burger, and Justice Stevens) recognized this fact and took the majority to task for its less than "meticulous" use of precedent.[9]

Justice Rehnquist leveled harsh criticism at the majority's opinion in all of its various parts. The dissent first noted that the Supreme Court has long recognized air rights as property rights and that it is constitutionally irrelevant that the property rights interfered with had not been actually and physically used at the time they were interfered with.[10] The dissenting justices also pointed out what had been a long-standing—and should have been an unexceptionable—principle: property has been taken whenever "inroads have been made upon an owner's use of it to an extent that, *as between private parties*, a servitude has been acquired."[11] Although Justice Rehnquist did not appear to be aware of the fact, his statement treating the government as any other party (for the purposes of determining whether a taking had occurred) was consistent with the view of the power of eminent domain taken by Blackstone in his *Commentaries*. That is, when acting under its power of eminent domain, government "is now considered as an individual, treating with an individual for an exchange. All that the legislature does [that is unique as compared to an individual] is to oblige the owner to alienate his possessions for a reasonable price."[12]

As to the majority's claim that no taking should be found when the owner has some remaining economically viable use, Justice Rehnquist pointed out the critical fallacy of the majority's position:

> The Court has frequently held that, even where destruction of property rights would not *otherwise* constitute a taking, the inability of the owner to make a reasonable return on his property requires compensation under the Fifth Amendment. [Cite omitted.] But the converse is not true. A taking does not become a noncompensable exercise of police power simply because the government in its grace allows the owner to make some "reasonable" use of his property. "[I]t is the character of the invasion, not the amount of damage resulting from it, so long as the damage is substantial, that determines the question whether it is a taking." [Cites omitted.][13]

The difficulties created by adopting the majority's position were also noted by the minority. For example, they noted that "[d]ifficult conceptual and legal problems are posed by a rule that a taking only occurs when the property owner is denied all reasonable return on his property."[14] Serious definitional problems exist under such an approach. Courts would be required to define "reasonable return" for numerous types of property such as farmlands and residential property, as well as commercial and industrial properties. Courts would also be required, the dissent noted, to "define the particular property unit that should be examined."

> For example, in this case, if appellees are viewed as having restricted Penn Central's use of its "air rights," all return has been denied. [Cites omitted.] The Court does little to resolve these questions in its opinion. Thus, at one point, the Court implies that the question is whether the restrictions have an "unduly harsh impact upon the owner's use of the property," *ante*, at 127; at another point, the question is phrased as whether Penn Central can obtain "a 'reasonable return' on its investment," *ante*, at 136; and, at yet another point, the question becomes whether the landmark is "economically viable," *ante*, at 138 n. 36.[15]

However correct the *Penn Central* minority's criticisms were, they—like virtually all other modern courts—failed to go back to origins. They did not begin their inquiry where all legitimate constitutional inquiries should begin: with a consideration of the language of the Constitution and Bill of Rights, with the historical context in which they were adopted, and the meanings assigned to those words by those who framed and ratified them. This is where I turn next.

7

THE MEANING OF PROPERTY

> *What Cardozo tells us is beware the "good result,"*
> *achieved by judicially unauthorized or intellectually dis-*
> *honest means on the appealing notion that the desirable*
> *ends justify the improper judicial means. For there is*
> *always the danger that the seeds of precedent sown by good*
> *men for the best of motives will yield a rich harvest of*
> *unprincipled acts of others also aiming at "good ends."*
>
> Chief Justice Warren Burger[1]

Since, by its terms, the takings clause applies only to private property,* whether a property interest is affected by regulatory action is the first inquiry to be made in any claim that a taking has occurred. If we examine the history surrounding the adoption of the Constitution, Bill of Rights, and the Fourteenth Amendment, along with the cases decided immediately after their adoption, we see that every specie of property was intended to be protected by the clause. Thus, their provisions were intended not only to protect real property, but also personal property, whether tangible property or intangible property. Intangible property includes such property interests as trade secrets, patents, and copyrights.

Similarly, regardless of whether tangible property is involved, the Con-

---

* The clause provides that "private property [shall not] be taken for public use, without just compensation." Hence, whatever mechanism exists to regulate the acquisition of property from public entities, such as state and local governments, it must be found elsewhere. While exploration of this question is beyond the scope of this book, it would be a fascinating study in itself. Does the power of eminent domain extend to the acquisition of property from governmental entities? If so, is it subject to the same limitations of just compensation and governed by the same rules as takings of private property. Does the specific limitation of the just compensation clause to interferences with private property imply a negative answer to that question?

stitution is concerned not only with the preservation of the owner's rights against a physical invasion or confiscation of that property or against the government's uncompensated acquisition of legal title, but also for full protection of the universe of rights that attend property ownership.

Modern courts have partially accepted the Framers' broad conception of property as embodied in the Constitution in the sense that those courts have consistently held that the takings clause was intended to protect every specie of property.*

Hence, we have such statements by the Supreme Court as that in *United States v. General Motors Corporation*, in which the majority rejected the notion that the term "property" for purposes of the Fifth Amendment was confined to "the physical thing with respect to which the citizen exercises rights recognized by law." Instead, they declared, the term "property" is more accurately viewed as "the group of rights inhering in the citizen's relation to the physical thing, as the right to possess, use, and dispose of it."[2] Modern courts have, therefore, held that "property" for purposes of the Fifth and Fourteenth Amendments includes such interests as trade secrets,[3] materialmen's liens,[4] interest accumulated on money deposited in an account pending resolution of legal claims against the money deposited in the account,[5] and a corporation's legal claim against the Republic of China.[6]

However, when it comes to protecting the full range of rights that an individual may have in any given item of any specie of property, modern courts have fallen far short of their responsibility to provide the protection intended to be given to property rights in the takings clause. Even to the extent that those courts have extended protection to property rights, that protection is not necessarily consistent. The modern judicial attitude toward what property should be affected and how before a "regulatory" taking should be found is somewhat schizoid and can be roughly described by dividing judicial responses into two categories. One is typified by Justice Holmes' position in *Mahon*. The other, espoused by Justice Brandeis in his dissent in *Mahon*, was more fully developed by the majority in *Penn Central Transportation Co. v. New York City*.[7]

The Holmesian view of property requires compensation for *any* interest actually taken from the property owner, without regard to the fact that some property interest or value remains in the hands of the affected party. That is, Holmes held that compensation is due whenever any one of the "sticks

---

* Whether modern courts would go so far as to include labor and personal services in their definition of property remains to be seen. Labor and personal services *were* deemed to be property subject to the power of eminent domain, and to the limitations on that power, in such preconstitutional laws as the Northwest Ordinance.

in the bundle of rights" that make up the relationship of individual to their property is taken by the public.[8] Holmes recognized that the concept of a partial taking, already well accepted in classical exercises of eminent domain and in inverse condemnation cases not involving regulation, such as that in *Causby*, is equally applicable when the taking is accomplished by regulation. As I noted in the preceding chapter, the coal company in *Mahon* complained that the Kohler Act, which in essence required the company to leave coal in the ground that it previously had the right to mine, worked a taking of its legal interest (the support estate), the value of which was the value of the remaining coal. Justice Holmes held that the Kohler Act had, in fact, worked a taking of the coal that the company was unable to mine, irrespective of the fact that some coal had already been profitably mined.

Justice Brandeis, on the other hand, would have compared the value of the coal left in place with the coal that had been or still could be mined. He would find no taking unless, on balance, the company had been denied economic use of the aggregate property. Brandeis' view ultimately prevailed in most post-*Mahon* regulatory takings cases. Thus it was that in *Penn Central*, the Court held that the application of New York City's landmark preservation ordinance to Penn Central's property was held not to be a taking because the Transportation Company continued to have some economically viable use of the property. In so holding, Justice Brennan proclaimed that

> "Taking" jurisprudence does not divide a single parcel into discrete segments and attempt to determine whether rights in a particular segment have been entirely abrogated. In deciding whether a particular governmental action has effected a taking, this Court focuses rather both on the character of the action and on the nature and extent of the interference with rights in the parcel as a whole.[9]

Curiously, Justice Brennan, writing for the majority, attempted to avoid a conflict with *Mahon* by characterizing the holding in *Mahon* as being based on a finding by the *Mahon* Court that the Kohler Act deprived the coal company of all of its reasonable, investment-backed expectations (that is, the support estate the Coal Company purchased) despite the fact that the term "reasonable, investment-backed expectations" was nowhere used by the Court in *Mahon*. Justice Brennan's remark demonstrates the intellectual foolhardiness of trying to draw such distinctions.

First, the term "reasonable, investment-backed expectations" is generally thought to involve factors other than ordinary property interests, although it is sufficiently imprecise to be endlessly flexible. Resort to such a mutable and indefinite term was not necessary in *Mahon*, however. The support estate purchased by the coal company, and retained by it when the

Mahons purchased the surface estate, was in fact a separate and distinct property interest in the same manner as are mineral rights, easements, tenancies-in-common, and a whole host of other property rights—each of which may be separately acquired, used, and sold.

While an entire discussion on general property law is beyond this book, it is entirely clear that whenever anyone acquires complete title to a property, that title carries with it the right to pull out strands of ownership, such as easements, and to sell those strands separately. The Penn Central Transportation Company purchased the air rights to the terminal property as clearly as the coal company in *Mahon* purchased the support estate when it purchased the property in fee. The term "fee simple" says it all. When New York terminated Penn Central's air rights, it terminated them all at least to the navigable air space. In my view, at a minimum, the city acquired an easement on Penn Central's property. The sole question in Penn Central should have been what, if any, compensation was due to Penn Central for the easement acquired. The minority agreed.[10]

The most charitable observation that can be made about Justice Brennan's rather remarkable statement about takings jurisprudence is that he paints with too broad a brush. Even today, taking jurisprudence frequently divides a single parcel into separate segments, particularly in nonregulatory cases and those cases involving regulations classified as resulting in a physical invasion and occupancy. In *General Motors*, for example, the Supreme Court specifically noted that

> When the sovereign exercises the power of eminent domain it substitutes itself in relation to the physical thing in question in place of him who formerly bore the relationship to that thing, which we denominate ownership. In other words, it deals with what lawyers term the individual's "interest" in the thing in question. That interest may comprise the group of rights for which the shorthand term is a "fee simple" or it may be the interest known as an "estate or tenancy for years," as in the present instance.
>
> * * * * * * *
>
> [In this case] the Government does not take [the person's] entire interest, but ... takes only what it wants ... and leaves him holding the remainder ...[11]

Justice Brennan fails to explain why his takings jurisprudence diverges from mainstream property law and classical eminent domain cases. In such cases, acquisitions of partial interests in property are and have been a common practice from at least the time of the Norman conquest. From the time of the Magna Carta, classical exercises of the power of eminent domain frequently focus on obtaining partial interests such as easements and leasehold interests. There is no principled basis for treating regulatory takings in any different manner.

There is certainly nothing to be found in the Constitution or in constitutional history to support the Brandeis/Brennan view. There has never been a serious suggestion, for example, that government need not pay for the acquisition of a right-of-way for a road simply because the owners of the land from which it was taken still have a significant portion of their property left. Nor has there been a serious claim that government could, without payment, take even 10 percent of an owner's 1,000-acre tract for the construction of much needed public buildings merely on the ground that the owner still has 900 acres left. Certainly, Justice Holmes had no problem in holding in *Mahon* that a taking had occurred even though only some of the coal owned by the company was affected, and properly so. To do otherwise elevates form over substance and leads to absurd results.

Neither can it be contended with any degree of accuracy that the Framers or postratification courts considering property rights claims would have found Justice Brandeis's view to be an acceptable one. First, the state laws (described in Part I) that prompted the Constitutional Convention delegates to abandon the Articles of Confederation in favor of the Constitution rarely, if ever, entirely destroyed the value of the property rights in the contracts at issue. Many of those laws that so incensed the delegates lowered the value of contracts, delayed payment due under them, or changed the terms upon which the payment had to be tendered. It was clear, however, that most or all of the contracts at issue remained economically beneficial to the creditors. They simply would not receive the full benefit of their bargain. The delegates were nevertheless deeply offended by such laws.

Second, classical takings cases that long preceded the adoption of the Constitution and Bill of Rights frequently involved acquisition of partial interests in property, such as easements and leasehold interests, as do modern *classical* takings cases. No one would suggest that compensation was not due in such cases on the grounds that the property owner has economically viable use of the remainder of the property.

Third, as discussed in Part I, the words of the writers and defenders of the proposed constitution, along with the sources they relied on in forming their view of property rights, establish that they had a broader conception of takings than that found in most modern regulatory takings cases. Blackstone's description of the absolute rights of property, for example, clearly contemplated that these rights include the power of "free use, enjoyment, and disposal of all his acquisitions, without any control *or diminution*, save only by the laws of the land."[12] Blackstone's importance as a legal authority and source of legal and social philosophy to the Framers and their contemporaries cannot be underestimated.[13] Madison, draftsman of the takings clause, commenced his definition of property with Blackstone's phrase that property means "that dominion which one man claims and exercises over the external things of the world, in exclusion of every other individual." He deliberately echoed, and later expanded, on Blackstone.

The laws of the land included natural laws that limit the authority of the legislature to acquire rights in private property by requiring that the legislature give its owner, "a full indemnification and equivalent *for the injury* thereby sustained."[14]* Natural law, in fact, would not authorize "*the least violation* of [the absolute rights of property]; not even for the general good of the whole community."[15] Locke echoed Blackstone, declaring that "[t]he supreme power cannot take from any man *any part* of his property without his own consent."[16] This view was also expressed by individual states in their takings law. The Delaware Declaration of Rights and Fundamental Rules, for example, declared that

> every Member of Society hath a Right to be protected in the Enjoyment of Life, Liberty and Property; and therefore is bound to contribute his Proportion towards the Expense of that Protection ... but *no part* of a Man's Property can justly be taken, or applied to public Uses without his own Consent or that of his legal Representatives.[17]

The former colonists (relying on Blackstone, Locke, and others) adhered to the view that the exercise of the eminent domain power gives the public no greater rights in an individual's private property than those enjoyed by another private individual with the single exception that the power of eminent domain confers an ability to force a sale that no private individual holds.

> [T]he public is now considered as an individual, treating with an individual for an exchange. All that the legislature does [that is unique as compared to an individual] is to oblige the owner to alienate his possessions for a reasonable price.[18]

Courts applying the clause following the adoption of the Constitution continued to follow this principle.

---

* In fact, it may legitimately be argued, and has been by the U.S. Supreme Court, that the power of eminent domain is not strictly speaking a legislative power and is, therefore, even more circumscribed. "To the legislature all legislative power is granted; but the question, whether the act of transferring the property of an individual to the public, be in the nature of a legislative power, is well worthy of serious reflection. It is the peculiar province of the legislature to prescribe general rules for the government of society; the application of those rules to individuals in society would seem to be the duty of other departments." *Fletcher v. Peck*, 10 U.S. (6 Cranch) 87, 135 (1810). If so, any deference that arguably is due to legislative actions would be inappropriate when a direct or indirect exercise of the eminent domain power is at issue.

> [The] right [of eminent domain] which every community must exercise, of possessing itself of the property of the individual, when necessary for public uses; a right which a magnanimous and just government will never exercise without amply indemnifying the individual ... perhaps amounts to nothing more than a power to oblige him to sell and convey, when the public necessities require it.[19]

Given the Framer's conception of the eminent domain power, it makes sense that they and their contemporaries would have expected the public to pay for any given interest it acquires.

Equally important in this analysis is the perception that the Framers and their contemporaries had of the role of private property in producing and maintaining economic prosperity. This view played no small part in the framing and defense of the proposed Constitution.

For example, Alexander Hamilton, in explaining the value of the commerce clause, observed that freeing individuals from commercial discrimination through state restraints on out-of-state goods stimulated productivity.

> By multiplying the means of gratification, by promoting the introduction and circulation of the precious metals, those darling objects of human avarice and enterprise, it serves to vivify and invigorate all the channels of industry and to make them flow with greater activity and copiousness. The assiduous merchant, the laborious husbandman, the active mechanic, and the industrious manufacturer—all orders of men look forward with eager expectation and growing alacrity to this pleasing reward of their toils.[20]

This view of the importance of private property to prosperity continued to be held after the ratification of the Constitution. Chancellor Kent of New York was among the many to note the importance of private property in stimulating human endeavor.

> The sense of property is graciously implanted in the human breast, for the purpose of rousing us from sloth, and stimulating us to action. ... The natural and active sense of property pervades the foundations of social improvement. It leads to the cultivation of the earth, the institution of government, the acquisition of the comforts of life, the growth of the useful arts, the spirit of commerce, the productions of taste, the erections of charity, and the display of the benevolent affections.[21]

This view argues against any claim that the Framers would have intended anything less than compensation for *any* interest obtained in the exercise of governmental authority.

Other contemporary legal and governmental scholars previously discussed confirm that Blackstone's understanding of property governed constitutional era thinking. Giles Jacob, for example, declared that "[p]roperty is the highest right that a man hath to lands or tenements, goods or chattels, which no way depends on another man's curtesy [sic] ..."[22]

The broad conception of property described by Jacob, Blackstone, and their contemporaries was not without support in practice either. The various provisions of the Magna Carta and British Acts (described in Part I) provided for protection of all species of property as did the later acts of the Continental Congress, the state legislatures, and the decisions of various American and British courts. For example, the Northwest Ordinance, enacted in the same year as the Constitutional Convention, provided that

> No man shall be deprived of his liberty or property, but by the judgment of his peers, or the law of the land, and should the public exigencies make it necessary, for the common preservation, *to take any person's property, or to demand his particular services*, full compensation shall be made for the same. And *in the just preservation of rights and property*, it is understood and declared, that no law ought ever to be made or have force in the said territory, that shall, *in any manner whatever, interfere with or affect* private contracts, or engagements, *bona fide*, and without fraud previously formed.[23]

James Madison, author of the takings clause and one of the multitude of spokesmen for the protection of property rights, defined property equally broadly. In so doing, he relied on Blackstone's specific words:

> [Property,] in its particular application, means "that dominion which one man claims and exercises over the external things of the world, in exclusion of every other individual." In its larger and juster meaning, it embraces everything to which a man may attach a value *and have a right*; and which leaves to every one else the like advantage. In the former sense, a man's land, or merchandise, or money, is called his property. In the latter sense, a man has a property in his opinions and the free communication of them. He has a property of peculiar value in his religious opinions, and in the profession and practice dictated by them. He has a property very dear to him in the safety and liberty of his person. He has an equal property in the free use of his faculties, and free choice of the objects on which to employ them. In a word, as a man is said to have a right to his property, he may equally be said to have a property in his rights.[24]*

The second half of Madison's description, emphasized above, should

---

* Not only does this statement reflect a common conception of property in Madison's day, it embodies a much greater concept of the value of property to both the individual and society and the vulnerability of the "property in rights" if the rights in property were subject to broad governmental control.

not be forgotten. It is not enough that one value some property or aspect of property. One must also have a right to it. The public, which with complete seriousness can be described as that group (regardless of number) having the loudest voice, may have an "interest" in the nonlegal sense in a multitude of things, but the public has no property right in those things. Thus, for example, the public may value a property that is privately owned and that provides a wildlife habitat, but it has no right in that property. If a private citizen owns a property, the mere fact of the public's "interest" does not convert that property into a public resource. I will explore this concept further in the chapter on wetlands regulation.

Madison, like many of his contemporaries and the courts interpreting the Constitution relatively soon after its adoption, was not inclined to narrow this definition for purposes of delineating the proper relationship between government and individual:

> Government is instituted to protect property *of every sort*; as well that which lies in the various rights of individuals, as that which the term particularly expresses. This being the end of government, that alone is a just government, which impartially secures, to every man, whatever is his own.
>
> * * * * * * *
>
> That is not just government, nor is property secure under it, where arbitrary *restrictions*, exemptions, and monopolies deny to part of its citizens that free use of their faculties, and free choice of their occupations, which not only constitutes their property in the general sense of the word; but are the means of acquiring property strictly so called.[25]

Madison was not willing to permit government to do indirectly what it could not do directly. In his view,

> a government ... which prides itself in maintaining the inviolability of property; which provides that none shall be taken *directly* even for public use without indemnification to the owner; and yet *directly* violates the property which individuals have in their opinions, their religions, their persons, and their faculties; nay more, which *indirectly* violates their property in their actual possessions, in the labor that acquires them their daily subsistence, and in the hallowed remnant of time which ought to relieve their fatigues and soothe their cares, the influence will have been anticipated, that such a government is not a pattern for the United States.[26]

The former colonists also had concerns about the effects of a failure to extend the protections Madison talked about on national economic ventures. Hamilton particularly noted that the failure of state legislatures to refrain from interfering with property rights severely affected the viability of commerce.

> Creditors have been ruined or in a very extensive degree, much injured, confidence in pecuniary transactions has been destroyed, and the springs of industry have been proportionately relaxed.[27]

Madison's sentiment about not allowing the indirect violation of property rights is consistent with the concepts of the broad definition and protection of rights and the notion that the takings clause applies to regulatory actions on the same principles as direct exercises of the power of eminent domain. Madison's proposition (that there are not only rights in property, but also property in rights) is similarly consistent with the view that protection of property is important for more than the recognition of abstract principles. His proposition also implicitly recognizes that unrestrained control over an individual's property jeopardizes all other rights. We have a wealth of information on the attitude of constitutional era Americans and their philosophical forebears toward the rights of individuals in their property. Among the sources of information available to us are the debates in the Constitutional Convention, the ratification debates, the historical precedents for the uses and limitations of the power of eminent domain, the early acts of Congress under the Articles of Confederation,[28] and the decisions in early cases considering property rights.[29] All of these establish that any claim that the government may abrogate any given right in property without payment because the owner retains some other value is inconsistent with the principles embodied in the takings clause. As Chief Justice John Marshall observed in *Fletcher v. Peck*,

> [t]he legislature is ... prohibited from passing a law by which a man's estate, *or any part of it*, shall be seized for a crime which was not declared, by some previous law ... Why, then, should violence be done to the natural meaning of words for the purpose of leaving to the legislature the power of seizing, for public use, the estate of an individual in the form of a law annulling the title by which he holds that estate? The court can perceive no sufficient grounds for making this distinction. This rescinding act would have the effect of an *ex post facto* law. It forfeits the entire estate of Fletcher for a crime not committed by himself, but by those from whom he purchased. This cannot be effected in the form of an *ex post facto* law, or a bill of attainder; why, then, is it allowable in the form of a law annulling the original grant?[30]

8

TAKINGS AND PUBLIC USE

The second issue in any just compensation clause case is whether the property at issue was "taken." If it has not been taken, not one of the remaining questions—such as whether a public use is involved or what compensation is due—arises. If the property has been taken, the next question that must be answered is if it was taken for a public use.

The question of whether a taking has occurred is the primary issue on which regulatory cases depart from other direct and inverse condemnation cases. In part, this issue is tangled up with the previously discussed issue of whether modern courts will recognize partial takings when regulations are at issue. However, because of judicial concerns about public policy, this issue is the one on which the courts are most likely to part company with the principles to be found in more traditional takings and inverse condemnation cases.

THE MEANING OF TAKING

Although no British or early American case conclusively defines the term "taking" as it pertains to the power of eminent domain (particularly in the regulatory context), the proper interpretation of the term can nevertheless be determined by looking to the plain meaning of the word, the broad meaning of the term "property," and the respect accorded property rights at common law and in statutory tradition. These sources of information, which I have described in only limited detail and on which the Framers relied, provide general principles to use as we apply the Fifth Amendment in concrete situations.

The American Heritage Dictionary of the English Language (New College Edition, 1976) defines the term "take" as meaning, among other things,

> to get into one's possession ... to seize authoritatively; confiscate ... to accept and place under one's care or keeping ... to appropriate for one's own or another's use or benefit ... to choose for one's own use; avail oneself of the use of ... to subtract (from) ... to use to one's advantage.

This same variety of meanings undoubtedly existed when the Constitution was adopted, although we need not limit our inquiry so.

Historical and constitutional era sources gave a legal definition to the term "taking," at least in some instances,[1] by reference to natural law,[2] although such definitions were not expressly made in the context of eminent domain cases. Natural law theory holds that an individual's rights in property can be interfered with only if compensation is provided except in the narrow circumstances in which the individual's use of his or her property worked an affirmative harm to other property owners or in which certain crimes were committed. Given this fact and the broad definition of property as a complex of rights, it follows that a taking may occur and has occurred whenever any discrete portion of an individual's relationship to a "property" (in its more restrictive sense) has been interfered with. This interpretation must be true even though the owner may have other rights (in the same tangible or intangible property) that have not been interfered with. Even modern definitions of the term "take" do not suggest that the whole of a tangible or intangible property need be interfered with before a taking has occurred.

Further, partial interests in properties are taken all the time by government and are recognized as takings. Indeed, private individuals frequently go to jail for interfering with another's rights in a property in even a limited fashion or for a limited time. The view that an interference with even one of a complex of property rights can be a compensable taking is consistent with the unchallenged view that is accepted even by modern courts outside the regulatory context—that a taking has occurred when even a portion of real property has been physically occupied by the government (permanently or temporarily), or where title has been taken to a portion of a property regardless of what other property rights may have been left to the owner. This interpretation is certainly consistent with the provisions of the various statutes, court decisions, and views of the legal authorities and scholars that I have described.

Hence, one can have the taking of an easement or a tenancy regardless of the fact that the property owner retains fee title and a reversion. It makes no sense—and would be thoroughly inconsistent with the original understanding of the *principles* of property rights that underlie the Constitution and Bill of Rights—to hold that government can do indirectly, by the simple expedient of labeling an action "a regulation," what it could not do directly. This is not to say that the government cannot regulate without causing a taking in every instance, but it does mean that the latitude given government under modern court decisions cannot be sustained.

THE MEANING OF PUBLIC USE

The next critical term in the takings clause is the term "public use." It is universally agreed that public use is a limitation on the power of eminent domain. It restricts the exercise of that power by allowing the government to acquire property interests only if the interest is acquired for public use. The general term is also composed of two more specific terms, "public" and "use." Arguments are frequently made that no matter what a challenged regulation does to an individual's property interests, the regulation does not constitute a use of any kind. Only if a court finds that a regulation amounts to a use of property does the issue arise concerning whether that use is a public one within the meaning of the takings clause.

To comprehend the meaning assigned by the Constitution's draftsmen to the word "use," we must understand that the protection of property rights against invasion was a major impetus for the adoption of the Constitution, that property is and was broadly defined, and that the colonists considered property rights to cover the entire gamut of actions that can be taken with respect to property (including use and enjoyment, and acquisition and disposal of all or any partial interest). Even modern Americans, like their predecessors, are experienced with and understand transferring and owning interests in property that are, in a sense, entirely passive. These interests include, for example, so-called negative easements which may consist of no more than a right in a third party to require the owner of a parcel of real property to refrain from making one or a number of uses of his or her property.* The term use obviously included the acquisition or holding of such property interests, which provides a benefit to the owner of that interest even though that person never set foot on the physical property to which the interest was attached.

Indeed, the terms "benefit" and "use" were constantly linked in Anglo-American law. In the sixteenth century Statute of Uses, for instance, the term "use" was synonymous with "benefit." Originally intended to abolish double ownership of the same property or property interest, the

---

* When considering this point, it is well to remember that—in the context of local real property regulation, for example—such regulatory schemes are called land use laws. The general plans and ordinances that effectuate those laws consist of determinations of what uses the public has decided cannot be made of land, although the determination is always couched primarily in terms of what uses are allowable. There is no better classic example of a negative easement.

Statute of Uses was ultimately held to legitimize the practice of having one person hold legal title to and administer property or one or more property interests for the benefit of a third party, so long as the holding party has active obligations to the third party. This practice would now be called a trust. In such situations, legal title vests in one individual while the equitable title vests in another. Another simple way to state this concept is that one person owns the property but has a duty to the third party to ensure that the benefits of the property are conserved and passed to the third party. Such a relationship was usually described by language conveying the property "to A to the use of B."[3]

Definitions of the term use, for example in the *Oxford English Diction-ary,*[4] relied on Blackstone and included the derivation of "revenue, profit, or other benefit" from property. Other sources may also be consulted for clues to the meaning of use in the Fifth Amendment, including the general principles underlying the takings clause.

While early statements regarding the power of eminent domain do not define the word use, we may find various statements in different sources about the power of eminent domain. These statements use different phrases to describe what seems to be the same concept, and they support the notion that use was employed in the commonly accepted broad meaning of the term rather than in some narrow technical sense. These statements also suggest that the terms "public use" and "public purpose" are arguably synonymous for taking purposes. Various state and federal constitutional provisions or statutes used phrases such as property taken "for public exigencies,"[5] or "for the use of the public."[6] Other formulations required that compensation be paid for property "taken, or applied to public Uses."[7]

If we look to judicial decisions, we see that early courts frequently used similar language. The court in *Vanhorne's Lessee* recognized that the "right of acquiring and possessing property, and having it protected, is one of the natural, inherent, and inalienable rights of man. ... No man could become a member of a community, in which he could not enjoy the fruits of his honest labour and industry."[8] The *Vanhorne's Lessee* Court held, therefore, that while "[e]very person ought to contribute his proportion *for public purposes and public exigencies*" no one could be required to give—without compensation—more than that proportionate amount."[9] Some reliable descriptions of the power of eminent domain went so far as to suggest that it could be invoked only when serious need existed. Pufendorf wrote:

> The third right is Eminent Domain, which consists in this, that when *public necessity* demands it, the goods of any subject which are *urgently needed* at the time, may be seized and used for public purposes, although they may be more valuable than the allotted share which he is supposed to give

for the welfare of the republic. On this account, the excess value should
… be refunded to the citizen in question."[10]

We may also look to the contracts clause, which forbids impairment of
contracts and appears to have been based on the same values and principles
as those underlying the takings clause. The contracts clause, as we have
seen, was considered by early courts to be part and parcel of the general
concept of the property protection that was the goal of the Constitution. As
we have also seen, courts established early on that contract rights are
property. Thus, for example, in *Hepburn v. Griswold*, the Court held that
requiring a payee under a contract to take money in paper instead of
specified coin offended not only due process but also the remainder of the
Fifth Amendment's property clauses. That is to say, the Fifth Amendment's
guarantees applied to the federal government with regard to contracts in
the same manner that the contracts clause applied to the states.

> The only question is, whether an act which compels all those who hold
> contracts for the payment of gold and silver money to accept payment
> in an inferior value deprives such persons of property without due
> process of law.
>   It is quite clear; that whatever may be the operation of the [Legal
> Tender Act], due process of law makes no part of it. Does it deprive any
> person of property? A very large proportion of the property of civilized
> men exists in the form of contracts. These contracts almost invariably
> stipulate for the payment of money. And we have already seen that
> contracts in the United States prior to the Act under consideration, for the
> payment of money, were contracts to pay the sums specified in gold and
> silver coin. And it is beyond doubt that the holders of these contracts were
> and are as fully entitled to the protection of this constitutional provision
> as the holders of any other description of property.[11]

The *Hepburn* Court's understanding regarding the Fifth Amendment's
application to federal impairments of contract rights was based not only on
judicial precedent but also on well-established principles of natural justice
and substantial evidence as to the Framers' intent. The *Hepburn* Court
understood that the Framers would certainly not have found such conduct
morally corrupt when carried out by state legislatures but morally acceptable if done by federal bodies.

To the extent that our observation that the contracts clause and the just
compensation clause embody the same values is valid, it suggests that the
terms "use" and "take" include the concept of impairment.* Impairment

---

* The contracts clause provides that "No State shall … pass any … Law *impairing* the Obligation of
Contracts."

was defined in eighteenth century literature as meaning "to diminish; to injure; to make worse; to lessen in quantity, value, or excellence."[12] Thus, for example, the Court in *Fletcher v. Peck*, in considering the validity of a legislative action declaring a grant of property void, remarked,

> It is, then, the unanimous opinion of this court, that ... the state of Georgia was restrained, either by general principles which are common to our free institutions, or by the particular provisions of the constitution of the United States, from passing a law whereby the estate of the plaintiff in the premises so purchased could be constitutionally and legally *impaired* and rendered null and void.[13]

Other courts, considering the effect of laws on contracts, as property, also found impairment of a property right to be violative of the Fifth Amendment.[14]

The Framers lived, as do we, in a universe of property laws and rights in which common practice involved selling various rights in property, many of which were nonpossessory and which might amount to no more than a grant of a power of the purchaser to prohibit the owner of the remainder from making particular uses of the property. In that universe and in an atmosphere in which the Framers and their contemporaries were no more inclined to permit the government to do indirectly that which they could not do directly by engaging in a labeling game, the terms use and take were unlikely to have been narrowly defined. Of course, the argument may always be made, with some justice, that use or even public use (as a limitation on the power of eminent domain) would be narrowly defined to keep the exercise of the power of eminent domain within proper bounds. More likely, however, use would be broadly defined to keep government from claiming that its action did not amount to a use, thereby bypassing the purpose of the limitation.

The term "public" in public use is more often at issue in a takings case. Unlike use, public was undoubtedly defined more narrowly to restrict the government's ability to simply redistribute wealth from one individual to another or from one group to another in the guise of serving some larger public need.

Most of the property rights violations that were a major factor in prompting the abandonment of the Articles of Confederation were of precisely the type that are commonly held to be acceptable exercises of governmental power by modern courts. They included "stay laws" (laws staying or postponing the payment of debts beyond the time fixed in contracts), installment laws (acts providing that debts could be paid in several installments over a period of months or even years rather than in a single sum as stipulated in the agreement), and commodity payment laws (statutes permitting payment to be made in certain enumerated commodities at a proportion, usually three-fourths or four-fifths, of their appraised value).[15]

The distaste for such laws enshrined in the Constitution prompted delegates to the Constitutional Convention to label them as "atrocious breaches of moral obligation and social justice."[16] Delegates considered these abrogated rights to be inalienable, that is, rights that could not even be given away in the social compact. Laws "adjusting the economic burdens and benefits of public life" by transferring property rights from one segment of society to another, thereby, represent the unbridled exercise of majoritarian power that the Constitution was designed to avoid. As Madison voiced it,

> In all cases where a majority are united by a common interest or passion, the rights of the minority are in danger. What motives are to restrain them? A prudent regard to the maxim that honesty is the best policy is found by experience to be as little regarded by bodies of men as by individuals. Respect for character is always diminished in proportion to the number among whom the blame or praise is to be divided. Conscience, the only remaining tie, is known to be inadequate in individuals. In large numbers, little is to be expected of it.[17]

Governmental actions taken for the purpose of merely transferring some economic or property benefit from one group of citizens to another were not, therefore, likely to be considered to have been taken for a legitimate *public* purpose. This is true even if the transfer would indirectly confer some benefit on the public by, for example, pumping additional money into the local economy.[18] The potential for abuse is far too great. Such action would, in fact, have been considered improper or wicked.

> A rage for ... an abolition of debts, for an equal division of property, or for any other improper or wicked project, will be less apt to pervade the whole body of the Union than a particular member of it, in the same proportion as such a malady is more likely to taint a particular county or district than a state.[19]

The term public, therefore, would unquestionably have been narrowly defined.* Without a narrow definition, the tendency noted by Justice Holmes in *Mahon* (to stretch concepts beyond any meaning originally attached to them) would defeat the limitation. Like the term harm, the term public can be argued to cover far more territory than was ever contemplated

---

* Eighteenth century dictionaries defined public as meaning "belonging to a state or nation; not private ... general ... regarding not private interest, but the good of the community." See, Johnson, *A Dictionary of the English Language* (2d Ed., 1755).

by the Framers. Just as we can argue that anything done by any one or group of persons can be said to harm someone else, so too we can argue that anything done by government can be said to serve some public purpose, however directly or indirectly, however intentioned or unintentioned.[20] This is not to say that the original concept of public use could never permit laws that had the incidental effect of transferring property rights from one person or group to another, but the concept does suggest that such laws would be subjected to close scrutiny by courts to prevent disguised improper transfers. Even then, of course, no such transfer could occur, however properly public, without compensation. Thus, transfers from one private party to another could not be legitimized because of an incidental benefit to the public.

Cases in the postratification period dealt primarily with the term public in the context of cases involving actions that typically would have been public functions. These actions include, for instance, construction and operation of ferries, roads, or toll bridges,[21] or those situations in which property is commandeered in time of war.[22] In fact, many of the first class of cases were not takings cases but taxation cases. Taxes, such cases made clear, could only be collected for and applied to public purposes. Some courts, at least, treated public as meaning the same for both the tax question and the taking question. This treatment may not be legitimate, particularly in regulatory settings where tax money (whether in cash or in the form of vouchers) is used as a subsidy. Subsidizing housing, for example, would be more in keeping with the intent of the Fifth Amendment than enacting rent control because the public as a whole would share proportionately in the burden of providing low-cost housing. With rent control, the entire burden is cast entirely on the property owner; with subsidized housing, owners are permitted to maximize the use of property without losing money.

The truly interesting thing about the cases in which property is commandeered for use in war is that they gave the courts considering them an opportunity to create a national emergency exception to the takings clause. The courts could have argued by analogy from the unprincipled but time-honored notion (questioned by Justice Holmes) that one can destroy a house to save all other houses from fire without paying the owner. They did not create such an exception.

In the public function cases, the property taken by the government was given to some private party to operate. For instance, the government might grant an exclusive franchise to an individual or business to operate a toll road or bridge. However, in each case, the property was open and available for public use and the use was regulated so that excessive tolls or fares could not be charged.[23] It was, in a manner of speaking, a method of contracting out the performance of public functions. On occasion, the converse occurred; the government took a privately owned and operated toll bridge or road and turned it into a free one. One of these cases, *West River Bridge Company*,[24] raises an interesting point. The claim was made in argument that because the franchise involved was issued by the state, the state could alter that franchise without running afoul of the Constitution. Justice McClean properly rejected such a claim.

> But it is said that the franchise of the plaintiff cannot be denominated property; that "it included the grant of no property real or personal; that it lay in grant, and not in livery." ... If the action of the State had been upon the franchise only, this objection would be unanswerable. The State cannot modify or repeal a charter for a bridge, a turnpike road, or a bank, or any other private charter, unless the power to do so has been reserved in the original grant. But no one doubts the power of the State to take a banking-house for public use, or any other real or personal property owned by the bank. In this respect, a corporation holds property subject to the eminent domain, the same as citizens. The great object of an act of incorporation is to enable a body of men to exercise the faculties of an individual. ... The franchise no more than a grant for land can be annulled by the State.[25]

I was confronted with the precise argument rejected in this case at a takings conference in Virginia. A representative of the Treasury Department had presented the view that because bank and savings and loan charters were granted by the state or federal government and because they were regulated so heavily, banks and savings and loans had no property rights that had to be paid for when the regulations changed, both because they could anticipate such changes and because they derived their very existence from the government. He was dubious about my challenge to that proposition.

The same logic applied to road and bridge cases was applied to cases in which the power of eminent domain or taxation was exercised in favor of, or sometimes delegated to, railroads.

> Whether the use of a railroad is a public or private one depends in no measure upon the question who constructed it or who owns it. It has never been considered a matter of any importance that the road was built by the agency of a private corporation. No matter who is the agent, the function performed is that of the State. Though the ownership is private, the use is public.* So turnpikes, bridges, ferries, and canals, although made by individuals under public grants, or by companies, are considered *publici juris*. The right to exact tolls, or charge freights is granted for a service to the public. The owners may be private

---

* This distinction is crucial. The fact that a private party provides a service important to the public is not an excuse justifying taking that privately owned property without payment to its owner.

companies, but they are compellable to permit the public to use their works in the manner in which such works can be used.[26]

One observation should be made about the issue of whether opening the use of the property to the public can be compelled. It seems clear that such regulation is clearly within the government's power when the property over which the road is to run was acquired by or under the government's eminent domain power. I question whether the government could compel a railroad to open its roads to the public without paying compensation when the property over which a railroad runs was not acquired by eminent domain (that is, a private railroad). Enthusiasts of the expansive definition of the commerce clause would have no problem saying that government could compel public use.

Soon the question was raised as to whether, at least as to exercises of eminent domain for these kinds of uses, the state could acquire an operating private road or toll bridge from one party and give it to another private party to own or operate. Any claim that this was a public use was quickly quashed.

> It is argued, that, if the State may take this bridge, it may transfer it to other individuals, under the same or a different charter. This the state cannot do. It would in effect be taking the property from A to convey it to B. The public purpose for which the power is exerted must be real, not pretended. If in the course of time the property, by a change of circumstances, should no longer be required for public use, it may be otherwise disposed of. But this is not likely to occur. ... If the use of the land taken by the public for a highway should be abandoned, it would revert to the original proprietor and owner of the fee.[27]

The last sentence quoted above most likely contemplates the situation in which the property taken for the road was an easement and not acquired in fee.

Like so many other holdings that properly applied the principles undergirding the takings clause, this holding was swept aside by later courts more insistent on deferring to legislatures.[28] Thus it was that in 1984 (a symbolic year), the Supreme Court, in *Hawaii Housing Authority v. Midkiff*,[29] sanctioned a scheme in which the state of Hawaii, deciding that it was unseemly for owners of large amounts of property to refuse to sell rental property to their lessees, devised a plan to force landowners to sell the leased land to their tenants. Clearly this transferred private property to private individuals, a fact that the *Midkiff* Court admitted as they labeled the action "a redistribution of fees simple."[30]

The Housing Authority's actions were justified by the Court as being for a "public purpose" because they benefited "the public." But these actions benefited the "public" only as *individuals*—individuals who wanted to buy the property they leased but whose lessors did not want to sell. This was in no way akin to the public transportation cases, in which the opportunity existed for any member of the public to take advantage of the property acquired on an equal and unhampered basis, coupled with a generalized enhancement of commerce and communication. There was, and could have been, no argument that the public needed to provide shelter for the homeless, for example, to prevent any one of a variety of public health and safety hazards that could arise therefrom. Every person who acquired property through the program was a tenant on the property. Tenants merely spent money each month on rent rather than paying a mortgage. Likewise, there was not even the argument that was successful in *Berman v. Parker*.[31] That case involved an urban renewal project, in which the actions complained of were taken as part of a generalized program to remove dangerous, unhealthy, and unsightly buildings and to replace them. The resulting development was expected to reduce crime and the factors that led to obsolescence and decay.

In short, Hawaii's program was no more than the taking of property "from A to convey to B" regardless of how many Bs and how few As were involved. While the justices were probably correct when they equated public purpose to public use in *Midkiff*, there is no doubt, if one is intellectually honest, that the action the Court sanctioned was *not* a public use within the meaning of that limitation in the takings clause. I seriously doubt that constitutional-era Americans—given all we know about their beliefs and attitudes—would have accepted the premise that a purpose is public simply because it benefits large numbers of individuals.

The truly central question in the debate over what is or is not a public use (which is really what these latter day cases illustrate) is much the same as in each other area of property and economic liberties law. Who gets to decide whether, in fact, a use is public or is a mere transfer from one private party to another? Because the Constitution assigns the role of constitutional guardian to the courts, that obligation should fall on the judiciary. The question of whether a use is truly public is a matter of constitutional fact. That is, whether the Constitution's limitations have been exceeded depends on the existence or nonexistence of that fact. If the legislature is to be the sole judge of whether a use is public, the Fifth Amendment is meaningless as a check on the legislative branch and on the popular passions that the Constitution was designed to control.

Certainly, earlier courts, such as the Supreme Court in *West River Bridge Company* quoted above, seemed to believe that the requirement of public use must be given substance and could not be avoided by mere labeling.[32] Similarly, Justice Holmes in *Mahon* had no difficulty giving the legislature's claim of public purpose close scrutiny. He struck down that part of the Kohler Act that he deemed to have a private purpose. Even one year later, in 1923, Justice Sanford, speaking for the Court in *Rindge Co. v. Los Angeles County*, refused to apply a statutory presumption of correctness of a legislative finding of public purpose. In his opinion, Sanford affirmed that "[t]he nature of a use, whether public or private, is ultimately a judicial question."[33] He was willing to give great, though not conclusive, weight to the judgment of a state *court* on the question, however. (The action complained of in *Rindge* was not federal.) He based this deference on the Court's knowledge of local conditions. We may question even that degree of deference, however, because local judges are supposed to base their judgments not on their own perceptions of local conditions in their everyday life but on the evidence presented to them. The reviewing Court can examine that evidence equally as well.

By the time of *Berman* (1954) and *Midkiff* (1984), however, any pretense by the judiciary that it would give meaningful scrutiny to legislative claims that their takings were for a public purpose was gone. The Courts merely declared that if the legislature says it, it must be so "unless it is shown to be an impossibility."[34] This standard seems even more lenient than the rational basis test discussed previously. The *Berman* and *Midkiff* Courts justified application of this test on the ground that to do otherwise "would result in courts deciding what is and what is not a governmental function."[35] The difficulty with this statement is that determining such functions is precisely the role of the courts under the provisions of the Constitution and the Bill of Rights. The *Midkiff* Court's attempt to find historical support by reference to statutes pertaining to removal of feudal incidents on property[36] is unavailing. While a full discussion of the flaws of the Court's reference is beyond the scope of this book, one simple fact is clear, the incidents of which the Court speaks barred the owners of the property to which they were attached from alienating the property, and the owners wanted to have that power. The property owners in *Midkiff* could sell. They just did not want to.

We should remember that courts have no apparent difficulty making such judgments when they define the right involved as being fundamental. In such cases, this kind of lax scrutiny is not found.

9

JUST COMPENSATION

THE CONCEPT OF JUST COMPENSATION

The issue of compensation is at the heart of the debate over recognition of property rights. It is not at the heart of the debate because there is any fundamental disagreement over the meaning of the term or the measure of compensation that is to apply. It is at the heart of the debate because the argument is constantly made by opponents of property rights that honoring the compensation requirement will make it all but impossible for government to function. For this reason, my discussion of the just compensation requirement will not focus on the details of the development of the law defining the proper measure of compensation to be paid once a taking is found. Instead, I will focus on the general concept of compensation and the mechanisms that may be used to provide compensation under the principles on which the takings clause rests.

The argument that adhering to constitutional guarantees will impair government efficiency is raised whenever the effect of a governmental action on individual liberty is at issue. This argument arises regardless of whether the right at issue is speech, religion, freedom from compelled testimony, due process, freedom from unreasonable searches and seizures, or any other constitutional right. Because of its superficial appeal, perhaps the most dangerous argument that can ever be raised is that governmental efficiency requires modifying constitutional guarantees. The U.S. Supreme Court has readily and repeatedly recognized the ubiquitous nature, fundamental fallacy, and great danger of this argument. For example, in *United States v. Lee*[1] the Court, when confronted with an argument that enforcing the Fifth Amendment would cause untold mischief, thoroughly rejected the claim.

> Hypothetical cases of great evils may be suggested by a particularly fruitful imagination in regard to almost every law upon which depend the rights of the individuals or the government, and if the existence of laws is to depend upon their capacity to withstand such criticism, the whole fabric of the law must fall.[2]

The *Lee* Court quickly recognized the slippery-slope character of such an argument. It also recognized the serious risk of the erosion of rights and liberties, as well as the severely heightened potential for tyranny if such arguments were accepted without reflection.

> The evils supposed to grow out of the possible interference with the exercise of the powers of the government essential to some of its most important operations, will be seen to be small indeed compared to this evil, and much diminished, if they do not wholly disappear, upon a recurrence to a few considerations.[3]

In many instances, modern courts have resisted the seductive nature of this argument and have held that efficiency, cost, and administrative convenience are insufficient reasons for ignoring or weakening constitutional guarantees.

In one case in which military dependents' benefits were at issue, *Frontiero v. Richardson*,[4] the Court refused to accept an invitation to permit governmental efficiency to interfere with the Court's concept of equal protection. The military would automatically provide benefits to male service members who claimed female dependents and those men would not have to demonstrate that the claimed dependent was truly dependent. The costs of investigating such claims was significantly greater than losses because of fraudulent claims. On the other hand, women service members were required to substantiate all claims that a male was a dependent because the costs of investigation were less than the amounts lost in fraud. This was certainly a rational assumption on which to base the rule, could be proven, and was intended to ensure cost-effective administration. The Court would not permit such claims of cost-effective administration to prevail, however. For the Court, at least, money was no object.

In the context of property rights and economic liberties, however, modern courts have unquestioningly accepted the efficiency argument, primarily because of their own notions of sound public policy. The California case of *Agins v. City of Tiburon*[5] is a classic case in point and is well worth a brief discussion.

Agins v. City of Tiburon

Donald and Bonnie Agins owned extremely valuable property on a hill in the City of Tiburon. The city wanted the property for a park, or at least wanted to keep it free of development because of its attractive nature. Tiburon had, in fact, instituted condemnation procedures at one point, but abandoned the condemnation attempt because the city decided it could not afford the property. Instead, it zoned the property to keep development to an absolute minimum. When the Aginses sued, alleging that the regulations deprived them of all economically viable use of their property, the California Supreme Court held that property owners could not obtain compensation even if the government's action was, in fact, sufficiently severe as to be a taking. Instead, said the Court, the Aginses were limited to asking the court to invalidate the offending regulation. The *Agins* majority made its determination not on constitutional principles but on public policy grounds.

Before addressing the real source of its opposition to the compensation obligation, the Court developed its own unique view of *Pennsylvania Coal Co. v. Mahon* in an attempt to avoid the clear language of the Fifth Amendment. The *Agins* Court depicted Justice Holmes's statement in *Mahon* that regulation "which goes too far ... will be recognized as a taking" as not meaning that compensation would be required. Instead, the Court said,

> This Supreme Court opinion [*Mahon*] has generated some confusion and has even been cited erroneously for the proposition that inverse condemnation is readily available as a remedy in zoning cases because of Justice Holmes' statement that "[t]he general rule at least is, that while property may be regulated to a certain extent, if regulation goes too far, it will be recognized as a taking." [cite omitted]. It is clear both from context and from the disposition in *Mahon*, however, that the term "taking" was used solely to indicate the limit by which the acknowledged social goal of land control could be achieved by regulation rather than by eminent domain.[6]

Of course, nothing of the kind was clear and the U.S. Supreme Court ultimately overruled *Agins*,[7] but not before considerable mischief had been done. The *Agins* Court tried to bolster its argument by saying that "[t]he high court [in *Mahon*] set aside the injunctive relief which had been granted by the Pennsylvania courts and declared void the exercise of police power which had limited the company's right to mine its land. The Court did not attempt, however, to transmute the illegal governmental infringement into an exercise of eminent domain and the possibility of compensation was not even considered." The *Agins* majority was suggesting that the *Mahon* Court, had it truly meant that regulations can cause a taking within the meaning of the Fifth Amendment, would simply have ordered compensation. This is not supportable. What was clear was that the *Mahon* Court did find that a taking, within the meaning of the Fifth Amendment, had occurred, and they invalidated the taking because the taking was not for a public use. The taking was instead a transfer of a private property right to another private party. As such, that portion of the Kohler Act was an invalid exercise of eminent domain power.

> If we were called upon to deal with the plaintiffs' position alone, we should think it clear that the statute does not disclose a public interest sufficient to warrant so extensive a destruction of the defendant's constitutionally protected rights.[8]

The reason for this was obvious.

> This is the case of a single private house. No doubt there is a public interest even in this, as there is in every purchase and sale and in all that happens within the commonwealth. Some existing rights may be modified even in such a case. [Cites omitted.] But usually in ordinary private affairs the public interest does not warrant much of this kind of interference. A source of damage to such a house is not a *public* nuisance even if similar damage is inflicted on others in different places. The damage is not common or public.[9]

This holding raises the issue of the difference between the due process and the takings clauses, a difference that seems to have been lost on most, but not all, courts. The due process clause may be envisioned as a proposition of "Can the government do it at all." If the governmental action fails to meet procedural requirements, is arbitrary or irrational, or violates any of a number of substantive rights, the government may not undertake the action at all and may be liable in damages. The just compensation clause, however, comes into play only if the government's action was otherwise permissible; that is to say, the action was authorized by some governmental authority, such as the commerce clause, *and* it satisfies due process. If these two conditions are met, then the government may undertake the action. However, whether the government must pay compensation is a separate question; post-*Mahon* courts will not invalidate governmental actions amounting to a taking unless the government refuses to pay compensation.[10]

To the extent that the due process and takings clauses overlap, this is so only because the "law of the land" includes the requirement that the public pay for otherwise legitimate takings. A refusal to pay is, therefore, violative of due process. Nevertheless, the obligation to pay must be considered separately. The difference between the two clauses is well demonstrated in *Nollan v. California Coastal Commission* and by *Department of Agriculture and Consumer Services v. Mid-Florida Growers, Inc.*[11] In the latter case, the Florida Supreme Court upheld the authority of the Florida Department of Agriculture to order the destruction of trees that were not infected by citrus canker, so the department could be on the safe side in its pest control program.

The Court remarked that the department could rationally have decided to play it safe, but declared that, nevertheless, Florida had to pay under the takings clause.

Despite the *Agins* Court's claim to the contrary, it was not necessary for the *Mahon* Court to either enjoin the Kohler Act or order compensation as to that portion of the act said to protect public property because (while Pennsylvania had joined the action and raised the question of whether the Kohler Act would cause a taking if enforced to protect public property) the Act was not being enforced to protect public property in *Mahon*. The Court did reach the question of whether the Kohler Act would cause a taking even where the protection of public property was involved, however, because Pennsylvania raised the question and the Court believed it was best to dispose of that question for all time rather than to wait for further litigation to raise the question again. The Court held that

> The rights of the public in a street purchased or laid out by eminent domain are those that it has paid for. If in any case its representatives have been so short sighted as to acquire only surface rights without the right of support, we see no more authority for supplying the latter without compensation than there was for taking the right of way in the first place and refusing to pay for it because the public wanted it very much. The protection of private property in the Fifth Amendment presupposes that it is wanted for public use, but provides that it shall not be taken for such use without compensation. A similar assumption is made in the decisions upon the Fourteenth Amendment.[12]

There was no logic or history behind the *Agins* Court's assertions that the remedy for a regulatory taking is limited to invalidation of the offending regulation. If regulations can rise to the level of a taking within the meaning of the term, as originally intended, then the express language of the takings clause unequivocally requires compensation. If property was taken, it was taken. Giving it back after using it for a time does not change the nature of the government's action. Numerous cases involving physical invasion or occupancy attest to the well-established principle that a taking remains a taking, however temporary, whether accomplished by an express exercise of the power of eminent domain, such as the acquisition of a leasehold interest,[13] or by inverse condemnation.[14]

What the *Agins* Court stated next, however, revealed that its decision did not rest on an analysis of takings clause principles but rather on the Court's own view of the effect enforcing the constitutionally mandated remedy would have on public policy goals it favored.

> We are persuaded by various policy considerations to the view that inverse condemnation is an inappropriate and undesirable remedy in

cases in which unconstitutional regulation is alleged. The expanding developments of our cities and suburban areas coupled with a growing awareness of the necessity to preserve our natural resources, including the land around us, has resulted in attitudes toward the regulation of land use.

* * * * * * *

In combination, the need for preserving a degree of freedom in the land-use planning function, and the inhibiting financial force which inheres in the inverse condemnation remedy, persuade us that on balance mandamus or declaratory relief rather than inverse condemnation is the appropriate relief under the circumstances.[15]

The *Agins* Court, in other words, had decided that the express command of the Fifth Amendment was an impediment to achieving public goals it valued. Enforcing the constitutional remedy of payment for a regulatory taking, in the Court's mind at least, "would have a chilling effect upon the exercise of police regulatory powers at a local level." The Court view was that the "threat of unanticipated financial liability will intimidate legislative bodies and will discourage the implementation of strict or innovative planning measures in favor of measures which are less stringent, more traditional, and fiscally safe." Judicial enforcement of the compensation remedy "would pose yet another threat to legislative control over appropriate land-use determinations."[16]

At a minimum, these are peculiar statements for a body to make when it is charged with protecting constitutional rights. A major purpose of constitutional provisions is to limit governmental power and to chill excessive governmental zeal, however well- or ill-intentioned, a fact seemingly ignored by the Court. The *Agins* Court seemed to feel that its role was to protect legislative bodies against a court-perceived inability on the part of legislatures to adequately assess the risk that their actions may have financial consequences. This role is the opposite of ensuring that constitutional guarantees are observed. Nevertheless, the *Agins* Court insisted that constitutional guarantees could not be allowed to stand in the way of what it saw as legislative prerogatives.

> We envisage that the availability of an inverse condemnation remedy in these situations would pose yet another threat to legislative control over appropriate land-use determinations. It has been noted that "[t]he weighing of costs and benefits is essentially a legislative process. In enacting a zoning ordinance, the legislative body assesses the desirability of a program on the assumption that compensation will not be required to achieve the objectives of that ordinance.[17]

The Court did not explain why it should indulge the legislature in that assumption, however, especially given that it could easily remedy that defect in legislative reasoning by putting legislative and administrative bodies on notice that they may have to pay for their regulatory actions. Had the Court done so, legislative and administrative bodies could carry out appropriate cost–benefit analyses. The Court was not finished, however. It continued,

> Determining that a particular land-use control requires compensation is an appropriate function of the judiciary, whose function includes protection of individuals against excesses of government. But it seems a usurpation of legislative power for a court to force compensation. Invalidation, rather than forced compensation, would seem to be the more expedient means of remedying legislative excesses.[18]

The Court again failed to explain why this was so. Clearly, legislative bodies could, if they chose, factor into their decision making the possibility that in at least some cases a successful action could be brought that would require the government to pay compensation. Then the legislature would have had every opportunity to exercise its judgment in deciding to proceed in the face of its risk assessment.

The Court went on to express its concern that the legislature was not the only body that could not be trusted to exercise adequate judgment in determining whether to take the risk that any given action might result in the government's being required to compensate a property owner. The Court argued that the people (although apparently competent to vote on spending initiatives) were not competent to adequately assess financial risk in property regulation.

> Other budgetary consequences reveal themselves when the land use control is exercised by means of the initiative. "Legislation in the nature of zoning can be and has been enacted by the people through a direct initiative. Are the voters, through the initiative power, also to have this unwelcome power to inadvertently commit funds from the public treasury? The logical extension of requiring compensation for the mere enactment of a harsh zoning measure indicates that the answer would be in the affirmative. The potential for fiscal chaos would be great if this were the result" [cite omitted].[19]

Other observations present themselves. First, the *Agins* Court declared that legislative bodies have the responsibility for weighing costs and benefits, which we might assume includes possible costs and benefits. Then the Court demonstrated that it believes that legislative bodies are incapable of doing so and need the Court to protect them from themselves. Thereby, the Court usurps the very function that it has identified as being a legislative one. Second, in making this argument, the *Agins* Court missed an important function of the takings clause that will be discussed in greater detail below. For now, I will say only (a) that resources, whether privately or publicly owned, are not infinite and (b) that so long as the public thinks it is acquiring private resources for public use without cost, it will not have the incentive necessary to ensure that it adequately considers whether those resources are better put to one use or another.

By bringing the cost of acquiring the resource into the picture, the takings clause forces the decision-maker, whether a legislative or administrative body or the public at large, to perform a more careful assessment. The *Agins* Court argued that the fact that "the legislative body assesses the desirability of a program on the assumption that compensation will not be required to achieve the objectives of that ordinance" should permit the Court to indulge that assumption. This argument makes little sense.

The effect of such an attitude by the courts was accurately forecast by Justice Clark, who dissented in *Agins*. His observation is pertinent to any claim that governmental efficacy will be harmed by respecting individual rights. Unlike the majority, Justice William Clark concerned himself with the constitutional rights of affected parties and understood that invalidation of the "offending" regulation would be "a nonremedy for an aggrieved [property owner]."[20] During the substantial amount of time, usually years, it takes to challenge a regulation, the owner loses use of the property and incurs considerable legal and other costs such as consultants fees, interest, taxes, and lost opportunity costs. Even if the property owner wins, the involved government body can (and usually does) modify the ordinance or other regulation and reimpose it. Property owners rarely, if ever, have the financial or emotional resources to sustain themselves through multiple challenges to the same essential program. The *Agins* decision enhanced the likelihood of such successive measures because the government faces no financial risk for imposing such measures. As Justice Clark observed in dissent, "Many landowners—particularly small ones—will be economically unable to challenge even a confiscatory enactment, being compelled to walk away from their properties."[21]

Moreover, there are more practical considerations and disturbing consequences than the potential for government to inadvertently acquire financial obligations. Exercise of the land use control power without the restraints imposed by observing constitutional requirements will ultimately affect people other than the individual property owner. Use of such power deprives those who could otherwise be property owners of that opportunity, a particularly egregious outcome given present day concerns over the availability of adequate housing and the lack of opportunity for economic advancement by minorities and people with little or moderate means. Schemes like the one in Tiburon "will price properties within [the city's] control out of reach of most people. Only the most wealthy will be able to afford purchase of and construction on lands in such areas."[22]

This latter observation touches on at least two important and sensitive points. The first is the potential for unscrutinized property regulation to be used to discriminate against economically disadvantaged or minority people as well as people who displease the relevant agencies. The second is the tendency for such regulations (when adopted without the careful consideration that enforcing the compensation obligation would encourage) to have serious adverse effects on important public goals. I will address both of these issues in more detail below.

The result of allowing schemes such at that created by Tiburon in *Agins* is to disproportionately benefit "that wealthy landowner, whose home will be surrounded by open space, unobstructed view, and unpolluted atmosphere."[23]

The true tragedy in the *Agins* decision is that it was based on a flawed premise: that preserving the individual's right to compensation is incompatible with effective governmental decision-making processes. First, of course, the fact that compensation may be due is a powerful incentive for governmental bodies to carefully tailor their actions to actual needs. This incentive prevents wasteful use of public and private resources, a fact that will be discussed in more detail in Part III. In this regard, the takings clause will make government *more* cost efficient, not less. It also encourages regulatory bodies not to unreasonably delay decisions, again aiding efficiency.

Second, and most important for this discussion, adherence to the obligation to pay just compensation when property is taken by regulation does not necessarily require an outlay of treasury funds. More innovative mechanisms are possible if governmental bodies would exercise the same degree of creativity to meet the compensation obligation as they use to avoid it.

ALTERNATIVE COMPENSATION

The second edition of Johnson's *Dictionary of the English Language*, issued in 1755, defined "just" as meaning "exact; proper; accurate; ... equally retributed ... complete without superfluity or defect" and "compensation" as meaning "something equivalent; amends." Precisely these concepts underlay the takings clause. The authorities on which the Fifth Amendment was based, as well as discussions in the Constitutional Convention, the ratification debates, various acts of Congress, and the postratification courts, demonstrate this fact beyond question. The Northwest Ordinance, for example, specifically required that "*full* compensation" be made for the taking of "any person's property, or ...

particular services."[24] This position was in full accord with Blackstone's admonition that the absolute rights of property were to be maintained by paying compensation for any interference with those rights, even if the deprivation of any right is accomplished "for the general good of the whole community."[25]

The compensation owed, said Blackstone and his latter day adherents, is "a *full* indemnification and *equivalent* for the injury thereby sustained."[26] However, nothing in any writing or discussion requires that the compensation be in cash, although that was the usual method of providing compensation. The most fruitful area for exploration in considering the takings clause is the question of what coin must be used to provide compensation.

Reciprocal or Compensating Benefits

Various mechanisms are available to provide compensation, a fact that courts have at least dimly recognized. However, they have groped toward this concept more in an attempt to find that no taking has occurred in the first place rather than in consideration of whether there was a taking but compensation had already been paid. This approach generally can be found in court attempts to define and apply such concepts as "reciprocal benefits," also known as "compensating benefits," in cases such as those cited in *Mahon*.

> It is true that in *Plymouth Coal Co. v. Pennsylvania*, 232 U.S. 531, it was held competent for the legislature to require a pillar of coal to be left along the line of adjoining property, that, with the pillar on the other side of the line, would be a barrier sufficient for the safety of the employees of either mine in case the other should be abandoned and allowed to fill with water. But that was a requirement for the safety of employees invited into the mine, and secured an average reciprocity of advantage that has been recognized as a justification of various laws.[27]

It is worth noting here that Oliver Wendell Holmes, author of the *Mahon* opinion, had not intended to suggest that "average reciprocity of advantage" was a valid general rule for avoiding compensation, but he used it, as he later explained, only to "explain a certain class of cases."[28]

In *Plymouth Coal*, each mine was protected against flooding by requiring each mine owner to leave a pillar of coal in place. That which was "taken" by requiring that the last few feet of coal stay in place was repaid by requiring the owner of the adjoining mine to do the same. This requirement gave mine owners insurance against flooding that they would not otherwise be entitled to, and the value of that insurance was at least equal to the value of the coal left in place. As the brief for the coal company in *Mahon* pointed out, the general practice then was for the mine owners to agree to remove the pillar, and each miner would get the economic benefit from the coal.

The concept of compensating benefits is a valid one if properly applied in the correct situations. There are two general flaws in application, however. The first is in applying the concept to determine whether a taking has, in fact, occurred. In reality, the compensating benefits doctrine actually deals with the issue of whether just compensation has been given. This flaw is more than quibbling over form. Judicial insistence on using the doctrine to determine whether a taking has occurred unnecessarily clouds the issue of what constitutes a taking and causes needless confusion. In most cases involving reciprocal benefits, the proper way to state the Court's conclusion is not that a taking has not occurred but that just compensation was inherent in the regulatory scheme.

I do not agree that most cases that found no taking would have been justified in saying that the "reciprocal benefits" were truly reciprocal or had adequately compensated the owner. In fact, I would say the opposite. Courts far more often are incorrect in so assessing the regulatory scheme. This point is amply demonstrated by the *Penn Central* dissent, discussed *supra*, involving New York City's landmark preservation ordinance in which the majority claimed that owners of Penn Central Station had not suffered a taking under the ordinance because there was a reciprocal benefit to landmark designation.

> Of the over one million buildings and structures in the city of New York, appellees have singled out 400 for designation as official landmarks. The owner of a building might initially be pleased that his property has been chosen ... for such a singular distinction. But he may well discover, as appellant Penn Central Transportation Co. did here, that the landmark designation imposes upon him a substantial cost, with little or no offsetting benefit except for the honor of the designation. The question in this case is whether the cost associated with the city of New York's desire to preserve a limited number of "landmarks" within its borders must be borne by all the taxpayers or whether it can instead be imposed entirely on the owners of the individual properties.[29]

The second flaw in applying the reciprocal benefits principle is that courts that even come close to considering the issue assume, without analysis, that the reciprocal benefits are equal to that which was taken. In fact, they rarely are. At a minimum, if the doctrine is to truly fit the purpose of ensuring just compensation, it must be understood to require that the affected party be at least as well off after the governmental action as it was before the action. At present, the test of reciprocal benefits is more often treated as being satisfied if the property owner gets any degree of benefit greater than zero. This notion is at odds with the originally intended requirement that compensation be a full and complete indemnification for that taken. This is not to say that the equivalence must be calculated to the last decimal place, at least where not feasible, but it most certainly requires that a gap be filled between the value of the reciprocating benefit and the value of that taken.

Justice Brennan's dissent in the 1987 Supreme Court case of *Nollan v. California Coastal Commission*, discussed below, is a prime example of the approach taken by those courts that assume that any benefit resulting from governmental action entirely and automatically offsets any loss to the property owner. The Coastal Commission attempted to impose a condition on granting a coastal development permit that would require the Nollans to dedicate an easement across their private beach to allow the public to cross their property on the way from a public beach south of the Nollans' property to one north of their property in exchange for allowing the Nollans to replace a dilapidated rental bungalow with a liveable residence. The Nollans ultimately refused, claiming that the condition was a taking. The majority of the justices agreed with the Nollans.

In his dissent, Justice Brennan argued that since other property owners had given an identical lateral easement across their private beaches, the Nollans received a counter-benefit by being allowed to walk across their neighbor's property.[30] Further, he argued, the Nollans also received an offsetting benefit since they were allowed to build a livable residence on the property, which he clearly did not consider a right, thus enhancing their property's value. The dissent was not correct, however, for two reasons other than that the right to build a house is not a government-bestowed benefit. The first is that the commission should not be able to take advantage of the fact that it was able to successfully extort, as the Court put it, such an easement from others to justify further extortions. The second reason, more pertinent to this discussion, is that the dissent missed the point that persons other than the Nollans' neighbors will also—and in the real world will most likely be the only ones to—use the easement across the Nollans' and their neighbors' property. Therefore, the benefit is not truly reciprocal. Also, it is doubtful that the Nollans, or any other private beach owner, felt especially privileged at being given the opportunity to walk to the nearest public beach.

Compensation in Exaction Cases

Nollan is an exaction case. In exaction cases, a governmental body requires property owners to provide some property or other concession in exchange for a permit to undertake the requested use of their own property. Most often, exactions occur in land use cases, or when a permit is requested pursuant to Section 404 of the Clean Water Act in the "wetlands" preservation context.[31]

In the typical land use exaction case, the permitting body requires the property owner to donate land for a public facility such as a park, hiking trail, school, firehouse, or police station, or to provide money for some municipal service or other. Often, as the *Nollan* Court stated, the reputedly "voluntary" donation is acquired by a none-too-subtle form of extortion. The justification for the exaction is generally that the development will put such an additional strain on community services or resources that it is only fair that the property owner provide for the additional need—a proposition innocuous in itself, but deadly in practice.

In reality, most often there is no close relationship between the likely impact of a proposed use and the dedication or exaction imposed on allowing that use. In some cases, there is no relationship at all between actual impacts and conditions imposed. In other cases, the exaction or dedication is disproportionate to actual impacts, even if only roughly calculated. In those cases in which there is no relationship or in which the required dedication or exaction is disproportionate to actual impacts on public facilities, the imposed dedication or exaction actually bestows benefits on existing residents and should create an obligation in those residents to compensate the property owner for what they have received. For example, if property owners seeking to develop their property are required to dedicate land for school facilities that will serve not only the new residents but also the existing residents by relieving the burden on preexisting facilities, those developers should be compensated for the property dedicated to the extent that the existing residents will benefit. The same should apply if the school facilities will benefit future residents of other existing or future developments. Similarly, if landowners must dedicate a park, hiking trails, pedestrian walkways, or bicycle paths that will be used by more people than the residents of the new development, which is usually the case, then that requirement should oblige payment to the owners to the extent that dedication of that land exceeds the actual burden that the development creates on public resources.*

---

* As I will discuss in detail in the next chapter, requiring owners to dedicate land or pay an exaction for the impact of their activities on public facilities is different from requiring owners to fulfill such conditions on the ground that their use of their property will have an impact on the resources present on their own property. Yet dedication or exaction conditions are often imposed on landowners for just that reason. Landowners are frequently, if not invariably, required to pay fees or dedicate land as "mitigation compensation" in the context of the Endangered Species Act, for example. The justification offered for such conditions is that the owner's land serves as actual or potential habitat for some endangered plant or animal species. In such cases, some segment of society values the owner's property as a wildlife refuge and insists that the owners must, if they wish to use that property, acquire some other property and turn it into a habitat for the species. The very notion that owners must compensate the government for being allowed to use their own land turns the just compensation clause on its head.

On the other hand, requiring a property owner to construct a sewer system that clearly serves only the residents of a proposed development should not give rise to an obligation to pay the developer compensation. The dedication serves only the new homes, enhances their value, and covers no more than the impact of that development—and only that development—on community-owned resources.

Mechanisms other than cash can be used to provide compensation. Many states and the federal government have substantial public land reserves and are capable of working equivalent land transfers when they wish to acquire property for such purposes as wetlands preservation, endangered species habitat, open space, or recreational resources. The acquisition of easements instead of fee simple interests or of temporary rights instead of permanent interests can reduce costs while providing flexibility. More careful land use planning, which is tailored to specific impacts on truly public resources (as opposed to resources that the public may covet but which are currently owned by private parties), may avoid takings liability for regulatory action altogether. Such planning will do this either by preventing the action from rising to the level of a taking in the first place or by reducing or eliminating the amount of compensation due.

TRANSFERABLE DEVELOPMENT RIGHTS—PAYING WITH STOLEN MONEY

One noncash compensatory scheme advocated by many land use planners, the so-called transferable development right (TDR) deserves particular mention as an example of what cannot be done in the search for flexibility. The basic concept of a TDR is that property owners who are not allowed to fully develop their property because of a government-imposed limitation on its use are "compensated" for that taken by allowing the owners to exceed development limitations on a second property. Aggrieved property owners may or may not own the second property at the time that their rights in the first property were taken.

The second property is generally burdened with a restriction of either the same or another type as the first property. Thus, for example, the owners of property being developed for residential purposes subjected to an extremely low-density restriction are compensated with a TDR that allows them a bonus density on land similarly restricted elsewhere. Similarly, as in *Penn Central*, an owner of valuable air rights that have been restricted in a manner sufficient to amount to a taking may be given a TDR allowing that owner to avoid a height restriction elsewhere. The question that immediately comes to mind when considering TDRs of this nature is how allowing a bonus density or abrogation of a height restriction can be valid if the restriction on density or height was appropriately tailored to a governmental need to begin with.

The concept of the TDR appears relatively simple, but it can swiftly become enormously complex. The TDR is subject to inherent limitations and flaws that make it an unworkable and even dangerous concept.

First, one jurisdiction, such as a city or county, cannot give a TDR that is effective outside its boundaries, that is, in a different city or county. If aggrieved property owners do not already own other property in the jurisdiction granting the TDR, they must buy another piece of property subject to some limitation that the TDR can be used to remove (which adds to the cost, offsetting the value of the TDR), or they must sell the TDR to a third party. There may or may not be a market for the TDR. To the extent that there is a market, the TDR's value on that market may be far less than the loss suffered by its owner from not being able to use the right on the property to which it was originally attached. If so, and if we assume it was valid compensation to begin with (which is not a fair assumption), the TDR is not just compensation as mandated by the Constitution. On the other hand, the aggrieved party may already own a property in the jurisdiction to which the TDR may be applied, but the increase in value of the second property is not sufficient to completely make up for the diminished value of the first property. If so, just compensation has again been denied unless the lost value is supplemented.

For example, in the first situation, owner A has two properties, Blackacre and Whiteacre, each burdened with a potential density restriction. A applies to develop Whiteacre but is limited to an extremely low density. A is given a TDR allowing use of Blackacre at a higher density than would otherwise be allowed. The value of the TDR can be ascertained with some degree of certainty, and A can determine whether he has been adequately compensated for his loss on Whiteacre. (Although, by the time A is in a position to develop Blackacre, the dynamics of the local market may have changed sufficiently so that the TDR's value has been either diminished or increased, adding uncertainty.) Thus, A does not incur additional costs in acquiring a second property to which he can attach the TDR (which cost must be subtracted from the value of the TDR to determine A's net compensation) nor is he subjected to the uncertainties of the marketplace.

In the second situation, A owns only Blackacre and must spend money to acquire property on which the TDR may be used, or must sell the TDR. In either case, the value of the TDR is rendered speculative; therefore, the TDR is inadequate and unjust compensation. If this discussion makes the concept of TDRs seem fuzzy, that is because it is fuzzy.

Others have struggled to explain this problem. Judge Breitel of New York, for example, explained it this way:

> In an attempt to preserve the rights, they were severed from the real property and made transferable to another section of mid-Manhattan in the city, but not to any particular parcel or place. There was thus created floating development rights, utterly unusable until they could be attached to some accommodating real property, available by happenstance of prior ownership, or by grant, purchase, or devise, and subject to the contingent approvals of administrative agencies. In such case, the development rights, disembodied abstractions of man's ingenuity, float in a limbo until restored to reality by reattachment to tangible real property. ... [T]he development rights are a double abstraction until they are actually attached to a receiving parcel, yet to be identified, acquired, and subject to the contingent future approvals of administrative agencies, events which may never happen because of the exigencies of the market and the contingencies and exigencies of administrative action. The problem with this arrangement ... is that it fails to assure preservation of the very real economic value of the development rights as they existed when still attached to the underlying property. ... By compelling the owner to enter an unpredictable real estate market to find a suitable receiving lot for the rights, or a purchaser who would then share the same interest in using additional development rights, the amendment renders uncertain and thus severely impairs the value of the development rights before they were severed.

The second flaw in the TDR concept is even more unsettling. Ultimately, the concept of a TDR rests on an invalid premise: that one may compensate a property owner by taking with one hand and giving back with the other, or worse, by taking from one person to compensate another person with what amounts to stolen money.

This scenario is not difficult to imagine. The governing authority simply makes a practice of heavily restricting property use (such as by decreasing allowable density, imposing height restrictions, or designating more property as open space). Then it later reduces or removes the restriction on one of the two parcels of property as compensation for retaining the restriction on the other.

It is this concept that makes the TDR dangerous by encouraging the government to engage in its very own pyramid scheme. The public takes a right in at least two pieces of property. Then it gives the right back in one property as compensation for retaining the right it took in the second property. Unless the aggrieved party owned both pieces of property at the same time, the rights transferred to owner A are likely to have been taken from owner B. Such "robbery under the forms of law"[32] is not to be tolerated. We must find other ways to preserve the constitutionally mandated balance between private rights and public needs, a balance that requires just compensation in some form.

The *Nollan* Court expressed similar reservations in a related context. The

Court was faced with the Coastal Commission's argument that the imposition of a condition on granting a use or building permit was a voluntary exchange because the owner was free to accept or reject the condition. Of course, rejection meant either a new round of administrative proceedings (adding more delay and cost) or, more realistically, denial of the permit. The Court termed this practice an out-and-out plan of extortion and observed that:

> One would expect that a regime in which this kind of leveraging of the police power is allowed would produce stringent land-use regulation which the State then waives to accomplish other purposes, leading to lesser realization of the land-use goals purportedly sought to be served than would result from more lenient (but *nontradeable*) development restrictions. Thus, the importance of the purpose underlying the prohibition not only does not *justify* the imposition of unrelated conditions for eliminating the prohibitions, but positively militates against the practice.[33]

10

PROPERTY RIGHTS-DEFEATING DOCTRINES

> *I have often thought that old Harlan's decision in* Mugler
> v. Kansas *was pretty fishy.*
>
> Oliver Wendell Holmes[1]

In addition to eroding the basic concepts of the takings clause, modern courts have created two other doctrines. When combined with the constitutionally unwarranted deference given by the courts to the actions of legislative and administrative bodies, these two doctrines have rendered the takings clause virtually meaningless, even within the confines of its altered definitions. The first of these doctrines is the so-called police power exception. The second is the doctrine of "ripeness" or "exhaustion of administrative remedies."

THE MYTH OF THE POLICE POWER EXCEPTION

The police power of the government is its general power to act to protect the health, safety, and welfare of the people.* In the states, according to generally accepted theory, the police power is inherent and unlimited except as limited by a state's own laws and constitution or by principles of natural law. For this reason, state governments are considered general governments. The federal government, on the other hand, has no police

---

* In former times, the police power was said to exist to include the power to safeguard the health, safety, welfare, and *morals* of the people. The term morals has been dropped in most modern formulations.

power, in theory. It is, therefore, a limited government and has only those powers expressly granted to it by the Constitution. The Tenth Amendment was added to make this clear.

In real terms, however, the obverse is the case. Early on, the Supreme Court interpreted two critical provisions of the Constitution—the commerce clause and the necessary and proper clause[2]—much more broadly than was ever intended. The Court's interpretation gives the federal government the virtual equivalent of the police power and, by virtue of the supremacy clause, allows it to override state decisions if it so chooses.*

Since everything the government does is ultimately a police power exercise, it is not hard to see the practical consequences of a doctrine exempting exercises of the police power, or its federal equivalent, from the dictates of the takings clause. *No* governmental action could *ever* constitute a taking. The action would either be irrational, and therefore invalid under modern reinterpretations of the due process clause (which would never happen under the rational basis test) or it would be rational and the government need not pay. Clearly, the Constitution was not intended to permit such a result, nor is it what generations of precedent have established as the law.

The historical and constitutional limitation of the use of property is narrow. The government can step in only to prevent affirmative and significant harm amounting to a public nuisance. The scope of this limitation was confirmed by *Mahon*. And yet, even after *Mahon*, the notion became increasingly popular that any action taken pursuant to the police power could not be a taking. This notion, which became known as the police power exception, eventually became firmly entrenched in cases like *Goldblatt v. Hempstead*.[3]

Goldblatt is a perfect example of the lengths to which the deference given to legislative and administrative actions, when combined with the breadth of the police power exception, goes to defeat clearly established property rights. The Goldblatt property was a quarry that, like most such quarries, had a deep pool of water at its bottom. The Town of Hempstead forbade further quarrying on the site, ostensibly to prevent children from drowning in the deep water. Goldblatt complained that the Town of Hempstead had taken its property because quarrying was the only use to which the property could be put. Goldblatt argued that the town could have required any number of other steps to protect children. These other options

---

* The supremacy clause is found at Article VI. It provides, "This Constitution, and the Laws of the United States which shall be made in pursuance thereof; and all treaties made, or which shall be made, under the Authority of the United States, shall be the supreme Law of the Land, and the Judges in every State shall be bound thereby, any Thing in the Constitution or Laws of any State to the contrary notwithstanding."

would work to protect the children and would leave the owners with the existing, economically viable use of the property. Hempstead could, for instance, have required effective fences or around-the-clock security guards. It was clear that preventing Goldblatt from adding a few more feet of depth to its already deep quarry would have little, if any, impact on the rate of drownings in the quarry. Nevertheless, the *Goldblatt* Court held that no taking had occurred because the town's determination that banning further quarrying would keep children from drowning was a rational conclusion, or at least was not wholly irrational.

The attractions of a police power exception are obvious. Since virtually any action can be justified as being for the public health, safety, welfare, or morals of the people, the public can easily acquire resources that clearly would have required compensation to private property owners under traditional takings rules. This excuse is being used with disheartening frequency. Local land use planning bodies customarily require property owners to dedicate land for a variety of traditional public uses, such as parks, roads, schools, wildlife refuges (presently called "habitats"), and other public amenities on the theory that any development imposes burdens on existing facilities.

One problem already noted is that such exactions consistently exceed any actual burden posed by the individual development and are sometimes entirely unrelated to any impact of the given development. Planning agencies have demanded, for example, that a property owner who wants to renovate a factory construct a bicycle pathway, although renovating the factory did not generate bicycle traffic or otherwise create a need for such a pathway. The federal government does likewise in its administration of Section 404 of the federal Clean Water Act, which I will discuss in more detail later. Another problem I will examine is that the impacted facilities are often privately owned resources and not public facilities at all.

The source of the difficulty, as in other aspects of takings law, lies in the judiciary's reluctance to exercise its role as constitutional guardian and in the individual judge's own concepts of proper public policy. The judiciary has been, by and large, a champion of such governmental activities as land use planning, environmental protection, and provision of housing. These are not unworthy goals in themselves, but it is not the province of courts to decide whether these are worthy goals. In this, the courts are correct. It *is* their province, however, to determine whether the means chosen to accomplish those goals comport with the dictates of the Constitution.

By creating a police power exception to the Fifth Amendment and a deferential attitude toward governmental actions, courts have avoided having to take positions that might interfere with what their judges conceive of as good governmental policy. To the extent that the collective attitude of any governmental branch can be analyzed, it appears that the judiciary at large is concerned that (a) requiring the government to pay compensation might cripple the government's ability, and therefore willingness, to undertake such programs; and (b) ruling otherwise will invalidate actions the courts believe desirable. This latter concern, if it is a belief held by members of the judiciary, is a particularly unfortunate one. Unless the action falls afoul of the requirement that a taking be for public and not private use, a governmental action is not invalid unless government refuses to pay in some acceptable manner.

If there is an exception to the just compensation principle, it must be found in those cases in which the individual's property use actually does amount to a public nuisance; that is, that the use results in an actual, significant, and demonstrable harm to a significant proportion of the general public. Harm must be narrowly defined for these purposes. We have already seen how easy it is to change definitions. It is not hard to imagine that virtually anything may be called a harm, since virtually every human activity will affect some other person in a way that the other person would prefer not to be affected. To characterize such adverse effects as a nuisance for takings purposes would nullify the takings clause, which would be an indefensible result.

A complete discussion of the nuances and subtleties of nuisance law is beyond the scope of this book, although nuisance law itself raises many questions, some of constitutional dimensions. For example, one such question involves an historically recent doctrine: people accused of maintaining a nuisance cannot use the defense, however true, that their activity was not a nuisance until the complaining party moved next door (a defense called "coming to the nuisance"). The following typical situation illustrates this doctrine. A person operates a private heliport well away from any residential or other commercial enterprises. The heliport, as might be expected, is noisy, with helicopters regularly taking off and landing. Then a developer constructs an apartment complex next door. The heliport's new neighbors complain about the helicopter noises and demand that the heliport be shut down and that the owner compensate them for the "damages" resulting from the noise. Modern courts would find the heliport operation to be a nuisance, notwithstanding the fact that the neighbors decided to move next door knowing that the heliport existed and could easily have anticipated the present problems and that the heliport might increase operations in the future.

In discussing the nuisance exception, we should examine a minimum of three particular questions. The first question is, Who should determine whether a property use is a public nuisance so that no compensation should be paid for taking what amounts to a negative easement? The second is, What constitutes a nuisance sufficient to bring such an exception into play? The third is related to the second: What is the breadth of the exception?

The answer to the first question is straightforward, or should be. In all other cases in which the constitutionality of a governmental action rests on the existence or absence of specific facts (called constitutional facts), the judiciary has recognized that it has the ultimate responsibility for determining whether those facts exist. That obligation was placed on the judiciary by the Constitution. If the Constitution is to have any meaning, courts cannot extend deference to the decision of the legislative or administrative body as to the existence of constitutional facts. In the context of the takings clause, that means that the Court cannot properly defer to the judgment of the legislative or administrative body that made the initial determination of nuisance. In some cases, however, the judiciary did abandon that role and improperly deferred to the judgment of the legislature on that issue. *Mugler v. Kansas*[4] (referred to by Justice Holmes in the quote at the beginning of this chapter) was just such a case and is often cited for the proposition that a nuisance exception exists.

In *Mugler*, the owner of a brewery sued for a taking of the brewery when Kansas declared potable alcohol to be a noxious substance. The Supreme Court deferred to that judgment. To defer to such administrative or legislative judgments where the issue is one of constitutional fact, however, is not only constitutionally indefensible, it encourages governmental bodies to engage in the labeling game just described, a game at which those bodies are particularly adept. I am not suggesting that the Court need not have deferred to the legislature's judgment about *whether* to ban alcohol, only that it could not constitutionally defer to the legislature's decision on whether alcohol constituted a public nuisance for the purposes of deciding if compensation was due. The two inquiries are not identical for constitutional purposes.

Answers to the second and third questions are more complex. In most areas of constitutional law, mere administrative convenience is insufficient to support an action that intrudes on constitutionally protected rights. When the rights involved are those deemed fundamental by the courts, the government must, as previously described, demonstrate that its interest is compelling or, in some formulations, significant. It must also show that its actions are closely tailored to protecting the governmental interest and that they do not unduly intrude on the rights involved.

There is, however, no constitutional principle or historic basis for applying any different standard when property rights or economic liberties are at issue. If courts apply, as they should, a unified constitutional rights approach to property rights consistent with the principles underlying the takings clause, they would: (a) require that the government affirmatively demonstrate significant harm to a governmental interest; (b) show an actual, nonspeculative connection between the property use that the government wishes to ban or control and the harm claimed to flow from that use; and (c) demonstrate that the action taken to abate or prevent the harmful activity is closely tailored to the actual demonstrated harm.

Under such ordinary circumstances the government would not be required to compensate the owner for its action. The definition of harm is appropriately limited to actual harm to public health and safety, that is, to direct threats to the well-being of humans. Such a standard would permit the government to regulate without payment, for example, a use that poured chemicals of verifiable and significant toxicity into ground or surface water. It would not permit the government to take regulatory or legislative actions that are the equivalent of acquiring a resource, such as the acquisition of open space or habitat, without paying compensation to the owner of that property.

I say "under ordinary circumstances" because of the third question regarding the breadth of the exception. That question considers the issue of whether the exception still applies where the use that is barred by the government is the only use that can be made of the owner's property. Justice Holmes in *Mahon* properly questioned the validity of a rule that requires individuals to give up their entire interest in a property, even to prevent a use that the public at large considers a nuisance. The Supreme Court, although it habitually speaks of the nuisance exception with approval, has yet to invoke the exception in a case where the property in question has absolutely no other use left.

THE DOCTRINE OF EXHAUSTION
OF ADMINISTRATIVE REMEDIES

The second doctrine, the rule that property owners must exhaust their administrative remedies before bringing a suit for compensation, is also spoken of as the ripeness doctrine. In practice, it requires owners of regulated property to make every effort to get the regulating body to approve some development of the property in question or to excuse the particular property from the regulation said to give rise to a taking—even where the owners have already, in their judgment, determined that nothing less than the use they applied for will give them economically viable use of their property.

On the surface and in some cases the doctrine of exhaustion is a reasonable proposition. Property owners should determine what use of their property will be allowed before claiming that the property has been taken. Only after doing so can the owners determine what and how much has been taken, if anything. However, this doctrine clearly should not apply in those cases in which (a) the regulation or statute is so restrictive and inflexible in its terms as to work a taking of property by its very existence (as in *Mahon*); or (b) where, for whatever reason, any attempt to qualify under the terms of the statute or regulation would be a waste of time (the futility doctrine). The difficulty with the ripeness doctrine is in its execution at the hands of modern courts.

In practice, property owners are often obliged to make not one but several efforts to obtain governmental approval before the courts will hear claims that their property has been taken. This leaves property owners at a distinct disadvantage. They may be kept in the application process indefinitely, requiring them to spend enormous amounts of money to revise their applications. Such costs include processing fees, consultants' fees, legal fees, carrying costs on the land, taxes, and other items. These costs place enormous pressures on property owners to accept limitations and conditions that have a severe impact on their rights and that they would otherwise find unacceptable, but they do not have the resources to resist.

In all, this doctrine poses an all too often insuperable obstacle to property owners seeking to vindicate their rights in the administrative process and in litigation. The administrative process is generally clumsy and favors the discretion of the regulating body. Unlike a court proceeding, the fact-finding process in administrative proceedings depends on testimony of individuals who (a) rarely have expertise on which to base opinions, (b) have a vested interest in keeping neighbors from using their own land, and (c) are not subject to the rules of evidence that a court must apply. Thus, the entire administrative process is weighted against the property owner. It is this last fact (that agencies are not bound by the rules of evidence) that militates, along with other factors, against the practice of according judicial deference to administrative and legislative determinations. As was aptly stated by the Supreme Court in *Fletcher v. Peck*, "If the legislature be its own judge in its own case, it would seem equitable that its decision should be regulated by those rules which would have regulated the decision of a judicial tribunal."[5]

If the ripeness doctrine is to be a just doctrine and if the private property owner and the government are to be placed on equal footing, then the ripeness doctrine must be properly confined, the futility doctrine must be appropriately recognized, and deference to the decisions of regulatory bodies must be eliminated.

PART III

THE CALCULUS
OF FAIRNESS

11

RECENT COURT RULINGS: A CASE FOR HOPE

If you make the law the palladium of the freedom and property rights of all citizens, and if it is nothing but the organization of their individual rights to legitimate self-defense, you will establish on a just foundation a rational, simple, economical government, understood by all, loved by all, useful to all, supported by all, entrusted with a perfectly definite and very limited responsibility, and endowed with an unshakable solidity.

If, on the contrary, you make of the law an instrument of plunder for the benefit of particular individuals or classes, first everyone will try to make the law; then everyone will try to make it for his own profit. There will be a tumult at the door of the legislative chamber; there will be an implacable struggle within it, intellectual confusion, the end of all morality, violence among the proponents of special interests, fierce electoral struggles, accusations, recriminations, jealousies, and inextinguishable hatreds; ... government will be held responsible for everyone's existence and will bend under the weight of such a responsibility.

Bastiat[1]

An honest appraisal of the Constitution and the Bill of Rights and the circumstances surrounding their formation will demonstrate that they were intended to establish a boundary over which the government cannot step in pursuit of its own ends—no matter how legitimate those ends may be. The same appraisal makes it clear that the Fifth Amendment's property clauses were no less intended to set such boundaries than were the First Amendment's religion and speech clauses, the Fourth Amendment's search and seizure provisions, or any other of the panoply of the Constitution's structural and substantive provisions.

What could be more calculated to stand in the way of the legitimate goal of societal control over violent criminal behavior, for example, than limiting the ability of government to search or seize one's home, person, papers, or effects; prohibiting the government from coercing individuals to be witnesses against themselves; or obligating the state to permit accused persons to directly confront their accusers? Could any limit on governmental action be more likely to make the prevention of noxious philosophy impossible than the First Amendment's speech clause? It would be disingenuous to suggest that the people responsible for the Constitution and the Bill of Rights were not aware of the plain meanings of the provisions they adopted or the retarding effect those provisions would have on the accomplishment of legitimate societal goals. But they emplaced such limits precisely because they understood the historical and inevitable tendency for governments to endlessly expand their powers and their authority over individuals. The Framers and their contemporaries understood equally well the proclivity of the government and segments of the public to justify such expansion by claims, however honestly made and however well-intentioned, that expansion is necessary for the common good. A discussion of this point was raised by those fearful of the potential strength of the proposed federal government. In his Essays, constitutional critic Brutus (who was probably Robert Yates), expressed this fear clearly.

> It is too often the case in political concerns, that men state facts not as they are, but as they wish them to be; and almost every man, by calling to mind past scenes, will find this to be true.
>
> * * * * * *
>
> It is natural for men, who wish to hasten the adoption of a measure, to tell us, now is the crisis—now is the critical moment which must be seized, or all will be lost: and to shut the door against free enquiry, whenever conscious the thing presented has defects in it, which time and investigation will probably discover.
>
> The government would always say, their measures were designed and calculated to promote the public good; and there being no judge between them and the people, the rulers themselves must, and would always, judge for themselves.[2]

Brutus's observations were valid. Limitations were placed on the means government could use to accomplish appropriate societal purposes precisely because the founders of the United States feared the potential for abuse in such claims and decided that less efficiency in government was an acceptable price to pay to safeguard liberties they had fought to preserve.

The Constitution's general mechanisms were well-devised by the Framers to avoid a diminution of other civil rights and liberties. These mechanisms include division of governmental power between three distinct branches of government, establishment of the judiciary as a bulwark against invasions of individual rights,* and establishment of a nonexclusive reservation of rights in the Bill of Rights and in the body of the Constitution. However well the Framers' general mechanisms have worked so far in protecting such rights as speech, they have failed in the property rights context, at least temporarily. As we have seen, modern court decisions have deviated significantly from the principles embodied in the Fifth Amendment. Definitions of the fundamental concepts of the takings clause have been distorted almost beyond recognition. Modern courts have supplanted a narrow limitation on the principle of just compensation—the concept that owners may not use their own property in a manner harmful to the rights of others—with the notion of a broader police power exception. That exception, combined with the unwarranted deference given by courts to the actions of legislative and administrative bodies, virtually eliminated the takings clause as a meaningful limitation on government power.

In 1987, however, after scrupulously avoiding any substantive decision in a takings case for more than half a decade, the Supreme Court issued three significant regulatory takings opinions that at least open the door for a restoration of balance in property rights litigation: *Keystone Bituminous Coal Association v. DeBenedictus*,[3] *First English Evangelical Lutheran Church v. County of Los Angeles*,[4] and *Nollan v. California Coastal Commission*.[5]

The first of these cases, *Keystone*, was a replay of the *Mahon* case, except that this time the government rather than the property owner won. Once again, Pennsylvania enacted an antisubsidence statute. The statute did not differ from the Kohler Act, which was the subject of the *Mahon* case, in any significant respect except it contained a preface that provided a laundry list of what public purposes the law was intended to serve.

On the surface, it appeared to be a run-of-the-mill modern takings case

---

* Unlike Judge Bork, I am not particularly concerned about the courts usurping legislative power or the democratic will of the majority so long as the courts confine the exercise of their power to invalidating unconstitutional acts. The courts overstep their bounds only when they take the next step and affirmatively direct the government as to what it must do instead. In the context of the takings clause, this is not a problem, since the clause itself provides the answer to what government must do. The judiciary's only obligation is to enforce that prescription.

in which a claim that the statute worked a taking on its face failed, although the *Keystone* decision stopped short of repudiating *Mahon*. As is typical in such modern cases, the majority was reluctant to find a statute to be a taking by its mere existence. To avoid doing so, the Court relied on extremely dubious distinctions between the new Antisubsidence Act and the Kohler Act. Also, as is typical of Supreme Court cases of any kind, the *Keystone* opinion had two footnotes that may ultimately prove more important than the body of the opinion.

Footnote 16[6] rejected the notion that courts should defer to legislative statements of purpose and declared that courts should examine the "operative terms" of the statute (which presumably would apply as well to regulations promulgated by administrative agencies) to determine what the statute really does. This note suggested a higher level of judicial scrutiny than had been applied for almost sixty years, scrutiny that emerged in fact in *Nollan*. Footnote 20[7] repudiated the notion of a broad police power exception. It referred to a statement in the earlier case of *Midkiff* that the police power and public use were synonymous and, hence, that to accept a police power exception would be to destroy the takings clause.

The *First English* case involved a development moratorium that at least temporarily prevented a church camp from rebuilding camp buildings destroyed by a flood. The *First English* majority applied traditional takings principles to discard California's *Agins* rule. *Agins* had limited the property owner's remedy for regulatory takings to invalidation of the regulation. Before *First English*, the Supreme Court had not addressed the *Agins* rule, although it had heard the Aginses' claim that their property had been taken. But the Court never reached the remedy question because it held that the ordinance complained of did not cause a taking by its mere existence. The Court then applied the ripeness doctrine to hold that the Aginses had to apply for a specific use to determine whether the ordinance worked a taking "as applied" to their property.[8]

Now the Court held that the government must pay compensation for the use of the property during the time its regulation amounted to a taking, although the government could *limit* the amount of its liability by rescinding regulations found to be a taking. The decision also established that regulations can result in temporary takings of property just as physical occupancy can. The decision also raised the issue of whether unreasonable or abnormal delays in permit processing time could rise to the level of a taking.

The crown jewel in the 1987 trilogy was the *Nollan* case. In it, the Court confronted the question of what conditions could be imposed on granting a governmental permit to use property. The California Coastal Commission took the position that since it had the power to grant or withhold a permit, it could impose any condition it chose upon granting a permit. The commission, in typical fashion, argued that its grant of a permit was the grant of a governmental benefit. The commission sought to bolster its argument by characterizing the transaction between the owner and the commission as a voluntary trade. After all, the commission argued, the owner was free to reject the proposed condition that the owner allow the public to pass to and fro along a strip of the property. The Court scornfully rejected this characterization, noting that far from being voluntary the condition amounted to virtual extortion.[9] It then laid out several principles to be followed in future cases.

First, the Court held that to *build* on one's property was a right that could not remotely be considered a governmental benefit or privilege, although it could be subjected to some reasonable regulation. This holding directly confronted two of the most pernicious doctrines to face property owners: (a) the notion that private property owners, whether of real or other property, were more caretakers of their property than owners and their use of property was, therefore, subject to the unlimited control of the public through its governmental agencies, and (b) the related doctrine that holds that property owners' sole right is to use their property in its natural state. Equally important, the Court held that government could impose no condition at all if it could not have prohibited the use applied for without causing a taking. This last is a commonsense ruling, of course. If one could not prohibit a use, what right can one have to extract a price for allowing it?

Next, the *Nollan* Court held that even if a condition could be imposed that condition must relate to the reason the proposed use could have been denied. That is, there must be a connection or "nexus" between the condition imposed and the purpose that denial of a permit would serve, such as denying a permit to build on an unstable slope because the building could cause a landslide. In this example, a permissible condition would be one that requires that engineering steps be taken to stabilize the slope. An impermissible condition would be one that requires the owner to dedicate land for a park.

It was not enough, however, that a permissible nexus be present. The condition also had to substantially advance that purpose: the condition imposed had to really work.[10] This point is perhaps one of the most significant in *Nollan*. The phrase "substantially advance" had been used in takings cases before, but in practice was no more significant a review than that contained in the so-called rational basis test described in Part II. This time, the Court said in essence, "When we say substantially, we *mean* substantially." In so saying, the Court specifically disapproved of one of the most troublesome cases in takings jurisprudence, one that reinforced the notion of a general police power exception in which the government's action is subjected to virtually meaningless judicial review (the *Goldblatt* case, that was described previously).[11]

In rejecting *Goldblatt*, the Court for the first time began to draw a wholly appropriate distinction between the due process clause and the takings clause. The majority gave the Coastal Commission's claims of governmental purpose what virtually amounted to strict scrutiny. It rejected the commission's asserted rationale and gave substance to suggestions contained in the *Keystone* footnotes. The Court was not through here, however. It raised two other issues: economically viable use and proportionality.

As previously pointed out, a belief has grown up that no taking can be found in a regulatory takings case unless the owner is left without economically viable use of the property. In *Nollan*, however, the Nollans clearly had economically viable use of their property. They were, after all, able to build a livable residence on their property, which, being a beach front home, was extremely valuable. Nevertheless, the Court found a taking of a partial interest in the property or, stated differently, a complete taking of one of the multitude of traditional interests in the property, in this case, an easement. Their ruling, as far as it went, was utterly consistent with the original meaning of the just compensation clause.

Although the Court did not decide the issue because it was not raised by the Nollans, the Court did, in a footnote, raise the issue of proportionality. The commission had claimed that allowing the Nollans to build their house would block the view of the ocean from the Coast Highway that runs through the Nollans' neighborhood and would deprive passersby of psychological access to the beach. Thus, the condition requiring grant of a lateral easement was necessary to remedy this problem.

In my view, it is cases such as *Nollan* that ultimately demonstrate the serious potential for abuse of the Court's prior rulings. The commission's argument of a psychological barrier to the beach meant that persons driving by would not know that the Pacific Ocean was nearby and would not realize, therefore, that there might be public beaches in the area on which they could frolic. The easement was necessary in the commission's view so passersby would see people walking up and down the beach and would know there was a beach nearby. We can imagine the *Nollan* majority mentally holding their heads in their hands at the mention of psychological access. They did not want to deal with such a concept, and they did not.

I have seen photographs of the Nollans' neighborhood. Their house was next to a vacant lot. It is clear from the photographs that people driving on Route 101 could not have seen anyone walking on the demanded easement in any event. Neither did the commission explain how motorists would be able to see people walking up and down the beach, even if they could have ordinarily, if the Nollans were allowed to build their house.*

The Nollans' house would have been, in the commission's estimate, the last brick in a wall of homes in the coastal area. The Court, saying that it was not deciding the issue, opined that a condition requiring one or a few property owners to solve a problem caused by the concerted actions of many would place a disproportionate burden on those few property owners. Requiring the Nollans to remedy a jointly created problem would, it seemed to the Court, violate not only the takings clause, if the condition were not paid for, but also the due process and equal protection clauses. The Court's footnote is a practical invitation to bring such a case.

These cases are significant for another reason. Particularly in *Nollan* and *First English*, the defendants and their supporters raised objections that were made in *Agins*. In these two cases, the defendants argued that to increase the risk that a taking would be found (*Nollan*) and to hold that government must pay if it regulates to the point of causing a taking (*First English*) would chill regulatory zeal. The *First English* Court agreed, but specifically pointed out that:

> [S]uch consequences necessarily flow from any decision upholding a claim of constitutional right; many of the provisions of the Constitution are designed to limit the flexibility and freedom of governmental authorities and the Just Compensation Clause of the Fifth Amendment is one of them. As Justice Holmes aptly noted more than 50 years ago, "a strong desire to improve the public condition is not enough to warrant achieving the desire by a shorter cut than the constitutional way of paying for the change."[12]

These decisions raise hopes that some measure of balance may be returned to takings law. Indeed, subsequent lower court and state court decisions, while not uniform, suggest that the pendulum is, in fact, swinging back to a more balanced position.[13] They also raise some issues that will be at the forefront in future litigation. Cases involving these issues offer the best hope of restoring property rights to their appropriate place among the other civil rights. What these cases do *not* do is ensure that the trend they appear to represent will continue. These cases immediately came under fire from municipalities and other governmental entities and were discounted

---

* I have lived in California for more than ten years, and everyone I know knows that the Pacific Ocean is there. Further, anyone driving anywhere near a public beach is confronted with large green signs pointing the way to the nearest public beach. The commission's asserted rationale simply, if the reader will excuse the pun, does not hold water. The frightening thing is that the dissent found the commission's rationale plausible.

by other interested groups who saw in them a threat to their own particular interests and who, therefore, sought to minimize the impact of such cases.

The potential scope of these decisions was immediately clear, however. On March 15, 1988, President Reagan issued Executive Order 12,630,[14] which requires federal departments and agencies to consider the takings implications of their regulatory actions and to act to minimize their interference with private property rights to the extent permitted by law. The subject of the last part of this book is how to ensure that the opportunity posed by this shift in the courts' view can be cemented into a jurisprudence of regulatory takings consistent with the intentions of the Framers and ratifiers and with the principles they embodied in the takings clause. Doing so is critical. Some courts, particularly those in California and in the Federal Court of Appeals for the Ninth Circuit, have worked hard to undercut these revolutionary 1987 cases and to relegate them to obscurity.

12

A STRATEGY TO
RESTORE PROPERTY RIGHTS

If we accept the premises that the level of protection that property rights were intended to have has declined and that there is a value to restoring an appropriate level of protection, then the question that remains is how to accomplish this repair. Despite the successes of the 1986–1987 Supreme Court term and despite an improvement in judicial treatment in the wake of these decisions, property rights advocates have certainly not been enormously successful in reversing generations of bad law. Developing a successful strategy requires us to examine how takings law got to be in its present state.

MAJOR FACTORS LEADING TO
DISREGARD OF THE FIFTH AMENDMENT

Language and Definitions

The first major factor affecting public debate on any topic is who captures the language in which the debate will be conducted and who first applies the most attractive label to themselves. This tactic is not exactly new. It was used even during the Constitutional Convention and ratification debates. The proponents of the Constitution immediately called themselves "Federalists," hence the titles "The Federalist Papers" and the "Antifederalist Papers." The problem with their using the name "Federalist" is that they were nothing of the kind. The term "federal" is derived from the word "confederation," which refers to a loose organization of independent states. Such a structure was set up by the original Articles of Confederation. Each state retained its sovereignty and independence. The Constitution was intended to set up not a confederation but a strong central government. It created a new single sovereign, and individual states were subordinate to the central government. If the people had any doubt about this observation, it vanished during the Civil War when the southern states were forcibly prevented from withdrawing from the Union. Use of the term "federalist" was a deliberate public relations ploy intended to garner public support for creating a new nation and to put the Federalists' opponents at a disadvantage. Their opponents, after all, became the "antifederalists."[1] The tactic worked.

Words are constantly redefined either by the legislature or by courts sympathetic to a particular policy. Meanings are given to common terms that are grossly at odds with the commonly understood definition of the words. In fact, statutes and cases plus the regulations interpreting them are often so much at odds with the plain meaning of the words they use that they mock the adage that one is presumed to know the law. Between the sheer volume of regulation and the abstruseness of the language, it is virtually impossible to keep up with the state of the law. This problem became particularly acute when the law moved away from regulating conduct that violates clear moral precepts and that truly threatens other people to a state in which even the minutiae of personal conduct are regulated. When the law becomes so pervasive, those responsible for it have an obligation to make that law as clear as possible—not to cloak it with meanings that the average person cannot guess without the aid of a lawyer.

What we find instead is the use of terms that carry one emotional connotation and that provide the voter with a particular image of what is intended. However, those terms carry an entirely different meaning in the regulation. This use of words is of singular importance in environmental regulation. In public debate about a proposed governmental policy, both sides often engage in vicious distortions of the purposes and effects of the policy. Both sides use simple terms to discuss highly technical issues. This tactic is used heavily, especially in states like California where a direct vote of the populace can enact laws and amend the state Constitution.

California's Proposition 65, for example, was labeled the Safe Drinking Water Act. It was passed by a majority of the very small percentage of registered voters who went to the polls in that election, but most of its provisions have little to do with safe drinking water. Instead, those provisions require manufacturers and suppliers of goods and services, office space and residential buildings, among others, to label their products and services with a warning that their products or services expose the user of the product or service to substances "known to the state" to be carcinogens or reproductive toxins.* The initiative's provisions are so confusing, however, that nobody is quite sure when the warnings are required or what the contents of the warning must be to comply with the law. Nor is it clear who is responsible to provide the warning in any given instance. If this sounds confusing, it is.**

Crisis Mode

The second factor affecting public debate is the use of the argument that a crisis exists and that immediate action is required to avert utter disaster. The contention is put forth that the crisis is so severe that only the most drastic measures will serve to abate it; there is no time for leisurely debate or further study. Action must be taken now or it will be too late. If the measures taken turn out to have been unnecessary, the argument goes, the measures adopted can be rescinded.

However, there can be no greater fallacy than the notion of a temporary regulation. Statutes are still on the books from the depression—measures that remain in effect more than fifty years after the crisis has passed that justified their passage as temporary measures. Statutes and regulations tend to have lives of their own and are rarely repealed unless replaced with a new and more stringent regulation of the same type.

In a crisis mode, the public is asked to trust the advocate of the policy

---

* From a scientific standpoint, the term "known to the state" is a ridiculous statement. A competent researcher will admit that research never proves or disproves any theory. It either lends support or removes support from the theory. Very few substances are actually "known" to be human carcinogens with any degree of scientific certainty, although many are suspected of so being. If, in fact, the variety of suspected carcinogens were actually to be significant factors in producing cancer, virtually everyone in the United States could be expected to require chemotherapy at some time or another.

**Proposition 65 also provides an example of self-defeating environmental regulation. To avoid being prosecuted for failing to warn, manufacturers and suppliers of products label virtually everything in sight. They are not sure what products actually contain the substances in amounts sufficient to pose the statutory level of risk. The problem with such labeling requirements is twofold. First, if it appears that every product contains a warning, then people have no incentive to avoid a product that actually may pose a health risk because all products seem to be dangerous. Second, where warning labels seem ubiquitous, users of products may unreasonably assume that a given use of a particular product is safe if the product contains no warning to the contrary.

Warnings for every remote danger associated with a product cannot be feasibly provided. Not only can every misuse of a product not be foreseen, there may be dangers associated even with normal use that cannot be foreseen until the product has been in use for a time. Further, if every danger, however remote, was warned about on a package or in a package insert, the warning may become so clumsy, amounting to a book, that it will not be read carefully. A truly important warning may be missed if it is buried in a mass of warnings about remote dangers. Finally, it is virtually certain that the warnings will be written in bureaucratese as their authors attempt to cover every known contingency to minimize risk of liability. Such obtuse language cannot be reasonably understood by many. The result will be that users may proceed on a false assumption and will not exercise their own judgment in using the product, even as to obvious dangers. This result is one of the many hazards of relying on the government as a superprotector.

because there is no time to do anything else. Those who counsel caution are often vilified and characterized as harboring ulterior motives. This too is not a new tactic. In fact, this very objection was raised in the constitutional ratification debates.

> It is natural for men, who wish to hasten the adoption of a measure, to tell us, now is the crisis—now is the critical moment which must be seized, or all will be lost: and to shut the door against free enquiry, whenever conscious the thing presented has defects in it, which time and investigation will probably discover. This has been the custom of tyrants and their dependents in all ages.[2]

The crisis argument is seductive and, hence, dangerous for two reasons. First, it appeals to human fears and thereby clouds reason and the dispassionate judgment needed to assess the true measure of risk and to devise appropriately tailored responses, that is, responses that are not excessive. Second, a sufficient number of instances do require near immediate action to lend plausibility to all crisis arguments, even where haste is not warranted. However, true crises requiring immediate response do not occur nearly as frequently as the argument is called upon.*

The Ability to Take the Initiative

A third major factor affecting public debate is the varying ability of parties to organize support and take the initiative. Observers saw a perfect example of the importance of being first to capture an issue and to be proactive in the 1988 presidential campaign. Then Vice President Bush took the initiative on the environmental issue in Governor Michael Dukakis's own backyard by announcing his "no net loss of wetlands" position. The erosion in the level of respect for property rights is as much a failure of property rights advocates to be proactive in educating the public and in advancing a coherent approach to property rights in litigation, regulation, and legislation as it is a result of any other factor. On the other hand, opponents of property rights, however fallacious their arguments, have been remarkably successful in acting together and in advancing positions rather than defending against attacks.

---

* The term for this kind of response is "superstitious reinforcement." The concept is best explained by example. Gamblers are frequent victims of superstitious reinforcement. Such a gambler may have a shirt that is distinctive in some manner, enough so that he recalls wearing it. Our gambler wears it one day while gambling and has a very good day. He associates the shirt with his success. The next time he wears the shirt gambling, he wins again. He is now convinced that the shirt is lucky. In the future, even though the gambler wears the shirt constantly, he wins only as frequently as the odds say he should. Nevertheless, he wins sufficiently frequently while wearing the shirt to associate it with winning. The association is even stronger if, for example, on the third occasion, he wore a different shirt and he lost.

Failure to Address Stated Goals

A fourth and extremely important factor affecting public debate is related to the third. It is the failure of property rights advocates to address the *stated* goals of the opponents of property rights. This failure is most evident in the area of environmental protection. There are, without question, environmental problems that must be solved because they pose substantial and genuine threats to human health and safety. One particularly outrageous example is the Cuyahoga River, which once became so contaminated with chemicals that its surface became flammable. Local residents and tourists would crowd the river banks to watch the river burn.

Because the most effective environmental groups have often taken outrageous, often wholly fallacious positions, and have done so with stridency, there is a natural tendency for property rights advocates to discount any position advanced by any person claiming to have a concern for the environment. The tendency to disregard the claims of environmental groups is entirely understandable. The following example perfectly illustrates why frustration levels are so high when we deal with any special interest group, regardless of whether environmental issues are involved.

In 1989, shortly after Christmas, a local radio talk show in Northern California got onto the topic of whether Christmas trees were an environmentally sound idea. The discussion began when a caller opined that cutting down Christmas trees was bad for the environment because they would no longer contribute to the ecology. Every additional caller, all appearing to be intelligent, articulate, and well-intentioned people, agreed. Not one caller pointed out (a) that Christmas trees are *farmed*; (b) that except for the farming, these trees would not have been grown at all; or (c) that Christmas trees are a renewable resource because new trees are grown to replace each tree cut down for Christmas. If it were not for the demand for Christmas trees, the land used to grow these trees would have been used for some other purpose that might have been environmentally harmful or environmentally neutral. Had the callers thought the problem through, they would not have responded as they did. If anything, this episode emphasizes the need to treat such concerns seriously and to educate those concerned as to what actually happens rather than to discount their concerns and rail against them.

As a practical matter, it does not pay to discount another's stated concerns, even where the statement of concern may mask other motivations and may be based on distortions and untruth. We should take seriously each statement of concern and should attempt to counter the concern. Even where the speaker is not genuinely motivated by the stated cause, others will accept the speaker's statement at face value and will act upon it unless given a reason not to. In open debate where genuine matters of concern are raised, the issue is what means should be used to address the problem unless the problem is wholly illusory. Otherwise, the person who raises the question of property rights in public debate can be improperly discounted in turn as being no more than an insensitive advocate for special interests.*

The falsity of the charge of insensitivity is irrelevant. Perception is far more important. This does not mean that every concern raised should be treated as true, but if it is not, or if it is exaggerated, the advocate must be prepared to show why it is not wholly accurate.

When confronted with an inaccurate claim, it is not enough for a proponent of property rights to provide the facts and figures that demonstrate the actual state of affairs. However accurate the advocate's information, a purely factual and rational discussion will not have the emotional impact necessary to carry the information home so that it will be acted on. For instance, consumer advocates claiming that a product is "unreasonably dangerous" (a term of art) do not merely recite the facts and figures stating the mortality and morbidity rates resulting from the use of the product. Those statistics will sometimes support and other times refute their contentions. These advocates will instead bring in pictures or models that create a graphic impression, regardless of the accuracy of the assumptions underlying the model. When this happens, it will not matter that the product may have a societal value that far outweighs its risks. What is remembered is the photograph or the model. Property rights proponents must be willing and able to paint the same kinds of pictures, backed up by solid facts.

A STRATEGY FOR PROPERTY RIGHTS RESTORATION

No single approach will suffice to restore an appropriate level of respect for property rights. The erosion of property rights protection occurred through a complex of mechanisms and must be revitalized in the same fashion. The strategy must involve at least four approaches. The first and perhaps most important approach is education of all involved parties. Education will affect the degree and durability of any renaissance in property rights protection. The second approach is participation in the legislative process. The third is participation in the administrative process. The fourth approach, and the one on which the remainder of Part III will focus most heavily, is litigation.

---

* I define a special interest group as any group to which the speaker does not belong.

Public and Legal Education

The fight to restore an appropriate level of protection for property rights must begin with education in the broadest sense of the term. As noted previously, whether any right will be respected depends ultimately on the willingness of the general public to respect the rights of others, the willingness of legislatures and regulatory agencies to be sensitive to those rights while designing or implementing legislation intended to address issues of public concern, and the willingness of the judiciary to fulfill its constitutional role as protector of those rights regardless of the judges' own views as to the correctness of the given legislative policy at issue.

To the extent that anyone's willingness to accept and act on any proposition can be ensured, that willingness can be ensured only if those who are in a position to affect rights understand the value of doing so. Otherwise, such people will view property rights as mere impediments and as valueless. No amount of abstract theory or historical analysis will encourage those people to accept occurrences or outcomes that may on occasion conflict with what they would personally find desirable. At the same time, those who are already familiar with and support the concept of property rights must be given the tools with which to act to protect those rights.

To be sure, some critics of property rights will continue to object strenuously to measures taken to protect those rights. Their criticisms are presently couched in bitter and absolute terms. In the view of these critics, any conflict, real or apparent, between individuals' rights in their property and the attainment of any of these goals is not to be tolerated. Such persons will regard any discussion of the merits of recognizing property rights with grave suspicion. The facts and simple logic and experience speak for themselves, although they must be presented in a manner that lends emotional impact to that information. Every effort should be made to bring those facts to the attention of those who have the power to influence the future course of events.

Property rights education must be pragmatically oriented; it must focus both on the nature of property rights as civil rights and on the positive effects to be derived from giving those rights the same degree of protection given to other civil rights. Educational efforts must also focus on the means and methods by which property rights protection can be achieved. What must be made especially clear in the effort to restore respect for property rights is that the phrase "it's only property" is not relevant to the debate. It is not the property that is at issue; it is the rights that are important.

The link between property rights and other rights is a concept that, with a little reflection, is readily apparent. It will take more effort to convey the connection between protection of property rights and accomplishment of other social goals. With this thought in mind, it becomes clear that property rights education must involve more than education about property rights *per se*. It must also involve education about public issues that are likely to have an impact on private property. Targets of property rights education must be exposed to information about the problems that may raise questions about private property so the people being educated can properly evaluate the claims of competing parties.

PUBLIC EDUCATION

Who are the most appropriate targets for property rights education? The answer is both simple and complex. The simple answer is everyone. Without large-scale understanding and support by the members of the general public, people who have a philosophical or political stake in minimizing the protection of property rights will be able, through modern techniques of mass persuasion, to defeat any legislative or administrative effort to achieve property rights reform. Members of the public generally understand property rights protection on an individual level. That is, they understand that property rights are at issue when their own property is directly affected. However, when the issue is distant from any person's daily life, it becomes more difficult for that person to see the ramifications of regulatory conduct, particularly when there is a superficial appearance of benefit. The first aspect of public education is to assist members of the general public to be more critical of claimed benefits and to analyze for themselves the actual costs, probable benefits, and likely risks of a proposed program.

A second aspect of public education is to provide members of the public with access to information they need to make a decision in an individual case. Such information is frequently denied them or is misrepresented by interested groups. For example, California voter's pamphlets contain a legislative analyst's summary of initiatives on the ballot. Such summaries often declare that a given initiative has no public cost. This statement is invariably incorrect. Every public measure has administrative costs. Such costs are unavoidable and are generally considerable. Also, there will almost invariably be costs to the public and the individual in terms of increased prices or adverse impacts on the availability of public goods and services. The public should be made aware of these costs. When answering abstract survey questions, members of the public frequently state that they are willing to pay more money for certain programs. However, if they are privy to all the facts in the individual case, they are reluctant to pay more when confronted with a concrete set of circumstances.

This premise was demonstrated in the 1990 election in California. Virtually every environmental initiative on the state ballot in California failed, including one being watched carefully across the country, the so-called Big Green initiative. Big Green was a massive environmental initiative that would have significantly increased regulation of virtually every aspect of California's commerce and would have had equally massive impacts on local and even on national economies. The initial advertisements opposing Big Green focused on the notion that such regulation was important but argued that Big Green "tried to do too much." If polls were to be believed, no voters seemed to be much swayed by this proposition. Later advertisements, however, focused on the potential economic impacts of Big Green and were much more successful in capturing the voters' attention. The initiative lost by a far greater margin than had been predicted in last-minute polls.

A separate sector of the public that needs to be a special target for property rights education is the property owner, particularly the real property or business owner whose property is most often going to be the target of excessive or inappropriate regulation. The reason for this is manifest. If a regulation will likely result in a taking of property, it will do so before a lawyer becomes involved in the individual case. In the present regulatory climate in which courts defer to administrative determinations, the creation of the administrative record is of paramount importance.

When faced with a confusing administrative process, an unsophisticated property owner is at a distinct disadvantage. If such owners are to have a chance of being able to protect their property interests, they must be knowledgeable enough to understand what they are up against and what steps they must take in their own behalf. If they can do so, they stand a better chance of not having to decide whether to take the risky and expensive step of litigating against an agency who they believe has taken their property.

FOCUSED EDUCATION

The second part of the answer about whom to educate is more complex. We must consider not only who is to be educated but also how they are to be educated. One obvious and important group for whom a balanced and effective property rights education must be provided is law students. Lawyers, for better or worse, occupy extraordinarily important positions in virtually every part of American society. They comprise by far the greatest percentage of legislators. They make law in courts as lawyers, head up and staff some of the most prestigious public policy institutes, and become the judges who will decide questions of property rights in the future. If there is to be any hope of a sustained renaissance in property rights protection, lawyers must understand the historic and practical bases of property rights protection. The place to start this education is in law schools. Those institutions long ago passed beyond being institutions designed to train practical lawyers and became public policy institutions instead. Whether this transformation is good or bad is irrelevant. It exists, and some of the most crucial property rights debates will occur in those schools.

Another sector requiring education is the private plaintiff's bar. Most property rights litigation is not initiated by law professors or lawyers whose practice consists exclusively of property rights work and who have years of education and experience in that area of law. Much of property rights litigation and administrative practice is done by lawyers whose practice is multisubject, even if the overall practice area is property law. Even experienced property rights attorneys cannot acquire all the experience that enables them to face every situation with an equal degree of knowledge. A lack of experience in the small nuances of administrative or litigation practice may spell the difference between success or failure.

Among the important aspects of property rights representation that property rights lawyers must know, aside from substantive property rights law, are (a) how to select cases, (b) how to make the administrative record, (c) how to present the best case before either the administrative body or the court, and, perhaps most important, (d) how to deal with the psychology of administrative agencies. Understanding how administrative personnel think and how they are likely to react to a given proposal is as important as a practitioner's knowing any area of law, particularly if the property owner wants to stay out of court.

Knowing the appropriate targets for property rights education is necessary but insufficient to ensure some measure of success in restoring property rights. Education is not, after all, a universal panacea. It is a necessary condition to improvement, but improperly designed educational programs can be worse than no programs at all. The appropriate means of providing necessary information must be selected, and the means must be tailored to the message. Opponents of property rights use multiple channels for their educational efforts. They use every medium from television commercials, billboards, and pamphlets to computer games, "message movies," and even children's cartoons.* Proponents of property rights and intelligent decision making must do likewise.

First and foremost, we need more public debate on the issue of property

---

* The use of children's programming to pass environmental and other social messages is a particularly virulent and obnoxious form of "educational" effort. While as a general proposition we may applaud the notion of socially conscious programming, these children's programs give no facts and do not teach intelligent decision making.

rights. It is not enough to discuss the issue in scholarly journals aimed at other professionals who are already engaged in the debate. For example, economists have debated the issue for years and, in a rare instance of near unanimity, have pointed out the fundamental defects in using rent control as a means of ensuring adequate and affordable housing. They have succeeded in communicating their message to almost no one. It is equally important to publish in popular literature at all levels. Articles on property rights and contemporary issues should be written for magazines such as *Regulation Magazine, New Republic, The Public Interest, Wall Street Journal,* or *Atlantic Monthly.* These publications should not only include articles linking important local and national issues and property rights, but also should include popularized versions of scholarly articles.

In line with previous comments about the need to capture not only the intellect of the public but also its emotions, property rights advocates should use the popular press and should supply anecdotal evidence about the fiefdoms created by property regulators and their potential for political corruption and extortion, not to mention their absurdity.*

Above all, members of the public must be educated about how the failure to protect property rights can have a direct impact on them as well as on issues of public importance. Among those issues of public importance in which the protection of property rights plays a part are the need for adequate and affordable housing and the effect that regulations have on the ability of the United States to compete in the world economy.

Participation in the Legislative and Administrative Processes

Most property owners become involved in the issue of property rights protection only when a regulatory scheme is implemented against their property. Typically, this occurs when owners decide to sell their property and the purchaser wants to know what zoning rules affect the property or

---

* My favorite story is one I first heard at a conference in San Francisco. On hearing it, I was sure that the story was apocryphal because it seemed so absurd. Later, however, as I was telling the story as an apocryphal one in a public speech, an attorney in the audience volunteered the information that his client was the owner of the property and that the story was true. I have since confirmed its authenticity through multiple sources including Frank Dunkle, who was Director of the Fish and Wildlife Service of the U.S. Department of the Interior at the time of the incident. The story involved a piece of coastal property that was partly upland and partly wetland. The owner decided to develop all of the property and sought a Section 404 permit to fill the wetland area of the property. The Fish and Wildlife Service examined the wetland portion and found that the Salt Marsh Harvest Mouse, a protected species, lived in the wetlands. The service then designated the *upland* portion as a critical habitat. The reasoning was as follows: We may be having a global warming trend, the agency asserted. If so, the ice caps may melt. If they melt, the sea level will rise. If the sea level rises, the wetland portions of the property will be inundated. If that happens, the mouse will want to move. Where will it move? To the upland portions of the applicant's property, of course.

whether the property is a toxic waste site. Their exposure to property regulation may also occur when owners decide to subdivide or develop their property. Property owners may similarly become entangled in the administrative process or litigation when they find out that they were required to obtain a permit to deposit fill on their property or were required to keep records of waste disposal that they never knew they had to keep.

When this happens, the owners' options are limited. They must either accept the dictates of the agency or be willing to litigate to protect their rights. In the present regulatory climate, neither choice is attractive, but in most instances the litigation option is the least attractive of the two. In either case, an owner is likely to have obtained an expensive lesson.

The only way to minimize the chances of becoming involved in this kind of Catch-22 is to participate in the administrative or legislative process early on, before the regulation has been promulgated or the statute passed. The cost of doing so and the complexity of the administrative process, however, inhibits property owners. Often, individual property owners recognize that it may cost them more to participate in a particular administrative proceeding than they lose by not doing so. Therefore, they will chose not to participate. This is, unfortunately, short-sighted, because the long-term costs will be greater when the regulatory scheme expands to cover more and more property, as experience shows it invariably will. The monetary and other costs of individual participation in administrative and legislative processes can be minimized if property owners act in concert in the most broad-based coalition possible. Only by doing so will those affected by regulatory action be able to make effective presentations before agencies and legislative bodies. In this, property rights advocates can take lessons from their opponents.

In either situation—before the adoption of a statute or regulation or when it is applied to the individual—the key to maximizing the chances of success is to make the most complete record possible before the governmental body. An owner certainly cannot depend on the agency to uncover all pertinent facts and information. Agencies may be understaffed or inefficient for any number of reasons. Their fact-finding procedures are usually inadequate; the agency depends on interested parties to bring information to their attention. Also, because both legislative and administrative bodies are politically sensitive, they will respond as much, if not more, to displays of support for a position as they will to facts. This response is unfortunate but accurate. It is also a fact that advocates of property rights can use to their advantage. If property rights advocates or property owners can show political support for their position equal to the support on the other side of the question, the governmental body will have to depend on individual facts to make a decision rather than on purely political considerations—an infinitely preferable state of affairs.

13

LITIGATION AND
THE RESTORATION
OF PROPERTY RIGHTS

If lasting change is to come in property rights protection, it will come from court actions that resolve questions that are presently unresolved. Legislation is too open to change whereas judicial rulings of constitutional dimension cannot be changed by the legislature, however imperfectly rendered.

On the other hand, litigation is the riskiest arena in which to attempt to bring about change. Litigation is an expensive alternative, both financially and emotionally. The outcome of a given case very often depends on how the judge views the equities of a case. More than one case that was perfectly sound on the basis of law has foundered because the judge took a dim view of the specific facts of the case.

If the case is at all significant, it is unlikely to end with a trial court ruling but will proceed through the courts of appeal. In fact, if the case does end at the trial court level, its value as precedent is limited. Further, modern courts, as we have seen, have not been generally hospitable to property rights claims. And, although the Supreme Court's 1986–1987 term, which saw what appears to be a potential counterrevolution in property rights protection, is likely to continue, that Court has not seized opportunities it has had since 1987 to further what it started. What appears to be a perfectly clear holding in a previous case is held by a later court to not say what it appears to say. Litigation is not, therefore, an alternative to be accepted lightly despite its ultimate importance.

Other factors make litigation a difficult route to achieve change. An attorney does not represent a philosophical principle in litigation but serves a client. Because the job of attorneys is to represent a client's interests, they cannot act in litigation to vindicate a principle where to do so would not serve the client's interest. Clients, and not attorneys, ultimately set the goals of litigation. Attorneys must not only respect the client's decision, they must affirmatively inform the client of the risks and benefits of taking a particular course of action.

CASE SELECTION

The greatest likelihood of achieving lasting success in litigation requires a property owner who is committed to the principles of property rights. People who have such a commitment often do not have the resources necessary to carry litigation forward on their own. On the other hand, people who have the resources are most often business people whose primary interest is in moving a stalled project forward and for whom vindication of principle is an important but secondary purpose. Even worse, if property owners have sufficient resources to withstand what may be years in litigation, and if they have a sufficient commitment to principle to be willing to sacrifice more immediate, legitimate interests, then they are sufficiently well-to-do to feed a public relations campaign aimed at painting them as wealthy developers or other persons or organizations that are perceived as being undeserving of sympathy. When this happens, it does not matter that the portrait painted is inaccurate or that the plaintiff's status is irrelevant to the question of rights. It is no accident that the major favorable takings decisions came out of cases like *Nollan*, which involved a single landowner who simply wanted to build a livable residence on his property, and *First English*, which involved a church camp.

A Robin Hood syndrome pervades the debate over property rights and makes achievement of unconscionable results possible. The theory is that a few greedy people who have no conscience are willingly abusing land and resources. Thus, people are justified in robbing the rich property owner to redistribute the wealth. Unquestionably, some people willfully abuse resources, but that abuse is more the exception than the norm. Ultimately, in civil rights, there cannot be one set of rights for one group and a second set for others. Either all rights are equal and entitled to equal protection, or there are no rights at all.

The image of Robin Hood is not entirely inapt, however, if we recall who Robin Hood was said to be and what he was actually said to have represented. The Robin Hood of legend did not simply "rob from the rich and give to the poor." He was a political rebel whose purpose was to free the Saxons from the conquering Normans who, under Prince John, were taxing the Saxons and seizing their lands for illegitimate purposes. According to the story, the taxes were taken to ransom King Richard, who had been taken hostage while returning from the crusades, but in fact they were being applied to other uses. In short, the Robin Hood of legend fought against the violation of rights, including property rights. The money and property that he robbed from the rich was, in legend, money and property that had been illegally taken from the Saxons; the poor to whom they were given were the Saxons from whom they were taken in the first place. In legend and stories, including modern retellings,[1] Robin Hood even recovered stolen property from people who had stolen it and gave it back to Norman nobles from whom it was stolen. So, in a sense, the analogy to the Robin Hood legend does provide a lesson in this arena. The lesson simply isn't the one popularly assigned to it.

An attorney who handles a case in litigation often has not been involved in the matter from its inception. Thus, the attorney has not had an opportunity to create the strongest record possible at the administrative level. If the record is not adequate, client and attorney work under a handicap from the beginning. If the client has a "hard case," one that makes "bad law," and insists on taking it forward, there is a significant likelihood that bad precedent will emerge. This precedent will make the job of moving the law in a positive direction more difficult.

BUILDING A COHERENT TAKINGS JURISPRUDENCE

The biggest single task reserved for litigation in the property rights context is to move the courts away from the utterly *ad hoc* approach to takings law that they now use. To do this, property rights advocates must persuade the judiciary to accept a coherent takings theory. That theory must be anchored in the principles of traditional exercises of the power of eminent domain and must revolve around the original meaning imbued in the takings clause by the Framers *and* in the purposes—historical and modern—for requiring payment of compensation. In particular, property rights advocates must show courts how the principles of the takings clause ultimately protect social values with which the courts can identify. A broad litigation strategy, as opposed to tactics in the individual case, must focus on at least three areas.

Broad Litigation Strategies

The first and most obvious strategy is to capitalize on the opportunities represented by cases like *Nollan*, *First English*, and the *Keystone* footnotes. The second strategy is, in appropriate cases, to slowly revisit the issues that have previously been decided and are adverse to the rights of property owners. This second strategy is necessary to restore some measure of balance. The best way to accomplish balance is incrementally and by demonstrating in each case (as must be done in capitalizing on more recent decisions) that the protection of property rights is not inimical to important public policies. Even if previously decided cases are helpful, there is certainly enough room to establish more uniform and proper regulatory takings standards. After all, previous cases have all, ostensibly, been decided on an *ad hoc*, case-by-case basis on the grounds that the courts "have been unable to discover" principles of general applicability. It is up to the property rights litigant to help courts discover such principles. In short, the courts have left an opening by intimating that such principles might indeed exist, but those principles must be discovered.

The third strategy is to lead the judiciary into considering issues of compensation in line with those discussed in Part II. The greatest area of concern leading courts to abandon their role as guardians of property rights and appropriate takings principles is their fear that to find takings requiring compensation will make the achievement of important public goals impossible. The result is that courts will distort the principles of takings law so they can avoid a finding that the particular type of action can give rise to a taking instead of focusing on the amount of compensation due. In many cases, regulations may cause a taking, but the value of the interest taken is *de minimis* and may be compensated for by provisions in the regulatory scheme itself. In other cases, the value of the interest taken may be large, but mechanisms other than cash can be used as a medium of compensation.

The belief that property rights protection is incompatible with important public goals is fallacious. Nevertheless, the perception of incompatibility exists and must be addressed. Ideally, the places to deal with this perception are in public and legal education and in working with legislators and administrative agencies to create alternative means of compensating property owners when a regulatory scheme has the potential to result in a taking of property. If litigation is necessary, several tactics may be useful.

Litigation Tactics

The most obvious litigation tactic is to bring the suit only for compensation and not to ask the court to invalidate the governmental action. Modern courts are loathe to invalidate governmental actions. They rarely do so. This has been particularly true after *Midkiff*, which declared that virtually any governmental action taken is supported by a public purpose. After all, the takings clause does not prohibit takings; it simply places limits on the exercise of the power to take. If the government wants to take property within those limits, it can. As a practical matter, however, if the government is told it must pay, it may find another, less intrusive means of accomplishing its end. It may willingly abandon the more intrusive measure to limit its liability. While most property owners would rather have their property than have the government take it, this is not likely to be accomplished by their asking the court to tell the government it cannot take their property. A court will probably invalidate a regulatory action only if the owners find themselves in the extraordinary situation in which the government's action is so obviously improper that a court will overcome its natural reluctance to invalidate a governmental act. The court would rather find no taking and allow the action otherwise.

In the more typical situation, property owners should carefully consider what, short of getting their property back, would be an appropriate level of compensation. It may be that, in reality, the government's action amounts to no more than the acquisition of an easement. It may be better for the litigant to claim that an easement has been taken, where that is the true effect of the government's action, and to sue only for that. The benefits of this tactic are at least three.

First, this tactic reduces the amount of relief asked for to a level that the judge may find more acceptable because the amount does not seem to be an attempt to gouge or place an undue burden on government. Second, this tactic takes advantage of the considerable body of law in traditional exercises of the eminent domain power for the acquisition of a partial interest in property. Third, if the plaintiff succeeds, the government will not acquire all of the plaintiff's property. The disadvantage is that one must deal with cases like *Penn Central* and *Keystone*, but these cases are already being dealt with in lower court decisions. For example, in *Loveladies Harbor*, among other cases, the Claims Court limited the possible scope of *Penn Central* by holding that a court could only consider the property owned by the plaintiff at the time of the government action said to give rise to a taking and not portions of the property that were previously owned but that had already been sold by the time the alleged taking occurred. At the time of this writing, this case is being appealed by the United States.[2]

There are a number of factual situations and types of regulations in which undecided and wrongly decided issues can be raised in future litigation with some hope of success. These regulatory schemes include wetlands regulation, endangered species regulation, rent and occupancy control, land use permit conditioning, landmark preservation, and temporary regulations. I have already discussed land use permit conditioning and temporary regulatory takings.

Rent control regulations and landmark regulations deserve special attention before I proceed to a discussion of wetlands regulation. Rent control is a particularly offensive form of property regulation in which the government essentially takes over operation of the owners' rental property, telling them how much they can charge to lease their property to tenants. The government frequently tells owners under what circumstances they can evict their tenants (occupancy control), when they may raise their rents, and even whether they can convert their property to another use. In such schemes, landlords are not only prohibited from evicting a tenant during the term of the lease, except for specific reasons stated by law, they are also often prevented from requiring tenants to leave at the end of their lease, which is what happened to Lena Schnuck whose story was told briefly in the introduction to this book. In other words, the tenant is given virtually a life estate in the property; in some schemes, the tenant gets even more.

Rent control is justified by analogizing it to price controls on other goods and services. But this analogy does not save the practice. Not only do the various rent control schemes fail to achieve their stated purpose, they have the opposite effect and simply entrench people who can often afford to pay market price. Occupancy control is even worse. Price control may have a valid purpose when prices are kept artificially high, such as in an anticompetitive setting. However, occupancy control is a pure usurpation of an estate from the property owner. It is no different than the state's condemning property for public housing. Like rent control, occupancy control has also been justified by a claim that owners are being compensated because they are being "allowed" a reasonable rate of return on their property. The fallacy in this argument is that the takings clause requires just compensation, which is appropriately defined as market value, or the difference between market value and what the owner is left with. Since the entire rationale for rent control is to keep rental prices from rising to where they would be except for the regulation (that is, market value), rent control falls short of just compensation by definition. This should not be taken to mean that providing housing for those who cannot afford market prices is an illegitimate purpose, but the rent control solution is not a legitimate means of achieving that purpose. If providing housing for those who cannot afford market rates is a legitimate goal, then people should have a more appropriate scheme to meet the housing need. This scheme should not violate the takings clause or distort the market, a paradoxical effect that is common to all rent control schemes. An appropriate scheme might be to directly subsidize the tenant by paying the landlord the difference between what the tenant can afford and what the property would rent for on the open market.

Landmark preservation ordinances are similarly obnoxious violations of the takings clause. Most landmarks began their lives as private property and remain so even today. There is no doubt that some historic landmarks, like some wetlands, are valuable and worth preserving. The problem is, as in wetlands, that they do not belong to the public but to their owners. It defies any sort of moral reasoning or logic to identify the point at which the property ceased to be private and became public because of who once lived there or because of the property's age. If the property remains private, the public cannot be deprived of it because the public never had it. The public merely wants the property and obtains it without cost by restricting its use and requiring its owner to spend money to maintain the property in an historic state. Thus, the public benefits without spending a single dime.

WETLANDS REGULATION
AND REGULATORY TAKINGS

Wetlands regulation provides the perfect example of litigation that can raise most if not all of the issues that can arise in a regulatory takings case. For this reason, wetlands regulation provides the perfect foil for discussing litigation strategy. The following discussion illustrates some of the issues that can be raised and how they should be resolved. It is not a litigation manual, and it does not suggest all the nuances that may arise in an actual case.

Section 404 of the federal Clean Water Act,[3] originally called the Federal Water Pollution Control Act, was intended originally to prevent people from polluting water by depositing pollutants in navigable waters. When enacted, it was not intended as a wetlands protection statute. Through judicial and regulatory amendment, however, the scope of the act was eventually expanded to include protection of wetlands for a variety of purposes, most of which have little to do with protecting water quality. As typically happens in such cases, legislators favoring the judicial amendment declare that what the court said was what they had in mind all along. Indeed, it is not an uncommon practice for legislators to vote for a bill they do not like because they expect that the courts or an agency will give the law the direction they had hoped for all along. In the case of the federal Clean Water Act, it is clear that wetlands preservation was not among the original purposes of the act. First, and most obvious, the bill was called the Clean Water Act, not the Wetlands Preservation Act. And before it was renamed, it was called the Federal Water Pollution Control Act. Second, the act as passed did not contain the word "wetlands" anywhere nor did it talk of "waters of the United States," but only "navigable waters." With time, and regulation, the definition of navigable waters was broadened to include nonnavigable waters. Third, the act, even today, does not prohibit dredging or draining wetlands, it only prohibits depositing fill in wetlands. If Congress had intended to protect wetlands, it would have prohibited drainage as well as fill.

The purposes assigned to the regulatory and judicial expansion of the act include the protection of habitat for wildlife; the preservation of the land in its natural state as a flood control device, as a water filtration device, and as food production land for wildlife; and the preservation of land for recreational uses and scientific research. All told, fifteen functions are commonly separately listed for wetlands. Some of the listed functions, however, are subsets of a larger category, such as flood control.

Administration of the act is divided between the U.S. Army Corps of Engineers and the U.S. Environmental Protection Agency. Section 404 of the act requires that an individual obtain a permit from the Corps of Engineers before depositing fill in navigable waters, now designated in Corps' regulations as a "water of the United States." The property owner applies to the Corps for a "404 permit" in much the same manner that property owners go to a planning commission or town council to obtain a conditional-use permit to develop their property. The application may be denied altogether, granted unconditionally, or granted with conditions. There are a few exemptions to the permit requirement and some so-called nationwide permits that modify this requirement, but even these exceptions may be overridden by the Corps or the EPA at each agency's discretion.

As in other regulatory schemes, the critical terms in Section 404 of the act have undergone definitional inflation. Wetlands were originally visualized as typical swamps, bogs, and other areas in which the soil was saturated with water most or all of the time.[4] In fact, the terms "swamp" and "bog" were specifically used to place limits on the type of property that could be regulated under Section 404 because the definition, which was based on the types of soil, plants, and hydrology, could be too loosely applied. The definition was further delimited by requiring that the "wetland indicators" be present under normal circumstances. In short, once wetlands came to be regulated under the statute, the language was intended to ensure that only true wetlands would be regulated.

This strict definition did not last. In short order, lands came to be regulated that under any commonsense definition of the term would not be considered wetlands. In 1989, the Corps, the EPA, and the Fish and Wildlife Service developed a wetlands delineation manual that broadened the definition of wetlands as a practical matter by broadening the classes of plants that could be considered wetland indicators and by eliminating the requirement of determining hydrology at all under some circumstances. That manual was revised under public pressure, but that revision is under attack from those who support the use of federal power for what is no more than disguised land use regulation. Even if the revised manual stands, while it may be helpful, it does not even begin to solve the Section 404 program's problems.

The definition of wetlands requires that three factors be present: (a) a predominance of wetland indicator plants, which are plants that are adapted to saturated soil conditions and that can and ordinarily do live in saturated soils; (b) hydric soils, which are soils that have been saturated long enough to produce a color change; and (c) wetlands hydrology, which means that the land has to be wet.

The various iterations of the delineation manual list five categories of plants. Plants in two categories grow either almost exclusively or more often than not in wetlands. Plants in the third category grow with equal frequency in wet or dry soils. Plants in the last two categories grow almost exclusively or more often than not in upland areas. Under the original delineation scheme, a property had a predominance of wetland indicator plants when 50 percent or more of the plants on the property belonged to the first three categories. This analysis was utterly insupportable. If a plant grows with equal frequency in upland and wetland soils, it should not be considered as either a wetland indicator or an upland indicator. A later delineation manual issued to federal regulators changed this delineation scheme to treat as wetland indicator plants those that grow with much greater frequency in upland areas but are occasionally found in wetland areas. Under this scheme, property owners could now have a field with nothing on it but this category of plant and be considered to have a field with a predominance of wetland plants. This iteration of the manual gave rise to the public outcry that led to the new delineation manual over which there is so much public controversy.

Like ordinary land use controls, the requirement that property owners obtain a 404 permit before being allowed to use their land not only has a significant impact on property owners but also can affect other public interests. For example, just as the denial or conditioning of a typical development permit affects the availability of land for housing purposes in a variety of ways, so too does the denial or conditioning of a 404 permit.

First, as in the local land use planning setting, Clean Water Act regulations increase the cost of remaining land by taking productive land out of the market. This occurs even if, as the Corps claims, more than 90 percent of all permit applications were approved. The Corps is playing with words when it makes this claim. An examination of Corps records shows that approximately one-half of the Section 404 permit applications submitted to the Corps are withdrawn by the applicants because the Corps has made it clear that the application as submitted will be rejected; 90 percent of the remaining applications are approved.

Although 90 percent of the remaining applications are granted, there is a net loss of productive land. Approvals of 404 permits almost invariably if not universally mean that another, often much larger, piece of property will be taken out of production as a mitigation measure. Mitigation or compensatory mitigation refers to the practice of requiring permit applicants to acquire nonwetland property to be converted to wetland to compensate the public for the applicants' being allowed to use their own land. Under a Memorandum of Agreement (MOA) entered into among the Corps of Engineers, the Fish and Wildlife Service, and the EPA, mitigation is an invariable requirement for granting any 404 permit. The mitigation required will often be at ratios significantly greater than 1:1, which the MOA states as the minimum mitigation allowable. For example, one developer in the San Francisco Bay area offered as much as 10:1 mitigation, an offer that was refused by the Corps as being insufficient.

There is something inherently disturbing about the requirement of compensatory mitigation. It turns the whole concept of the takings clause on its head. Under takings principles, the government should pay the property owner if it uses that owner's land for a public purpose. The wetland may indeed be a resource, but it is a resource presently owned by a private party; no amount of governmental statements about public resources can lawfully convert a privately owned resource into a public one.

The process of obtaining a Section 404 permit is expensive. It can be made even more expensive and is likely to interfere with other public goals if no meaningful restraints are put on the Corps' or EPA's ability to define terms and interpret statutes and regulations. Agency interpretations have virtually gutted specific exemptions, including a number of the agricultural exemptions that were meant to protect ongoing farming operations. Other federal statutes, like the National Environmental Policy Act[5] and the Endangered Species Act[6] also play a role in wetlands regulation.

Wetlands Regulation and the Nuisance Exception

Wetlands regulation is justified primarily on the grounds that wetlands serve important functions that benefit the public. Therefore, wetlands comprise important public resources. If the owners' use of their property changes the character of the property so that it no longer serves those functions, that use is said to deprive the public of those functions and that deprivation constitutes a harm to the public.* Therefore, we are told that if the owners' property presently serves as a habitat for an endangered specie, or could do so, and if the owners use that property for another purpose that destroys its value as a habitat, then the owners are depriving the public of the wildlife habitat. They are, therefore, harming the public. This reasoning has two flaws. First, in most instances, these resources happen to be owned by private parties. If we accept

---

* As we have seen, this same spurious reasoning is applied to historic preservation schemes.

the characterization of these resources as public merely because they can serve important public purposes, the takings clause disappears. Anyone's property can serve important public purposes.

The second flaw is in the reasoning that holds that a change in character that eliminates a function once served by the property thereby deprives the public. This is extremely slippery reasoning. Virtually anything that individuals do with their property and that changes its character will deprive the public of an opportunity to see the property used for some purpose that the public may prefer. The problem with this reasoning is that the public cannot be deprived of something that it did not own. Therefore, we must properly delimit the definition of what constitutes a harm. The distinction between preventing an affirmative harm and acquiring a public benefit lies at the heart of the nuisance exception.

Defining the nature and extent of the nuisance exception will be a major area of litigation in the foreseeable future. The *Keystone* Court appropriately rejected the notion of a broad police power exception to the takings clause's compensation requirement, albeit in a footnote. The fact that the Court's position was stated in a footnote, however, cannot diminish its importance; some of the most significant of the Supreme Court's doctrines have been announced in footnotes.*

In the *Keystone* note, the Court emphasized that the exception is a nuisance exception, not a police power exception. The Court did not decide how a nuisance is to be defined nor who gets to determine whether a given use constitutes a nuisance, however. As will be seen shortly, the wetlands regulation context provides the ideal setting to resolve these questions. Indeed, some federal trial and appeals courts have already considered the issue of whether wetlands regulations can give rise to taking and have concluded that they can. Two cases, *Florida Rock* and *Ciampetti v. United States* specifically addressed the issue of whether the government can defend against a taking claim by a blanket appeal to the nuisance exception and rejected that claim.[7]

In *Florida Rock*, the government expressly claimed that it acted to protect the public against pollution and its acts could not, therefore, be a taking. The Claims Court rejected this argument in a brilliant and forceful opinion that also rejected the Corps' claim that any pollution was caused by the proposed activity. The Claims Court's decision was challenged in the Court of Appeals for the Federal Circuit.[8] The lower court's decision

---

* One of the most influential Supreme Court-created constitutional doctrines of all time is contained in the famous footnote 4 in *United States v. Carolene Products*, 304 U.S. 144 (1938). Whole law school examination questions have been built around that footnote. The footnote itself consisted of a mere four sentences, exclusive of citations. Many thousands of sentences have been written about it since.

was reversed in part by the appeals court for two reasons. First, the appeals court held that the Claims Court erred in determining that there was no *de jure* pollution, that is, pollution "in law" within the meaning of the Clean Water Act. The existence of such pollution was necessary before the Corps had jurisdiction to regulate the land. The second reason was that trial court had to determine as a factual matter whether there was economically viable use left in the property. The appeals court did not accept the proposition advanced by the Corps that Congress's determination of pollution for jurisdiction purposes was binding for the purpose of deciding whether compensation was due, however.[9] The appeals court left the remainder of the trial court's opinion intact. The major flaw in the appeals court's decision was its holding that an owner of a wetland who was prevented from using it could, nevertheless, have economically viable "use" of the property if that owner might be able to sell it to a speculator who would be willing to buy and hold the property while waiting to see if the regulations would ultimately be lifted.

First, if selling the property to a speculator were to constitute economically viable use, the temporary takings concept found valid in *First English* would be a nullity. There is always a possibility that regulations may change. By definition, a temporary taking does not deprive a property owner of all economically viable use of the property. The measure of damages in most cases would likely be the rental value of the property.

Second, even if a buyer could be found, the price would reflect the uncertainty regarding the eventual removal of the regulation and would result in a hefty discount on the price. In other words, the owner would get less than the market value. Since the measure of just compensation is at least the market value of the property, owners would be required to accept less than what is due them. If the government were to condemn the property after it implemented a regulation that so decreased the value of the property, and if the government then attempted to pay only the diminished value of the property, it would violate the obligation to pay just compensation. Why should the government be able to achieve that result by forcing a sale to a private party at a severely discounted price?

Again, at a minimum, in cases such as *Florida Rock*, the government has either bought the entire property, subject to its right to convert the permanent taking into a temporary one, or, if a speculator's market exists, the government has acquired an easement that may be measured as the difference between full market price and the diminished value of the property with the regulation intact. Even then, the taking should be considered as a complete taking, whether temporary or permanent, unless the speculator's market is established as not being illusory. As noted previously, *Florida*

Rock ultimately went to judgment and a taking was found. The United States is appealing that judgment.

Despite numerous claims to the contrary, no federal case appears in which the nuisance exception was cited as a rationale in which *some* economically viable use, however minimal, did not remain. This observation includes *Mugler v. Kansas*,[10] the most-cited nuisance case, and *Keystone*. The *Ciampetti* court made the same observation and opined that even the abatement of a public nuisance would give rise to takings liability if all economically viable use of a property were destroyed. This court also refused to accept the government's claim of nuisance without a factual inquiry as it did in *Loveladies Harbor, Inc. v. United States*.[11]

The holdings of these cases relate to the second part of this question, previously discussed: Who gets to decide whether a use of property is a public nuisance? This raises the issue of what degree of deference is going to be paid to legislative determinations that a conduct constitutes a nuisance. The Claims Court's decisions just cited clearly take the position, discussed in Part II, that whether conduct constitutes a public nuisance is a constitutional fact to be decided by the court. You should also be aware that the nuisance exception was raised and rejected in a case involving the Surface Mining Control and Reclamation Act, *Whitney Benefits Corporation v. United States*.[12] In that case, the Claims Court rejected the government's claims that its actions were exempt from the just compensation clause because it was preventing environmental harm. The appeals court affirmed the trial court's judgment that awarded $60 million plus interest to the property owners, and the Supreme Court refused to hear the case, leaving the judgment intact.[13]

There is no doubt that some wetlands can serve valuable purposes and are worth preserving, although all wetlands, even properly defined, are not created equal. The real question is not whether some wetlands should be preserved but who must bear the cost of that preservation. That cost should be borne by the public as a whole if the public values the wetland, wants to preserve it, and derives benefit from the wetlands' functions. The owner derives no greater benefit from the property in its natural state than does any other member of the public. The only right remaining to the owner is to set foot on the property from time to time and to pay taxes on it.

While wetlands regulations can prevent or abate actual nuisances, they are most often used simply to preserve wetlands. More often by far, the purpose of refusing a wetlands permit, or of issuing a permit but with conditions, is not to prevent the commission of a genuine nuisance. The real purpose is to acquire what traditionally would be considered a public amenity, such as a wildlife refuge, flood control project, or water treatment plant. In the last two instances, the sole difference between acquiring land to construct a flood control project or treatment plant and prohibiting use of a wetland would be that rather than having to build a dam and levees or having to construct a treatment plant, the government acquires one that is already functioning. This fact was noted by the appeals court in *Florida Rock*. Denial of a permit, the court observed, would require Florida Rock to

> maintain at its own expense a facility, the wetlands, which by presently received wisdom operates for the public good, and benefits a large population who make no contribution to the expense of maintaining such a facility.[14]

Certainly no one has offered a convincing justification as to why the public must pay for land it takes to construct a treatment plant but need not pay if the land can be argued to serve that function naturally. No one has argued that the government would not have to pay for an artificially created, privately owned treatment plant simply because it already existed when the government decided to acquire it.

If neutral observers were to engage in an honest appraisal of wetlands regulations in operation, they would be forced to conclude that those regulations would, in most instances, be more appropriately labeled land use regulations and not environmental regulations. The term "environmental" leads people to believe that the issue at hand is toxic land, air, and water. In operation, however, the real issue is more often what use of a particular property is more valued by some segment of the public that has the know-how and the clout to enforce its will. A case in point illustrates the use of Section 404 as a land use device. A landowner intended to build a shopping center across the road from the Manassas Battlefield, a Civil War battlefield and national park. The owner's property was next to but not on the battlefield, which was immune from development because it was already a park. A local historical preservation society believed that such a development near a battlefield park was not appropriate, and the society wanted to keep the land undeveloped. The battle raged for some time, and it was becoming clear that the society or the government was going to have to buy the owner's land to prevent all use. Then someone noticed a small creek running through the land. The preservation group called the Corps of Engineers and asked that the Corps issue a cease and desist order and examine the creek to see if a wetland subject to Section 404 existed. Clearly, the development's opponents were not interested in preserving water quality but only in retaining an atmosphere that they treasured. This is not to say that there is anything wrong with their desire to protect that atmosphere, but their use of the statute was for a wholly different purpose from the one for which the statute was created.

Interestingly, the new attitude toward regulation has been captured in two stories published in the *Chemical Regulation Reporter*. The first story quotes EPA Deputy Administrator Henry Habicht II as saying that the EPA will regulate the use of dioxin in paper manufacture more stringently even though it is not a significant health or environmental threat.[15] The second article reported that the EPA's Science Advisory Board has concluded that the EPA is overly concerned with protecting human health. The board is apparently "recommending a shift away from human health concerns and into 'broader ecological issues'," even if those apparently have no consequences for human health.[16]

Indeed, although the Clean Water Act speaks in terms of prohibiting the discharge of pollutants into water, most of the time the fill deposited in a wetland area is not a pollutant that poses a hazard to persons on or off the owner's property. In fact, in many if not most instances, the fill is nothing more than soil that comes from other parts of the owner's property. The statute does not prohibit the deposit just of contaminated dredged or fill material; it prohibits all material.

Related to the question of whether wetlands regulation prevents a nuisance is the issue of whether property owners have the right to change the natural state of their property. Before 1987, a number of courts had developed the notion that property owners' rights to use their property were limited to the right to use that property in its "natural state." This view is expressed in typical fashion in the Wisconsin decision in *Just v. Marinette County*. In that case, the Wisconsin Supreme Court held that there was and could be no taking of the Justs' property if they were not allowed to build a home on the property because the public had "rights" in leaving the land in its natural state and that to allow it to be changed from its natural state would constitute a "harm" to the public.[17]

The *Nollan* decision's declaration that property owners have a right "to build" on their property invalidates the *Just* position. Wetlands cases, again, will provide the perfect laboratory for testing this proposition. The whole point of wetlands regulation is to keep property owners from changing the natural state of their property or to have them replace their property with other land converted to serve the same functions. Therefore, if wetlands regulation can cause a taking, then the *Nollan* language is accurate, and cases limiting the right to use property to the right to use it in the natural state are invalid.

Opponents of property rights have attempted to bolster their claim that the right to use property is limited to use in the natural state by raising a doctrine known as the "public trust doctrine." The public trust doctrine has its roots in the notion that certain real property, specifically land *underlying* navigable waters, cannot be subject to private control if that control would bar the use of the waters for commerce.[18] Property rights opponents have expanded on this concept and added dimensions that were never a part of the original doctrine and, worse, have attempted to expand its use to all property. For example, they argue, as did the *Just* Court, that the public trust doctrine permits the government to control private land not only to protect commerce along navigable waters but also to protect access to the water across land adjacent to the water for public recreational purposes.

Ultimately, property rights opponents argue, *all* land is impressed with a public trust that enables the government to limit the use of the property to those uses that the government deems to be consistent with some amorphous public good. Not only is there no historical basis for such an expansion, but broadening the public trust concept is antithetical to the fundamental notions of private property held by the Framers. If, in fact, such a doctrine were adopted, the Fifth Amendment would be meaningless.

Analysis of Wetlands Regulation Under *Nollan*

The Supreme Court's 1987 *Nollan* decision set forth principles that are more consistent with the original meaning of the just compensation clause than those decisions of previous years. If we analyze a typical wetlands case, we can see how these principles should work in practice if the Court adheres to the principles in future cases. This analysis is based on an assumption that the wetland property constitutes the entire property. What happens in cases in which the wetland makes up only a portion of the property will be discussed in the next section of this chapter because it raises entirely separate issues.

In a typical wetlands case, the Corps of Engineers either has determined to deny a 404 permit altogether or has conditioned the permit in a manner that is unacceptable. The conditions are designed to minimize, if not eliminate, the impacts of the use on wetland property. Where the impact cannot be eliminated, the Corps requires compensatory mitigation as described above. The questions are as follows: (a) is there a taking if the Corps denies a permit altogether, and (b) if the Corps does not deny the permit altogether, do the conditions the Corps imposes on the permit amount to a taking?

As previously discussed, the *Nollan* Court held that property owners have the right to build on their property. Appropriately interpreted and consistent with original meaning, that decision means owners have a right to alter the natural state of their property. The Court modified its statement by holding that the right to build may be subject to reasonable regulation. It did not, however, define the scope of that limitation. Modern cases before *Nollan* held that there was no taking if owners were left with economically viable use of their property, a proposition that is questionable under the original meaning of the takings clause unless the reciprocal advantages of the regulatory scheme amount to just compensation, as discussed in Part II. When considering this issue, we must remember that the potential for compensating benefits to equal just compensation is the factor that permits land use regulation. The government must simply be more careful in analyzing the need for regulation. It must then tailor the regulation closely enough to a significant need to provide compensating benefits that do not keep the regulation from being a taking but that balance the books by providing just compensation in the regulatory process itself.

In some regulatory schemes, as in the example used by the *Mahon* Court (in which the mine owners left a pillar of coal between their adjoining mines), it may be true that there are compensating benefits inherent in the regulatory program. In a wetlands regulation scheme, there is never a compensating benefit. Wetlands are scattered. Proponents of wetlands regulation have justified severe wetlands regulation by claiming that wetlands have been vanishing at an alarming rate since the colonization of America. However, their estimates are just that, estimates. Further, their calculations do not seem to account for the ongoing natural and artificial creation of wetlands. In any event, if we are to believe their estimates, only a small percentage of remaining land in the United States is wetland, which, if true, means that only a limited number of people will be directly affected by wetland regulation. Thus, there can be no reciprocity of benefit sufficient to be considered just compensation. The owner of the land designated as wetland gets no more benefit from the preservation of the land as wetland than any member of the public but pays the entire cost of maintaining it as a wetland.

Under a number of modern pre-*Nollan* cases, then, the question that would be asked is whether there was an economically viable use of the property. This, in turn, requires deciding what constitutes economically viable use and how much of a deprivation can exist before economically viable use can be said not to exist. These questions have never been resolved and will never be because they are, by their nature, too amorphous. A meaningful answer can come only from applying the principles of traditional eminent domain.

Those principles would lead us to conclude that the government has, at a minimum, acquired a partial interest in the property amounting to at least a conservation easement for as long as the use is denied. This brings the holdings of *First English* into play. *First English*, as observed previously, rejected the notion that a regulation could only be invalidated and could not give rise to an obligation for compensation. Instead, the Court held, the government must pay for a temporary regulation. Thus, unless the denial of the use could truly be said to be necessary to prevent or abate a public nuisance, it cannot be accomplished without payment of compensation. Even if conversion of the wetland is arguably a nuisance, under principles just discussed, complete denial of all use should be seriously considered as giving rise to an obligation to compensate the property's owner.

Nollan next held that no conditions could be attached to a permit *unless* the government could have prohibited the use altogether without causing a taking. The Court did not discuss what circumstances would permit flat denial without causing a taking. However, reason and the original principles of the Fifth Amendment suggest that the only circumstance that could support a complete denial would be that the use amounts to a public nuisance and that the owner would be left with other uses if the applied-for use were denied. If the use could have been flatly denied without causing a taking, the Court then held, it could attach conditions to allowing the use, but those conditions had to serve the same purpose as the denial. If the only reason that would support denial is that the use amounts to a public nuisance, the conditions that could be applied must be ones that mitigate the nuisance impacts of the use. Those conditions could not serve some other purpose. This limitation on imposing conditions would not prohibit the regulatory body from imposing conditions that mitigate the development's impacts on public facilities so long as these conditions did no more than balance the impact of that particular development on those public facilities. Such conditions fall more within the definition of taxes if they are imposed only to provide for needs actually generated by the development and if they are proportional to those needs.

The question of the impact of development on public facilities and of its potential as a nuisance raises a point not discussed in *Nollan*. Can the government prohibit a development because of its nuisance impact or its impact on public facilities if those impacts can be mitigated by conditioning? This is not an idle question. In the *Gilbert* case discussed in the introduction to this book, the rationale given for denying permits that would have allowed the Gilberts and other Bolinas landowners to build their homes was that the town did not have an adequate water supply. However, Bolinas still refused to allow landowners to build when the owners found ways to provide their property with an adequate and reliable water supply.

Under original principles of property rights and their constitutional protections, this action by Bolinas was wholly improper. Government cannot, consistent with these principles, be permitted to deny a property owner's rights when the reason for doing so can be eliminated.

Following the above reasoning, the only conditions that can be imposed in the wetlands context would be either those that would mitigate a true nuisance that would result from the use or the burdens that the development would generate on public facilities. Since the Corps has no jurisdiction over local facilities, such as schools or infrastructure, it could not impose a condition such as making the developer dedicate land for a fire department. The Corps can concern itself only with impacts within its jurisdiction.

In the case of wetlands compensatory mitigation, the Corps imposes conditions such as requiring the owner to purchase land elsewhere to turn into a wetland that serves the same function (often on an exaggerated acreage ratio). Compensatory mitigation, then, is imposed for impacts to the owner's *own* land, unless the use of the owner's land has a direct impact on enough other wetlands in the vicinity to be considered a public nuisance. We should remember that a nuisance, to come within the exception, must be a *public* nuisance, as required by *Mahon*. By definition, a nuisance is a use of one's own property that unreasonably affects others in the use or enjoyment of their property. An impact to one's own property cannot be a nuisance. Some proponents of wetlands regulation argue that changing the nature of the wetland so that it does not serve the wetlands function is an impact on other properties. However, this is false reasoning and requires that the definition of harm be stretched all out of proportion. Changing the definition of harm, in turn, requires the complicity of the courts, which means that the change is not impossible.

Assume, however, that the use would constitute a genuine nuisance. Perhaps the use is one that would, if poorly operated, result in toxic chemicals being released into the water supply. Under these circumstances, the Corps could condition the use, but the conditions under *Nollan* would be required to truly and substantially advance the purpose of preventing toxic spills. In such circumstances, the Corps could not require the owner to create a mitigation wetland elsewhere. The condition would have to be designed to prevent the toxic materials from entering the water and should be subject to a heightened level of scrutiny from the Court.

Finally, *Nollan* raised the question of proportionality without deciding it. Inherent in the concept of takings law, even under modern conceptions, is the notion that property owners ought not be required to bear burdens that rightfully belong to the public. Although modern courts have often recited this formula, they have not applied it according to its spirit. The wetlands protection arena provides a particularly good example of this problem. As already described in the preceding section on nuisance in the wetlands context, the basic nature of wetlands protection is to acquire or preserve resources that are presently in private hands so those resources may benefit the general public. Yet private property owners are the ones asked to bear the cost of providing those resources. Nothing could be more disproportionate. Therefore we must ask what is more than a rhetorical question. If wetlands preservation, or historical preservation, or any of a host of other goals are so very important, why is the public unwilling to bear its share of the cost for what it says it values?

The proportionality question arises in another way in the wetlands protection context. This question is closer to the one actually raised by the *Nollan* majority. If wetlands protection advocates are correct when they assert that wetlands preservation is now so important because of the vast losses caused by past activity, is it not disproportionate for the government to ask present wetlands owners to pay the cost for wetlands destruction that not only occurred in the past but also occurred because the government encouraged destruction of wetlands through its own programs? Remember that in *Nollan* the Coastal Commission argued that it needed to preserve psychological access to the beach because past development had reduced the existing psychological access. The Court appropriately raised the question as to why the Nollans or any small group of landowners should be required to shoulder the entire responsibility for remedying a problem to which numerous others contributed.

WETLANDS PROTECTION AND
TEMPORARY TAKINGS: REGULATORY DELAY

In considering the issue of temporary regulatory takings, the *First English* Court raised the issue of whether unreasonable delay in decision making might be held to be a taking that requires compensation. Unreasonable delay should be considered a compensable taking. To hold otherwise simply encourages regulatory agencies to accomplish their purposes by acting slowly. Those agencies should know that they will have to pay if they follow the simple expedient of acting slowly in the administrative process or of enacting temporary moratoria on development of permit issuance while they study a plan.

Any opponent of a project of any nature soon learns that delay can kill virtually any project. A project opponent can start either a court action or, more often, an administrative protest with the intention of causing a fatal time delay. For this reason, it is imperative that agencies be required to complete their review and decide in a specified time period or face the penalty of having the applicant's request automatically approved. In the absence of a hard deadline, agencies frequently use any opposition as a reason for delay or, acting in good faith, will dither about making a decision in order to avoid controversy.

Some states, including California, have statutes that provide for hard and fast deadlines.[19] These statutes not only will frequently provide for deadlines but also will contain provisions that will prevent the affected agency from avoiding the deadline by using such tactics as interminable requests for more information before deeming the application complete or such as blackmailing the applicant for more time. To force agencies to meet the deadline, these statutes provide that the agency can ask the applicant only for a single extension of a limited duration. These procedural innovations are extremely helpful to applicants, even when the application is denied, because the procedures permit applicants to know when they can challenge the agency's action. Otherwise, applicants hang in regulatory limbo while the agency makes up its mind. However, we should recognize that procedural safeguards are insufficient to ensure the protection of rights. An analogy to criminal procedure illustrates this point. Federal courts have created a process in which evidence is suppressed if it was obtained in violation of constitutional norms. However, in many instances, these court-created procedures do little more than teach some offending government officials to create convincing affidavits showing probable cause. Administrative agencies likewise learn quickly how to structure the administrative record to favor their decision, even when the facts, dispassionately examined, point in an entirely different direction.

The wetlands context is one area in which delay becomes an almost invariable feature of the landscape. Not only are wetlands regulating agencies no less prone to the problems of large administrative bureaucracies than any other agency, but also the sheer volume of agencies involved in the regulatory process and the need to comply with intersecting federal statutes, such as the National Environmental Policy Act, cause severe delays.

State agencies can also be involved. This raises another interesting issue that will have to be resolved—and soon: Who must pay for a taking when two or more levels of government are involved? For example, in the wetlands context, several federal agencies are involved and, in some states, so are state wetlands statutes and regulations. Next, we add local land use planning bodies. If all or some of these agencies deny their respective authorizations, sufficiently interfering with the property to cause a taking, who pays? All of them? The one who denied first? Does it depend on the degree to which one agency's action influenced the others? This is a complex issue, but one principle should predominate. The owner should not go remediless because more than one agency is involved. Perhaps we should borrow the most appropriate principle from tort law. Make each denying agency jointly and severally liable. Then the interest they acquire will be held as a tenancy-in-common.

Often, we find processing delays that result from inadequate staffing beyond the agency's control. However true this may be, the lack of adequate resources does not and should not be held to provide an excuse for unreasonable delay. As already noted in another connection, courts will not excuse other constitutional violations on the basis of inadequate funds. The applicant should not have to bear a loss because government creates an unwieldy process and then refuses to provide support for the programs it creates.

Wetlands Regulation and the Definition of Property

Although many subsidiary issues, even significant ones, could be discussed in this context, I will leave those for another time, except for a brief comment on the ripeness issue discussed in Part II. Recent Claims Court cases considering the question of wetlands regulation have applied the futility argument to Corps claims that an applicant should be required to come back with less ambitious plans for the wetlands in question. That all important document, the administrative record, made it clear that the Corps would refuse to allow any use.[20]

Therefore, one major issue remains to be explored in the wetlands regulation context. What happens when only a portion of the owners' property is wetland and they are able to develop all but the wetlands portion? Under cases like *Penn Central*, they would have no claim for a taking because they could develop the remainder of their property, assuming that development of the remainder constitutes economically viable use. Under cases like *Mahon* and under the original principles of the Fifth Amendment, however, the only portion of the property that should be examined is that portion for which a permit has been requested and denied. Even the *Nollan* case, which dealt primarily with the question of what kind of conditions can be imposed on a permit and when they can be imposed, found a taking despite the fact that economically viable use was left in the property. Lower court cases subsequent to *Nollan*, including *Florida Rock* and *Loveladies Harbor*, have refused to find that a taking has not occurred simply because the remainder of the property could be used.

Wetlands regulation unquestionably provides a microcosm of the regulatory takings debate. The likelihood that a significant wetlands takings case will be accepted by the Supreme Court in the near future (meaning within the next five to ten years) is high, and there is a substantial possibility that it will be resolved in favor of the property owner. To maximize that chance, proper case selection and presentation are essential because wetlands preservation is presently a highly sensitive subject. The task of the property advocate will be not only to show how takings issues arise and how they should be resolved but also to be sensitive to the Court's public policy concerns in what is legitimately an area of public interest. As in any regulatory takings case, one of the most crucial elements in presenting the case will be to demonstrate that applying sound takings principles will not jeopardize the goals of wetlands protection. Those principles only circumscribe the means by which wetlands protection can be achieved.

14

RESPECT FOR PROPERTY RIGHTS

Government can achieve the goals desired by the public, such as protection of wetlands and endangered species, through various measures without abandoning property rights protection and without straining government budgets. For example, in the context of wetlands and species preservation, government may indulge in land exchanges by trading government-owned nonwetlands or other land for privately owned wetland properties or for habitat rich properties of comparable value. In the land use arena, government can more carefully tailor regulations to significant, carefully defined governmental purposes that either will avoid takings liability altogether or will ensure that compensating benefits are provided to obviate the need for further compensation.

Whatever land use, environmental, commercial, or other regulatory schemes government ultimately uses, clearly some accommodation must be made that protects private property so the functions served by private ownership of property and by the takings clause may have their effect. The importance of this philosophy is illustrated by two headlines that appeared side by side in a San Francisco Bay area newspaper in July 1991. In one column of the front page, an article proclaimed a nationwide rise in unemployment, with the highest rise being in California. In the next column—directly across from the first article—a second article revealed the economic and social problems being caused in the West by regulations protecting the northern spotted owl. The protective regulation was throwing lumbermen out of work and was disrupting communities that were wholly dependent on timbering. Sadly, the paper was probably unaware of the irony and educational value of the juxtaposition of the two articles.

What is very clear after decades of experience is that regulatory programs more often than not exacerbate rather than solve the problems at which they are aimed. When this dichotomy happens, the rights of individuals in their property have been sacrificed for nothing. The sacrifice of civil rights of any kind is tragic, but the tragedy assumes epic proportions when it has been for nothing.

The full protection of property rights is not inconsistent with attainment of important public goals. Governmental bodies must be willing to respect property rights as they respect any other civil rights. They must also be willing to be creative in finding solutions to problems of public importance without sacrificing the rights of property owners. Property owners, in their turn, must be sensitive to the genuine concerns of members of the public, even when they believe those concerns to be unfounded. Property owners must rely as much as possible on working extensively with concerned parties and on educating the public wherever possible. This does not mean, however, that property rights advocates must accept the erosion of their civil rights any more than any other segment of the public must. When presenting their case to the appropriate parties, property owners must learn to use the same techniques, the same means of communications, and the same willingness to organize as those who oppose them.

Clint Bolick, in his most recent book, *Unfinished Business: A Civil Rights Strategy for America's Third Century,* outlined what he called "Ten Commandments for a Successful Public Interest Strategy." Briefly, those commandments are (1) articulate clearly defined long-range goals; (2) focus on direct litigation in federal cases; (3) develop a systematic, point-by-point strategy; (4) find sympathetic plaintiffs; (5) present unblemished facts; (6) find cases amenable to summary judgment; (7) generate scholarly support; (8) argue the case in the court of public opinion; (9) generate amicus support; and (10) separate fund raising from the case selection function. The reader should refer to Bolick's text for a complete explanation of these principles. They are of as much value and applicability when the civil rights at issue are property rights as they are concerning violations of the equal protection, expression, or religion clauses. But, as Bolick acknowledges, litigation is not enough.

We can hope that the executive and the legislative branches will be as assiduous in protecting property rights as they are in protecting other civil rights, but they will not do so unless the public insists on such legislative and executive action and the courts provide the underpinnings of appropriate constitutional jurisprudence. Executive Order 12,630 demonstrates that the executive can act to protect property rights. Recent moves in Congress, led by Senator Steve Symms and other Republican and Democratic senators, to lend legislative support to Executive Order 12,630 demonstrate that the legislature can be motivated to act on behalf of property rights. Before these efforts can bear fruit, however, people willing to take the political risks of defying property rights opponents must be given public support. It is the job of the property rights advocate to provide that support.

15

AFTERWORD

After this book was written, the U.S. Supreme Court decided two takings cases that had been under consideration during the latter part of the 1991–1992 court term. Both advocates and opponents of property rights have been awaiting the Supreme Court's next decisions in this arena since the landmark 1986–1987 term, when *First English*, *Keystone*, and *Nollan* were decided. Opponents of property rights were hopeful that the principles announced in the 1987 decisions would be limited or abandoned in subsequent cases but feared that the Court would instead uphold or even expand on the 1987 decisions. Property rights advocates, on the other hand, hoped that the Court would, at the very least, confirm those principles and, at best, would answer some of the questions raised but not decided in the three principal takings decisions.

The U.S. Supreme Court has seemed inclined to stand behind its earlier pronouncements. In *Preseault v. Interstate Commerce Commission* (1989), the Court rejected a decision by a federal court of appeals that had held in a sweeping opinion that a congressional scheme to transfer railroad rights-of-way to trail users could not be a taking of property because it was a valid exercise of the federal Commerce Clause power.[1] More recently, the Court let stand an appeals court decision that found that regulation of coal mining under the Surface Mining Control and Reclamation Act constituted a compensable taking. Significantly, in this latter case, *United States v. Whitney Benefits, Inc.*,[2] discussed briefly above, the United States had defended both on the ground that it was protecting the environment and on the ground that Whitney Benefits had economically viable use of the surface. As did the Supreme Court in *Nollan*, the trial court and the appeals court in *Whitney Benefits* went behind the government's statement of purpose to decide what the government was actually doing.

If *Preseault* and *Whitney Benefits* were any indication of the Supreme Court's thinking, property rights advocates had every reason to be optimistic that later cases would favor property owners. Still, courts have been known to abandon what appeared to be clear lines of precedent. Everyone was entitled, then, to worry about what the next round of decisions would bring.

The first of the two takings cases to be decided in 1992, *Yee v. City of Escondido*,[3] failed to give a clear indication of the Court's intentions with respect to the 1987 decisions. Yee claimed that a mobile home rent control scheme was a taking of his property because it authorized an unwanted physical occupancy of the property, relying on the *Loretto v. Teleprompter CATV* line of cases (see Chapter 6) in hopes of avoiding the balancing test that courts have applied in regulatory takings cases. The Court rejected Yee's argument, but in the same breath suggested that Escondido's scheme might be a *regulatory* taking of property. The Court refused to decide whether a regulatory taking had occurred because of a highly technical rule of court. This decision left property rights advocates disappointed and somewhat confused, but not without hope.

The second case to be decided was *Lucas v. South Carolina Coastal Council*.[4] Property rights opponents, predictably, discounted the decision, arguing that it was too narrow and fact-specific and that the set of circumstances to which it is to apply too rare in occurrence for the principles announced in the case to have much application. Curiously, many property rights advocates also reacted to the opinion by minimizing its importance. However, if one examines the majority opinion—and the dissenters' reactions to the majority opinion—carefully, it quickly appears that both property rights advocates and opponents seriously underestimate the importance of the *Lucas* decision. *Lucas* is an extremely significant decision, not only for what it directly decided but also for what it suggests the Court may do in the future.

Lucas involved a regulatory scheme that is typical today. Lucas purchased two parcels along the South Carolina coast together valued at just short of $1 million. When he bought the land, it was outside of the state's coastal area. As a result, he did not need to obtain a permit from the Coastal Council to build on the property. The parcels Lucas bought were flanked on either side by existing homes. After Lucas bought the land, however, South Carolina enacted the Beachfront Management Act. This act, which imposed a permanent and unvarying prohibition on the construction of any habitable permanent structures anywhere along the coast within a zone defined in the act, changed the state's coastal regulation scheme. In an attempt to prevent potential liability, the statute contained a laundry list of the purposes it was intended to serve. These purposes ranged from habitat preservation to protection against beach erosion, to preservation of recreational opportunities, to protection of public safety. Lucas challenged the scheme, alleging that the prohibition in the statute deprived him of all economically viable use of his property and was a taking of his property without regard to the validity of the state's police power rationale. The trial court agreed with Lucas and awarded him damages.

When the case reached the South Carolina Supreme Court, however, the tables had turned. That court held that it was bound by the legislature's determination that the prohibition was necessary to protect against harm and could not, therefore, be a compensable taking. While the case was pending before the state Supreme Court, the legislature amended the Beachfront Management Act to allow for applications for a variance from the flat prohibitions of the act. The state court refused to require Lucas to go back to apply for such a variance. Instead, the court ruled that the act could never be a taking because of its avowed purpose. Lucas filed a petition for *certiorari,* asking the U.S. Supreme Court to review the state court decision.

EXHAUSTION OF ADMINISTRATIVE
REMEDIES AND TEMPORARY TAKINGS

In the Supreme Court, South Carolina raised as a defense the fact that the state legislature amended the Beachfront Management Act while the case was pending in the state Supreme Court to allow some development on the coast. The state argued that this change obligated the U.S. Supreme Court to return Lucas to the Coastal Council with application in hand under the exhaustion doctrine (see Chapter 6) to determine what, if any, use the council would now permit Lucas to make of his property.

The Supreme Court refused to accept this invitation to avoid the takings issue. The majority first noted that the doctrine would have applied under ordinary circumstances, but since the state court refused to apply the doctrine in favor of making a decision on the merits of the takings claim, the federal court would not require Lucas to go back to the agency. The *Lucas* majority noted that the state court's decision that the act was not a taking, if not reviewed, would at the very least deprive Lucas of a claim for a *temporary* taking of his property for the years when the Beachfront Management Act prohibited all use of Lucas's land. By refusing to duck the case on exhaustion grounds, the *Lucas* majority reaffirmed its commitment to the principles it announced in *First English* and informed governmental bodies that they can, if they choose, convert a permanent taking of property into a temporary one by changing an absolute prohibition of use into a temporary prohibition, but they cannot avoid their constitutional obligations by altering their actions once it looks like payment will be required.

THE DEFINITION OF TAKING

The *Lucas* majority then explicitly recognized what was implicit in earlier decisions—that a deprivation of all economically viable use is only one way in which regulations can cause a taking. The Court placed regulatory schemes that deprive owners of all economically viable use of their property on the same level as those who have had their property physically invaded; that is, they deemed such regulations as "categorical takings" but then stated expressly that there are other ways in which regulations may take property, and noted that they will not always limit their consideration of takings to questions of whether a development right has been taken.

That something less than a deprivation of all economically viable use of a property can be a taking should have been obvious from numerous other cases. In *Nollan*, for example—a case the Supreme Court chose to treat as a regulatory case and not as a physical invasion case—there was no question that the Nollans had economically viable use of their property despite the imposition of a condition requiring them to dedicate a lateral easement across their private beach. After all, they had been allowed to build a liveable residence on oceanfront property in southern California. Developed oceanfront property in California is uniformly valuable. The *Nollan* Court listed several ways in which a regulation might cause a taking, only one of which was deprivation of all economically viable use. Likewise in *Kaiser-Aetna v. United States*,[5] the owner of a hotel located on a landlocked lagoon had unquestionably valuable use of the land even though the U.S. Corps of Engineers wanted to require the owner to make his lagoon open to public boating when it permitted the owner to open the lagoon to the sea. Some critics of this view have attempted to treat these two cases as "physical invasion" cases to avoid concluding that simply because economically viable use remains does not mean that a taking has not occurred. The fact remains, however, that the Supreme Court did *not* treat these cases as physical invasion cases, a fact emphasized when the *Yee* Court refused to treat a mobile home regulatory scheme as a physical invasion case despite the fact that the net effect of the scheme was to compel an unwanted physical occupancy.

The Supreme Court itself further emphasized this point when it declared that the rule it was announcing in *Lucas* was, at least for the moment, confined to cases in which the claim for regulatory taking was based on allegations that the regulation in question deprived the owner of all economically viable use. Clearly, if the only basis for a claim of regulatory taking is that property owners have been deprived of *all* economically viable use of their property, then a special statement confining the rule to one class of regulatory takings cases would hardly be necessary.

Lower courts also recognized this principle following the 1986–1987 Supreme Court term. In a number of cases, some of which were discussed in previous chapters, lower courts expressly found takings even though economic value remained in the property in question. In *Yancey v. United States*,[6] the U.S. Claims Court, followed by the U.S. Court of Appeals for the Federal Circuit, recognized that the existence of economically viable use of property is only one factor in deciding whether a regulation constituted a taking. In an even more significant case, *Whitney Benefits* (which the Supreme Court refused to review), these same two courts held that a taking had occurred even though Whitney Benefits had an economic use of the surface estate, because the regulation rendered mining of the subsurface coal uneconomical. The *Whitney Benefits* case, however, is more relevant to a different aspect of the *Lucas* case.

DEFINITION OF THE PROPERTY TO BE CONSIDERED

When the claimed basis for a regulatory taking is that the regulation deprived an owner of all economically viable use of a property, the appropriate question to ask is, What property? This question was discussed at length in Chapters 6, 7, and 9. The Supreme Court, in *Penn Central Transportation Co. v. New York*,[7] took the position—contrary to both the fundamental principles of the takings clause and over a century of experience in takings jurisprudence—that courts do not divide a property into segments and decide whether a particular segment has been taken but instead looked to the property as a whole to decide whether any economic use could be made of any part of it. As also discussed, the dissent, led by Justice Rhenquist, took the majority to task for its historically and legally insupportable position. The majority's position led to a legally and logically absurd result in which the government effectively acquired interests that, between private parties, would clearly have been considered easements and servitudes. Other inverse condemnation cases, such as *United States v. Causby* (see Chapter 5), illustrate earlier courts' adherence to the principle that *Penn Central* refused to recognize.

One of the most significant aspects of *Lucas* is the Court's signalling of its willingness to reconsider *Penn Central*. In footnote 7 to *Lucas*, the Court tempered its statement that the principle it announced in *Lucas* was limited (at least at this time) to situations in which the basis for the claimed taking was a deprivation of all economically viable use. After saying that cases of deprivation of all economically viable use were rare, the *Lucas* majority then acknowledged that the *Lucas* case only presented one example of a deprivation case, one in which all economically viable use of the entire fee interest was gone. They then said,

Regrettably, the rhetorical force of our "deprivation of all economically feasible use" rule is greater than its precision, since the rule does not make clear the "property interest" against which the loss of value is to be measured. When for example, a regulation requires a developer to leave 90% of a rural tract in its natural state, it is unclear whether we would analyze the situation as one in which the owner has been deprived of all economically beneficial use of the burdened portion of the tract, or as one in which the owner has suffered a mere diminution in value of the tract as a whole. (*For an extreme—and, we think, insupportable—view of the relevant calculus, see* Penn Central Transportation Co. v. New York [cites omitted], *where the state court examined the diminution in a particular parcel's value produced by a municipal ordinance in light of total value of the taking claimant's other holdings in the vicinity*).[8]

If the *Lucas* majority is to adhere to the principles of the Fifth Amendment, it must limit its consideration to the affected 90 percent. Critics of *Lucas* have already been quick to point out that many of the most significant features of *Lucas* are contained in footnotes and, therefore—they argue—are of little importance. Many of the Court's most important and adhered to rules have first made their appearance in footnotes. For this reason, footnotes in Supreme Court cases deserve careful examination and should be given full weight when considering the possible import of any given case. If the suggestion in this particular footnote is followed by future courts, the situation to which the main rule of the case is purportedly limited, deprivation of economically viable use, will become common rather than uncommon.*

THE NUISANCE EXCEPTION

The heart of the *Lucas* case—and the rule the Court is at least nominally restricting to the set of cases in which the claim for a taking rests on a loss of all economically viable use—involves the nuisance exception. As you will recall, the nuisance exception arose out of the notion that a person has no right to use his property in a way that deprives another person of his rights to use his own property. This concept was discussed at length in Chapter 10. Over time, the so-called nuisance exception came to be treated as a "police power" exception, and courts were prone to holding that a taking had not occurred because the action said to give rise to a taking was

---

* The majority refers to this situation as being rare. I disagree. In my experience, such situations in which all economically viable use of an entire property is gone are uncommon, but not rare. Situations in which all economically viable use of the major portion of any given tract is gone are extremely common.

a rational exercise of the police power (see Chapter 10). This broad conception of the police power exception was overruled in 1987, first in *Keystone* (where the Court made it clear that the exception, to the extent it exists, was a *nuisance* exception and not a police power exception) and again in *Nollan* (where the Court expressly overruled *Goldblatt v. Hempstead*, which had applied a rational basis test to decide whether a taking had occurred).

The questions that remained after *Nollan* and *Keystone* were whether the nuisance exception applied when the regulation in question left absolutely no economic use for the property in question, what constitutes a nuisance, and who gets to decide whether a prohibited use constitutes a nuisance. This last question is of particular importance. If courts must defer to a legislature's or administrative agency's determination of whether a use constitutes a nuisance, the takings clause is, for all intents and purposes, dead (see Chapter 10). *Lucas* appears to have considered and to have answered these questions, at least in part.

Persons attempting to use the nuisance exception have been prone to apply a "harm" label to the activities they wished to prohibit, such as filling a wetland or building homes on property that could perform habitat functions for some species. By playing this labeling game, property rights opponents hoped to avoid the strictures of the Fifth Amendment. The *Lucas* majority recognized the slipperiness of this concept. Expressly noting that "the distinction between 'harm-preventing' and 'benefit-conferring' regulation is often in the eye of the beholder," and that "[w]hether one or the other of the competing characterizations will come to one's lips in a particular case depends primarily on one's evaluation of the worth of competing uses of real estate,"[9] the Court announced that the legislature's "recitation of a noxious-use rationale cannot be the basis for departing from our categorical rule that total regulatory takings must be compensated."[10] Instead, the Court made it clear that the government can eliminate all economically viable use of land only if the prohibited activity was one that was "always unlawful" under principles of common law nuisance. This clearly would not ordinarily include such government regulatory schemes as wetlands or wildlife habitat preservation laws since such activities were without question not generally nuisances under common law principles.

Equally important, the Court appears to have recognized that courts cannot merely rely on governmental statements of purpose to find a nuisance basis (a principle announced as well in *Keystone*). In fact, the majority noted in a typically acerbic footnote, adopting a test that requires finding no taking if the government articulates a harm-preventing rationale would be no more than adopting a test of whether "the legislature has a stupid staff."[11] Leaving the decision as to whether a common law nuisance exists in the individual case in the hands of the court is not only consistent with the constitutional role of courts as finders of constitutional fact but also is consistent with the fundamental nature of the nuisance exception.

Although some courts have treated the nuisance exception as an integral part of the determination of whether a particular governmental action is a taking in the first instance, this treatment is wrong. The true nature of the nuisance exception is that of an affirmative defense.* It is not an exception to the takings clause as a whole but only to the compensation requirement. If the governmental action is not a taking in the first instance, then the nuisance exception is irrelevant. Whether the nuisance exception is an affirmative defense is important in only one respect—who must prove the existence or nonexistence of the defense? If the lack of the existence of a nuisance is an element of a taking, then the property owner must prove the lack of nuisance. If, on the other hand, the existence of a nuisance is an affirmative defense, then the government has the burden of showing that it was acting to prevent a nuisance. The property owner has to show that a taking did indeed occur, but if the property owner does make that showing, the government must show that it is, nevertheless, not obligated to pay because of some third factor—the prevention or abatement of a nuisance— this showing has traditionally been the burden of the government or private plaintiff in a customary nuisance case. The *Lucas* opinion, if it is to be read as it appears it should be, leaves that burden where it belongs.

UNDECIDED ASPECTS

Because of space and time limitations, all the dimensions of *Lucas* cannot be explored in this Afterword, even as to the information already discussed. I ask your indulgence for this summary treatment of what may be one of the more significant cases in this area of law to be decided in recent decades. However, I cannot leave this case without a word of warning. There are aspects to this case that are potentially troubling to property rights advocates if the Court follows them to their logical extreme in future cases. The one aspect of *Lucas* of most concern is the majority's apparent willingness to treat personal property as somehow different from real property for takings purposes.[12] For reasons already discussed, there is no constitutional or principled basis for distinguishing between real property and personal property in this regard. Certainly, the fact that government—and some courts—have ignored constitutional principles as to personal property for

---

* For non-lawyers, an affirmative defense is a legal defense in which the party otherwise meets all the requirements for liability but some additional factor mitigates the obligation to pay.

a long time does not justify courts in a continuing abandonment of those principles.

A second area of concern, though perhaps less so, is the majority's all too willing acquiescence in the claim that, prior to the 1922 case of *Mahon*, courts believed that only direct confiscations of property violated the Constitution's property protections. Though early courts did not always rely specifically on the takings clause in indirect interferences, the numerous cases and historical documents discussed here make it clear that—from the first—indirect invasions of property rights were in fact deemed improper unless compensation was forthcoming. Nevertheless, this lack of understanding by the majority as to the historical actions of the courts is mitigated by their willingness to recognize that the principles underlying the takings clause do apply regardless of the indirect nature of the taking.

Lucas, regardless of its flaws (such as treating regulatory takings cases as still being somewhat different in principle from so-called physical invasion cases), remains an important decision—far more important that it is given credit for—and is evidence that the courts are continuing to move in the right direction. Nevertheless, its flaws remind us that the fight to restore property rights to their rightful place in the constitutional scheme is not yet won. Property owners and other property rights advocates must continue to press forward on all fronts to ensure the meaningful protection of this most basic of civil rights.

NOTES

Frontispiece

1. Remarks to the National Federal Lands Conference delivered by the author in November 1990, citing *Loan Association v. Topeka,* 20 U.S. (Wall.) 655 (1874) and a letter from Justice Oliver Wendell Holmes to Harold J. Laski, October 22, 1922, reprinted in, 1 *The Holmes-Laski Letters* 457 (Howe, ed., 1953).

Introduction

1. Thomas Sowell, *Civil Rights: Rhetoric or Reality?* (New York: William Morrow, 1984), at 7.
2. San Rafael, CA (Marin Co.), *Marin Independent Journal,* April 14, 1990.
3. This information was derived from depositions, testimony, correspondence, and other documents filed in and relevant to the case.
4. "What's New in Greenwich Village? Private Property Rights," *Wall Street Journal,* Wednesday, June 13, 1990, p. A15.
5. *Ziman v. New York State Division of Housing and Community Renewal,* 544 N.Y.S.2d 147 (1989); "Live-in Nightmare on Dream Street", *Insight,* February 26, 1990; "What's New in Greenwich Village? Private Property Rights," *Wall Street Journal,*" Wednesday, June 13, 1990, p. A15.
6. Complaint for Declaratory Relief, Injunction, Damages for Violations of Civil Rights, *Schnuck v. City of Santa Monica,* (No. 87-05936)(C.D. Cal. September 4, 1987). This case provided the backdrop for *Are Landlords Being Taken by the Good Cause Eviction Requirement?* 62 So.Cal.L.Rev. 321 (1988).
7. *Surfside Colony, Ltd. v. California Coastal Commission,* 226 Cal. App. 3d 1260 (1991).
8. *Lynch v. Household Finance Co., Inc.,* 405 U.S. 538, 552 (1972). Interestingly, Justice Stewart also recognized that "a fundamental interdependence exists between the personal right to liberty and the personal right in property. Neither could have meaning without the other." *Id.* Unfortunately, the Supreme Court did not follow through on this principle when it devised its analytical scheme dividing fundamental rights from nonfundamental rights in deciding due process and equal protection cases.
9. Brief of the United States Opposing Certiorari.

10. *See, e.g.,* Anderson and Hills, *Birth of a Transfer Society* (1989).
11. The broader philosophical aspects of this issue are well discussed in Richard Epstein's pathbreaking book, *Takings: Private Property Rights and the Power of Eminent Domain* (Harvard University Press, 1985). I have chosen to limit the scope of inquiry in this book to the historical and political development of property rights law.
12. For a complete, revealing, and entertaining discussion about the growth of bureaucracy during the Roosevelt years, *see,* Higgs, *Crisis and Leviathan,* 159–195 (San Francisco: Pacific Research Institute, 1987).
13. *Barbecue Industry Association v. South Coast Air District,* Cal. Superior Ct., Los Angeles County, BS004212, April 17, 1991.
14. *Lynch v. Household Finance Co., Inc.,* 405 U.S. 538, 552 (1972).
15. Recent examples come readily to mind. The Supreme Court recently decided two cases involving flag burning: one considered a Texas statute forbidding flag burning; the second involved a federal statute enacted in response to the Court's first ruling. Both cases made national news. In each case, the Court held that the statute in question was invalid because it was aimed at "expressive conduct." It is not hard to predict that the outcomes may well have been radically different had the prosecution in the first case been based on a local ordinance that forbade open air burning of any object. The intent in prosecuting the defendant would have been the same in each instance: to punish the individual for expressing a particular viewpoint by burning the flag. But by couching the prosecution in different terms and giving a different rationale for pursuing the matter, the result would have been quite different.

   Another, even more compelling example also comes to mind. The federal government recently filed an indictment against one man for having filled a "wetland" without a permit required by Section 404 of the federal Clean Water Act, 33 U.S.C. § 1344. As part of the "plea bargain," to minimize the extent of the jail sentence he might otherwise receive, he was required to dedicate a "conservation easement" over his property to a nonprofit conservation group, prohibiting him from developing that property. Of course, if the government could lawfully have prevented him from filling the wetland and developing it without having to pay him in the first place, one wonders why it was necessary for him to give the easement. In any event, it is hard to imagine a more abusive use of the prosecutorial power than employing it to force an individual to give property to the government or its designee.
16. When I was with the United States Department of Justice I had the opportunity to author Executive Order 12,630 and its implementing Attorney General's Guidelines and tried to use this principle to encourage agencies to act responsibly. These documents require federal departments and agencies to do an analysis, called a takings impact assessment (TIA) whenever proposing or applying regulations or legislation. Agencies proposing or implementing regulations must consider the potential for their actions to result in a taking of property requiring compensation. The TIA must include an anaylsis of alternatives to proposed actions that will reduce interference with private property wherever possible. Where an alternative exists which will permit the agency to meet its statutory obligation while minimizing its property rights impact, the Order and Guidelines require that the least intrusive alternative be used.

   One suggestion I made in the discussions on the Order and Guidelines while they were being devised was to establish a mechanism whereby an agency against whom a takings award was levied could be required to reimburse the federal judgment fund, which would originally pay the award. I suggested this knowing that an agency would be more likely to make a good effort to do the required analysis if agencies knew that takings awards would affect their budgets. Legislation that would require such reimbursement was forwarded to House Speaker Thomas Foley on July 10, 1991, by the President's Council on Competitiveness, headed by Vice President Dan Quayle. The proposed legislation was accompanied by a letter from then Attorney General Richard Thornburgh and Treasury Secretary Richard Darman recognizing both the importance of constitutional sensitivity where property rights are involved, the importance of fiscally responsible behavior by agencies, and the role that a reimbursement requirement would play in encouraging responsible behavior. The letter also emphasized the role that reimbursement would play in putting the public policy ball back in Congress' court where it belongs, rather than leaving agencies to create policy through regulation.

17. The California Supreme Court in *Agins*, which will be discussed later, certainly recognized the truth of this assertion. It, however, chose to thwart this function of the takings clause by refusing to require the government to pay.

18. The major purpose of Executive Order 12,630 on regulatory takings, signed by President Ronald Reagan on March 15, 1988, was to bring this function of the takings clause into conscious operation at the federal level. It was particularly aimed at avoiding inadvertent fiscal liability for the government while ensuring a minimum of interference with private property consistent with the dictates of law.

   When the Order was signed, there were approximately $1 billion in outstanding takings claims against the federal government alone in just one section of one division of the Justice Department. Most of these claims were regulatory takings claims. This amount only accounted for the face amount of the outstanding claims. It did not include interest on the claimed amount that would have to be paid if the claimant were successful, nor did it consider the litigation costs that had been and would be incurred by the government or any of a host of other costs that would be incurred regardless of whether the government ultimately won. Neither did this rather informal survey include past recoveries, either in court or in settlement, or claims that were made or settled without a complaint being filed in court.

   If even 10 percent of those claims were paid, the amount would be $100 million, exclusive of interest, not an inconsiderable sum even today. In 1989, a single verdict was issued against the federal government in the *Whitney Benefits* case for $60 million plus interest, an amount sure to exceed $120 million. *Whitney Benefits, Inc. v. United States*, 18 Cl.Ct. 374 (1989), *modified* 20 Cl.Ct. 324 (1991). That decision was upheld on appeal before the Court of Appeals for the Federal Circuit. *Whitney Benefits, Inc. v. United States*, 926 F.2d 1169 (1991). The Supreme Court refused to hear the case, leaving the takings award intact and preserving the case's value as precedent. *Whitney Benefits, Inc.*, ___ U.S. ___, 112 S.Ct. 406, 116 L.Ed. 2d 354 (1991).

19. For a complete discussion of the various types of regulations affecting housing prices see, *Resolving the Housing Crisis*, M. Bruce Johnson, ed. (San Francisco: Pacific Research Institute, 1982).

20. *See, e.g., id.*

21. *See*, Mercer and Morgan, "An Estimate of Residential Growth Controls' Impact on House Prices," in *Resolving the Housing Crisis* 189 (Johnson, ed., 1982).

22. *See, e.g.*, Frech, *The California Coastal Commission: Economic Impact*, in *Resolving the Housing Crisis* 259 (Johnson, ed., 1982).

23. *Id.* at 266.

24. *Report of The President's Commission on Housing* at 180 (1982).

25. Report of the HUD Advisory Commission on Regulatory Barriers to Affordable Housing, "Not In My Back Yard" (1991).
26. *See, e.g.*, Hanke and Walters, *Social Regulation: A Report Card* (1990 National Chamber Foundation) and studies cited therein.

CHAPTER 1

1. Thomas Jefferson, *The Declaration of Independence*.
2. *See, e.g.*, Erich Fromm, *Escape from Freedom, passim* (1941); F.A. Hayek, *The Road to Serfdom* 71–72 (1960); Alexis DeTocqueville, *Democracy in America* 57 (Mayer, ed., 1969).
3. For an excellent discussion on the role of crises in the growth of government, *see*, Higgs, *Crisis and Leviathan: Critical Episodes in the Growth of American Government* (1987).
4. Clint Bolick, *Changing Course: Civil Rights at the Crossroads* xi–xii (San Francisco: Pacific Research Institute, 1988).

CHAPTER 2

1. Letter to Harold J. Laski, September 15, 1916, *reprinted in*, 1 *Holmes-Laski Letters* 21 (Howe, ed., 1953).
2. John Jay, Federalist Paper No. 2, *The Federalist Papers* 39 (Rossiter, ed., 1961). Admittedly, Jay was being somewhat disingenuous. The convention was called specifically to reform the Articles, not to scrap them.
3. *See, e.g.*, (Pinckney) *Notes* at 35; (Patterson) *Notes* at 95–96; (Lansing) *Notes* at 122; (Hamilton) *Notes* at 129–131.
4. *See, e.g.*, discussion infra, p. 48. For convenience and accuracy, further references to the Constitution will include the Bill of Rights unless some other reason exists for mentioning the bill separately.
5. Madison, *Notes of Debates of the Federal Constitution* 648 (Bicentennial Edition 1987) (hereinafter "*Notes*").
6. *Id. See, also, e.g., id.* at 299–300.
7. 5 U.S.C. section 552.
8. S. Rep. No. 813, p.9; *see, also,* H.R. Rep. No. 1497, p. 10.
9. *National Labor Relations Board v. Sears, Roebuck & Co.*, 421 U.S. 149, 150–151 (1975) (emphasis in original).
10. *See, e.g.*, Alexander Hamilton, Federalist Paper No. 70, *The Federalist Papers, supra*, at 424.
11. Lewis Caroll, *Through the Looking Glass*, ch. 6, p. 205 (1934).
12. As noted, volumes have been written about this topic. I will not, therefore, explore all dimensions of that debate here. For a good, brief summary of arguments supporting the notion that the original meaning assigned by the Framers and ratifiers to the Constitution may be safely ignored, and rebuttals of that proposition, *see*, Robert Bork, *The Tempting of America* 161–178 (New York: MacMillan, 1989).
13. *See, e.g.*, Madison, Federalist Paper No. 43, *The Federalist Papers* 278.
14. *See, e.g.*, Robert Bork, *The Tempting of America* 183–185 (1989).
15. Numerous scholars have explored this issue. *See, e.g.*, Epstein, *The Political Theory of the Federalist* (Chicago: Univ. of Chicago Press, 1984); Wright, *The Contract Clause and the Constitution* (Westport, CT: Greenwood, 1938), among many others.
16. The Fourteenth Amendment is discussed in more detail below.

17. Reprinted in *The Antifederalist Papers and Constitutional Convention Debates*, 219–221 (Ketcham, ed., 1986).

18. *See*, Bork, *The Tempting of America* 183–185 (1989).

19. *See, e.g.*, Letter of May 8, 1825, to Henry Lee, from *The Writings of Thomas Jefferson* (Ford, ed., 1892–1899), Vol. X at 343; *see, also, Notes* at 202, in which Luther Martin of Maryland cites Locke, Vattel, and others regarding natural rights.

20. Richard B. Morris (no relation) referred to Gouverneur Morris as "the stylist of the Constitution" (*see, e.g.*, Morris, *Witnesses at the Creation* 17 (1985)), and attributed much of the Constitution's "spare, eloquent language" to him. *Id.* at 207. Richard Morris also noted that it was Gouverneur Morris who made the fateful motion to supplant the loose confederation of the Articles with a national government. *Id.* at 223. Gouverneur Morris was equally active at pushing reforms before the convention. He, along with Robert Morris of New York (also no relation to either Richard or Gouverneur) had urged army officers who had remained unpaid since the end of the revolutionary war, to put pressure on Congress to do something about back pay. He reminded that august body that the soldiers had the swords. *Id.* at 141–143.

21. (Morris) *Notes* at 233.

22. *Id.* at 244.

23. *Id.* at 247, 247, 269, 278–279; Madison, Federalist Paper No. 10, *The Federalist Papers* 78; Federalist Paper No. 54, *id* at 339.

24. John Jay, Federalist Paper No. 1, *The Federalist Papers* 36.

25. Benjamin Wright, *The Contract Clause and the Constitution* 4–5 (1938). *See, also,* Nevins, *The American States Before and After the Revolution, 1775–1789,* at 836, 390, 404, 457, 525, 532–533, 537, 549, 570–571 (1924) for a survey of the various laws that concerned the delegates. This is not to say that the Framers were opposed to any legislation affecting contracts. Their concern was for legislation affecting *existing* contracts. *See, e.g., Notes* 543–544.

26. Alexander Hamilton, Federalist Paper No. 11, *The Federalist Papers* 87.

27. *The Papers of Alexander Hamilton* 479 (Syrett, ed., 1977).

28. Hamilton, Federalist Paper No. 7, *The Federalist Papers* at 65.

29. *Id.*

30. Madison, Federalist Paper No. 44, *The Federalist Papers* 282.

31. Hamilton, Federalist Paper No. 85, *The Federalist Papers* 522.

32. (Sherman) *Notes* at 208.

33. (Madison) *Notes,* at 76.

34. Madison, Federalist Paper No. 10, *The Federalist Papers* 79.

35. *Id.* at 81.

36. *Id.* at 84. The contagious disease metaphor was also resorted to in the Federalist Papers, for example in Paper No. 38, *The Federalist Papers* 234–235.

37. *Id.* at 78.

38. (Hamilton) *Notes* at 196. That this report reflected Hamilton's view is evident from Hamilton's contributions to *The Federalist Papers*.

39. *See, e.g.*, Hamilton, Federalist Paper No. 84, *The Federalist Papers* 513.

40. Madison, Federalist Paper No. 57, *The Federalist Papers* 353.

41. (Madison) *Notes* at 77.

42. (Hamilton) *Notes,* at 135.

43. *Id.*

44. Madison, Federalist Paper No. 51, *The Federalist Papers* 320.

45. *Id.*

46. Hamilton, Federalist Paper No. 85, *The Federalist Papers* 521–522.

47. *Notes* at 312.
48. (Madison) *Notes* at 312.
49. *Id.* at 338.
50. (Ghorum) *Notes* at 315.
51. Hamilton, Federalist Paper No. 71, *The Federalist Papers* 432 (emphasis in original).
52. Hamilton, Federalist Paper No. 15, *The Federalist Papers* 110–111.
53. Alexis DeTocqueville, *Democracy in America* 251, Meyer, ed. (New York: Harper and Row, 1988).
54. Letter No. I, October 8, 1787, *Observations Leading to a Fair Examination of the System of Government Proposed by the Later Convention; and to Several Essential and Necessary Alterations to It In a Number of Letters from the Federal Farmer to the Republican* (hereinafter, *Letters From the Federal Farmer*), *The Antifederalist Papers and Constitutional Convention Debates* (Ralph Ketcham, ed., 1986) at 259–260. Originally published in the *Poughkeepsie Country Journal,* November 1787 – January 1788 and in pamphlet form, authorship of the Letters has not been conclusively established. It is thought that they may possibly have been written by Richard Henry Lee or, as Ketcham believes more likely, by Melancton Smith.
55. (Morris) *Notes* at 339–340.
56. Hamilton, Federalist Paper No. 70, *The Federalist Papers* 423.
57. *See, e.g., Notes* at 485–486, 630.
58. *See, e.g.,* Hamilton, Federalist Paper No. 84, *The Federalist Papers* 513–515. In convention, for example, James Wilson of Pennsylvania objected to an attempt to include a provision barring the government from imposing *ex post facto* laws, arguing that "[i]t will bring reflexions [sic] on the Constitution—and proclaim that we are ignorant of the first principles of Legislation, or are constituting a Government that will be so." (Wilson) *Notes* at 511.
59. Hamilton, Federalist Paper No. 84, *The Federalist Papers* 513–515.
60. Letter from the Federal Farmer No. II, *The Antifederalist Papers and Constitutional Convention Debates* (Ketcham, ed., 1986) 266.
61. Essay No. II, The Essays of "John DeWitt", published in the *Boston American Herald,* October – December 1787, reprinted in *The Antifederalist Papers and Constitutional Convention Debates* 195–197.
62. *The Antifederalist Papers and Constitutional Convention Debates* 219–221.
63. *See, e.g., United States v. Lee,* 106 U.S. 195, 219 (1882).
64. *See, e.g.,* Federalist Paper No. 84, *The Federalist Papers* 513–514.
65. *See, e.g.,* (Gerry), *Notes* 652; 3 *Papers of George Mason* 991–993 (Rutland ed.), reprinted in *The Antifederalist Papers and Constitutional Convention Debates* 175 (Ketcham, ed., 1986); "Brutus" Essays I, VI, XI, reprinted in *The Antifederalist Papers and Constitutional Convention Debates* 271, 274–275, 280, 296.
66. *See, e.g.,* Madison, Federalist Paper No. 44, *The Federalist Papers* 285–286.
67. Hamilton, Federalist Paper No. 78, *The Federalist Papers* 466.
68. *Id.* at 466–467.
69. *Id.*
70. *Id.* at 467.
71. *Id.* at 469.
72. Hamilton, Federalist Paper No. 81, *The Federalist Papers* 482.
73. *Id.*
74. Id.
75. Id. at 470.

76. For a thorough discussion of the Ninth Amendment, see, Barnett, *The Rights Retained by the People* (Lanham. MD: University Press of America, 1989).
77. *Id.* at 470–471 (emphasis added).
78. *See, e.g., Notes* 317–318, 536–537; Hamilton, Federalist No. 79, *The Federalist Papers* 472–474.

CHAPTER 3

1. Felix Frankfurter, *Of Law and Men* 19 (1954).
2. *Lynch v. Household Finance Co., Inc.*, 405 U.S. 538, 552 (1972).
3. 28 Edw. III, Chapter 3 (1335), quoted in Corwin, *The Constitution and What It Means Today* (rev. by Chase and Ducet 1973).
4. *See, e.g.*, The Petition of Right (Pickering, ed., 1628), Statutes at Large VII, 317–320.
5. *See, e.g., Dr. Bonham's Case*, 8 Rep. 118a (1610).
6. Blackstone, *Commentaries*, *41.
7. *Id.* at *134.
8. *Id.* at 134. James Kent, another legal scholar much relied on in America, confirmed that the right to acquire and enjoy property is "natural, inherent, and inalienable." Kent, *Commentaries on American Law*, vol. 2, p.1 (1971)(reprint of 1827 edition).
9. Jacob, *New Law Dictionary* (9th Ed., 1772).
10. Declaration and Resolve of the Continental Congress (1774), *Documents Illustrative of the Formation of the American States (69th Cong., 1st Sess.)*, 1–5, reprinted in Swindler, 1 *Sources and Documents of the United States Constitutions* 292 (1982).
11. *Id.* at 10–17, Swindler at 307.
12. The Northwest Ordinance, *Documents Illustrative of the Formation of the American States (69th Cong., 1st Sess.)* at 47–54, reprinted in Swindler, 1 *Sources and Documents of the United States Constitutions* (1982).
13. 4 *The James Madison Letters* 478 (March 27, 1792), quoted in Siegan, *Economic Liberties and the Constitution* 58 (1980). This language appears in part as well in "Property," *National Gazette*, March 27, 1792, in 14 Madison, *The Papers of James Madison* 266 (Riland, ed., 1977).
14. *See, e.g.*, Madison, Federalist Paper No. 10, *The Federalist Papers* 79; (Hamilton) *Notes* at 196.
15. Jacob, *New Law Dictionary* (9th Ed., 1772).
16. Shepard, *Land Use Regulation in the Rhenquist Court: The Fifth Amendment and Judicial Intervention*, 38 Cath. U. L. Rev. 847 (1990).
17. *Fletcher v. Peck*, 10 U.S. (6 Cranch) 87, 137–138 (1810).
18. *See, e.g.*, discussion *infra*, notes 2, 8, 12, 27 and accompanying text.
19. *Dr. Bonham's Case*, 8 Rep. 118a (1610).
20. 3 U.S. (3 Dall.) 386 (1798); 2 U.S. (2 Dall.) 304 (1795); 58 Ark. 407, 415, 422, 25 S.W. 75 (1894); 113 Pa. 131 Pa. 431, 437, 6 A. 354 (1886); 98 N.Y. 98, 110 (1886). For an excellent and complete discussion of these and numerous other constitutional and pre-Civil War era cases and commentaries on the due process clause, *see*, Siegan, *Economic Rights and the Constitution* (1980).
21. Blackstone, *Commentaries* at *125, *130, *134.
22. Locke, *Two Treatises on Government* (1690).
23. Blackstone, *Commentaries* *121–122.
24. Locke, *Of Civil Government*, Second Treatise, ch. XI, sec. 137
25. *See, e.g.*, Bernard Siegan, *Economic Rights and the Constitution, supra*.

26. *See, e.g.*, Bolick, *Unfinished Business: A Civil Rights Strategy for America's Third Century* 73–76 (1990).

27. Van Bynkershoek, *Quaestonium Juris Publici* 218 (Frank Trans. 1930), quoted in Stoebuck, *A General Theory of Eminent Domain*, 47 Wash. L. Rev. 553, 557–569 (1972).

28. *See, e.g.*, Blackstone, *Commentaries* *135.

29. *Id.*

30. *Id.*

31. *Id.*

32. *Id.*

33. Samuel Pufendorf, *De Officio Homines et Civis*, Tit. II, ch. 15, Section 4. *See, also*, Pufendorf, *Jurae Naturaeet Gentium*, bk. VIII, ch. 5, sec. 7 (C. and W. Oldfathers, trans. 1934).

34. Grotius, *De Jure Belli et Pacis*, bk. VIII, ch. 14, sec. 7 (1625). and the like.

35. Stat. 6 Hen. 6, ch. 5 (1427). This statute and others dealing with the same subject matter (sewers) declared that appointed commissioners would have the power to take property where necessary to repair walls, ditches, gutters, lowlands, and bridges.

36. Stoebuck, *A General Theory of Eminent Domain*, 47 Washington L. Rev. 553, 576–577 (1972).

37. *See, e.g.*, Stat. 6 Hen. 8, ch. 17 (1514–1515); Stat. 31 Hen. 8, ch. 4 (1534).

38. *Vanhorne's Lessee v. Dorrance*, 2 U.S. (2 Dall.) 304, 311 (1795)

39. Stoebuck, *A General Theory of Eminent Domain*, 47 Wash. L. Rev. 553, 583 (1972). *See*, also, Grant, *The "Higher Law" Background of Eminent Domain*, 6 Wisc. L. Rev. 67 (1931) for a survey of federal and state cases considering the existence of a compensation obligation.

40. September 11, 1776, quoted in 5 *The Founders' Constitution* 312 (Kerland and Lerner, eds., 1987). Notice the suggestion inherent in this language that there may be a difference from the protection of individuals against intrusion on property by others and other more general public uses.

41. *Calder v. Bull, supra*, 3 U.S. at 386, 400 (1798) (Iredell, J., dissenting).

42. *Id.*

43. Siegan, *Economic Liberties and the Constitution, supra*, at 80.

44. *Cong. Globe*, 39th Cong., 1st Sess., 599 (1866) [emphasis added].

45. *Cong. Globe*, 35th Cong., 2d Sess. 983 (1859) [emphasis added].

46. *Cong. Globe*, 34th Congress, 3d Sess., app. 140 (1857).

47. *Cong. Globe*, 35th Cong., 2d Sess. 985 (1859).

48. *See, e.g.*, *Corfield v. Coryell*, 6 F. Cas. 546 (1823), which Representative Shellabarger relied on in drafting the Civil Rights Act of 1871. *See*, discussion *infra*.

49. *See, e.g.*, Statement of Representative Shellabarger (chairman of the committee drafting the 1871 Act), *Cong. Globe*, 42d Cong., 1st Sess., App.68 (1871). "The model for [Section 1 of the 1971 Act is] found in the second section of the act of April 9, 1866, known as the 'civil rights act.'"

50. S. Rep. No. 1, 42d Cong., 1st Sess., at II (1871).

51. *Cong. Globe*, 42d Cong., 1st Sess., App. 69 (1871).

52. 6 F.Cas. 546, 551–552 (1825).

53. *Cong. Globe*, 42d Cong., 1st Sess., 244 (1871).

54. *See, e.g.*, *Cong. Globe*, 42d Cong., 1st Sess., 332–334, 369–370, 375–376, 429, 448, 459–461, 475–476, 501, 568, 577, 607, 650–651, 653, 666.

55. 83 U.S. (16 Wall.) 36 (1872).

CHAPTER 4

1. 83 U.S. (16 Wall.) 36 (1872).
2. *Barron v. Mayor of Baltimore*, 32 U.S (7 Pet.) 243 (1833).
3. 10 U.S. (6 Cranch) 87 (1810)(John Marshall, J.).
4. 106 U.S. 195 (1882) (Miller, J.).
5. 6 F.Cas. 546, 551-52 (C.C.E.D. Pa. 1823)(No.3,230).
6. 2 F.Cas. 570 (C.C.W.D. Pa. 1865)(No. 827).
7. 75 U.S. 603 (1870).
8. 55 U.S. 538 (1853).
9. 79 U.S. 457 (1871).
10. 85 U.S. 129 (1873).
11. 13 NY 378 (1856).
12. 25 U.S. (12 Wheat.) 212 (1827) (John Marshall, J., dissenting).
13. 165 U.S. 578 (1897).
14. 17 U.S. (4 Wheat.) 518, 581 (1819).
15. 17 U.S. (4 Wheat.) 235, 244 (1819).
16. 1 S.C.L. (1 Bay) 252 (1792) (South Carolina Supreme Court).
17. 5 N.C. (1 Mur.) 58 (1805) (North Carolina Supreme Court).
18. 7 Johns (N.Y.) 477, 506 (1811) (Chancellor Kent).
19. 2 U.S. (2 Dall.) 304 (1795).
20. 27 U.S. (2 Pet.) 627, 657 (1829).
21. 3 U.S. (3 Dall.) 386 (1798).
22. 13 U.S (9 Cranch) 43, 50–51 (1815).
23. 87 U.S. (20 Wall.) 655 (1875).
24. 166 U.S. 226 (1897).
25. 164 U.S. 403 (1896).
26. 164 U.S. 403 (1896).
27. *Calder v. Bull*, 3 U.S. (3 Dall.) at 387–388.
28. *Id.*
29. *Vanhorne's Lessee v. Dorrence*, 2 U.S. (2 Dall.) at 310 (1795).
30. *Id.*
31. *Id.*
32. *Bank of Columbia v. Oakley*, 17 U.S. (4 Wheat.) 235, 244 (1819).
33. *See, e.g., Bowman v. Middleton*, 1 S.C.L. (1 Bay) 252 (1792) (invalidating an act of the colonial assembly taking away a freehold from one person and vesting it in another without any compensation or jury trial, "as it was against common right as well as against magna carta"); *Trustees of the University of North Carolina v. Foy*, 5 N.C. (1 Mur.) 58 (1805) (invalidating act revoking land grant to a University under a "law of the land provision" in the state constitution).
34. *See, e.g., Fletcher v. Peck*, 10 U.S. (6 Cranch) 87, 130 (1810) (Marshall, J.).
35. *Id.*
36. *Id.*
37. *Fletcher v. Peck*, 10 U.S. at 132–133.
38. *Id.* at 135–136.
39. *Id.* at 135–136 [emphasis added].
40. *Id.* at 142.
41. *Id.* at 144.
42. *Id.*
43. *Id.* at 138–139.

44. 7 Johns (N.Y.) 477, 506 (1811).
45. 6 F.Cas. 546 (C.C.E.D. Pa. 1823). *Corfield* was relied upon by the authors and ratifiers of the Fourteenth Amendment. *See infra.*
46. *Id.* at 551–552.
47. *Id.* at 657. *See, also, Terrett v. Taylor,* 13 U.S (9 Cranch) 43, 50–51 (1815); *Hepburn v. Griswold,* 75 U.S. 603, 624 (1870) (due process clause and other Fifth Amendment provisions operate "directly in limitation and restraint of the legislative powers conferred by the Constitution"); *Trustees of Dartmouth College v. Woodward,* 17 U.S. (4 Wheat.) 518, 581 (1819) ("By the law of the land is most clearly intended the general law; a law which hears before it condemns; which proceeds upon inquiry, and renders judgment only after trial. The meaning is, that every citizen shall hold his life, liberty, property, and immunities, under protection of the general rules which govern society. Everything which may pass under the form of an enactment, is not, therefore, to be considered the law of the land ..."); *Bank of Columbia v. Oakley,* 17 U.S. (4 Wheat.) 235, 244 (1819)("As to the words from Magna Carta, incorporated into the constitution of Maryland, after volumes spoken and written with a view to their exposition, the good sense of mankind has at length settled down to this: that they were intended to secure the individual from the arbitrary exercise of the power of government, unrestrained by the established principles of private rights and distributive justice"); *Bowman v. Middleton,* 1 S.C.L. (1 Bay) 252 (1792) (invalidating an act of the colonial assembly taking away a freehold from one person and vesting it in another without any compensation or jury trial "as it was against common right as well as against magna carta"); *Trustees of the University of North Carolina v. Foy,* 5 N.C. (1 Mur.) 58 (1805) (invalidating statute revoking land grant in face of a law of the land provision in state constitution).
48. *Fletcher v. Peck,* 10 U.S. (6 Cranch) at 133 [emphasis added].
49. *United States v. Lee,* 106 U.S. 195, 208–209 (1882).
50. *Id.* at 217.
51. *Id.*
52. *Id.* at 219.
53. *Id.* at 220–221.
54. *Id.* at 218. For an extensive discussion of these and other cases, state and federal, considering the treatment of property rights by courts during the first century of the postratification period, *see,* Siegan, *Economic Liberties and the Constitution, supra.*
55. *See, e.g., United States v. Locke,* 471 U.S. 84, 105 (1985).
56. *Fletcher v. Peck,* 10 U.S. (6 Cranch) 87, 137–138 (1810).
57. 75 U.S. 603, 624 (1870).
58. *Id.*
59. 475 U.S. 211, 223 (1986).
60. *Hadacheck v. Sebastian,* 239 U.S. 394, 410 (1915).
61. *Hadacheck v. Sebastian,* 239 U.S. 394, 410 (1915).
62. *Just v. Marinette County,* 201 N.W.2d 761 (1972).
63. *Id.* at 771 n.6.
64. *United States v. Lee,* 106 U.S. 195, 208–209 (1882).
65. 83 U.S. (16 (Wall.) 36 (1872).
66. 83 U.S. (16 Wall.) at 78.
67. *Id.* at 78. For excellent discussions of this case and the significant problems with the majority's opinion *see,* Bolick, *Unfinished Business: A Civil Rights Strategy for America's Third Century,* 7–8, 28, 60–70, 76–86 (1990); and Siegan, *Economic Liberties and the Constitution,* 47–53 (1980).

CHAPTER 5

1. Of course, the threat is even more apparent when the tendency to regulate is accompanied by a relaxed scrutiny by the judiciary.
2. 290 U.S. 398, 474 (1934).
3. This again demonstrates why the modern judiciary's claim that it is forbidden to interfere with legislative enactments affecting property and economic rights because it is forbidden to concern itself with the legislature's motivation is fallacious. The Framers were concerned about legislative interferences with rights and not merely with the motives that precipitated them.
4. 42 U.S.C. section 2000e-2(a).
5. Section 2000e-(2)(j).
6. 110 Cong. Rec. 1518 (1964).
7. 443 U.S. 192 (1979).
8. *Id.* at 216.
9. 80 U.S. (13 Wall.) 166 (1871).
10. *Id.* at 177–178 [emphasis in original].
11. 328 U.S. 256 (1946).
12. *Id.* at 259.
13. *Id.* at 259.
14. *Id.* at 261–262.
15. *Id.* at 262.
16. *Id.* at 261.
17. *Id.* at 265. [Emphasis added.] Contrast this statement with the Court's position in *Penn Central Transportation Co. v. New York City*, 438 U.S 104 (1978), discussed *infra*, in which air rights were also at issue.
18. 260 U.S. 393 (1922).
19. *San Diego Gas & Electric v. San Diego*, 450 U.S, 621, 652–653 (1981)(Brennan, J. dissenting)[emphasis in original].
20. *Id.*
21. *Id.* at 652.
22. To be specific, as the coal company noted, the relevant portions of the statute were described by the Pennsylvania Supreme Court:

    The statute is entitled: "An act regulating the mining of anthracite coal; prescribing duties for certain municipal officers; and imposing penalties."

    Section 1 provides that it shall be unlawful "so to conduct the operation of mining anthracite coal as to cause the caving-in, collapse, or subsidence of

    (a) Any public building or any structure customarily used by the public as a place of resort, assemblage, or amusement, including, but not being limited to, churches, schools, hospitals, theaters, hotels, and railroad stations;

    (b) Any street, road, bridge, or other public passageway, dedicated to public use or habitually used by the public;

    (c) Any track, roadbed, right of way, pipe, conduit, wire, or other facility, used in the service of the public by any municipal corporation or public service company as defined by the Public Service Company Law;

    (d) Any dwelling or other structure used as a human habitation, or any factory, store, or other industrial or mercantile establishment in which human labor is employed;

    (e) Any cemetery or public burial ground."

Sections 2 to 5, inclusive, place certain duties on public officials and persons in charge of mining operations, to facilitate the accomplishment of the purpose of the act.

Section 6 provides the act "shall not apply to [mines in] townships of the second class [i.e., townships having a population of less than 300 persons to a square mile], nor to any area wherein the surface overlying the mine or mining operation is wild or unseated land, nor where such surface is owned by the owner or operator of the underlying coal and is distant more than one hundred and fifty feet from any improved property belonging to any other person."

Section 7 sets forth penalties; and § 8 reads: "The courts of common pleas shall have power to award injunctions to restrain violations of this act." P.L. 1921, p. 1198. 274 Pa. St. 489, reversed.

Mahon, supra, 260 U.S. at 394.

23. *Mahon*, 260 U.S. at 406.
24. *Id.* at 394.
25. *Id.* 409.
26. *Id.* at 413.
27. Letter to Harold J. Laski, October 22, 1922, *reprinted in*, 1 *The Holmes–Laski Letters* 457 (1953). Holmes originally inserted these words in an opinion (*Knights v. Jackson*, 260 U.S. 12 (1922)), but he decided to remove them after it was suggested to him that to leave them in would not be in the best of taste. *Id.* The title of this book, in fact, is derived from Holmes's characterizations of the powers of government. Holmes, whose letters demonstrate a considerable personal bias toward private property, once cynically described the courts' use of tests for determining whether an action took property in a manner requiring compensation. He said that such use was really no more than "determining a line between grabber and grabbee that turns on the feeling of the community." Letter to Harold J. Laski, October 23, 1926, reprinted in, 2 *The Holmes–Laski Letters* 888 (1953). Holmes, never one to mince words, also found Justice Harlan's opinion in *Mugler v. Kansas*, 123 U.S. 623 (1887), to be "pretty fishy." Letter to Harold J. Laski, January 13, 1923, reprinted in, 1 *The Holmes–Laski Letters* 473 (1953). *Mugler*, discussed later, is the case most relied on for the proposition that compensation is not required if the government's action prevents a nuisance.
28. *Mahon, supra*, 260 U.S. at 413 [emphasis added].
29. *Mahon, supra*, 260 U.S. at 413.
30. *Id.* at 414.
31. *Id* at 416.
32. *Id.* at 413.
33. *Id.* at 414–415. [Emphasis added.]
34. *Id.* at 415.
35. *Id.* at 415–416.
36. *Id.* 416.
37. *Id.* at 414–415. [Emphasis added.]
38. *Id.* at 419.

CHAPTER 6

1. Letter to Harold J. Laski, October 23, 1926, reprinted in, 2 *The Holmes–Laski Letters* 888 (1953).
2. *See, e.g., Andrus v. Allard*, 444 U.S. 51 (1979).
3. *The Report of the President's Commission on Housing* 182 (1982).

4. "Not In My Back Yard," pp. 2-1–2-12, 4-1–4-11.
5. 438 U.S. 104 (1978).
6. *See, e.g., Penn Central Transportation Co. v. New York City*, 438 U.S. 104, 124 (1978).
7. *See, Loretto v. Teleprompter Manhattan CATV Corp.*, 458 U.S. 419, 434 (1982). ("[W]hen the 'character of the governmental action,' [cite omitted], is a permanent physical occupation of property," the Court has consistently found a taking.) Under these circumstances, no balancing of public benefit and economic impact on the property owner is made. *Id.* at 432, 434.
8. *See, e.g., Agins v. Tiburon*, 477 U.S. 255, 260 (1980); *Nollan v. California Coastal Commission*, 483 U.S. 825, 836 n.3 (1987).
9. *Agins*, 477 U.S. at 142 n.4 (Rehnquist, J., dissenting).
10. *Id.* at 143 n.5 and 6.
11. *Id.* at 146 [cites omitted, emphasis added].
12. Blackstone, *Commentaries* *135.
13. *Penn Central, supra*, 438 U.S. at 149–150 (Rehnquist, J., dissenting) [emphasis in original].
14. *Penn Central*, 438 U.S. at 149 n. 13.
15. *Penn Central*, 438 U.S. at 149 n. 13.

CHAPTER 7

1. *United Steelworkers v. Weber*, 443 U.S. 192, 219 (1979)(Burger, J., dissenting).
2. *United States v. General Motors Corporation*, 323 U.S. 373, 377–378 (1945).
3. *Ruckleshaus v. Monsanto*, 467 U.S. 986 (1984).
4. *Armstrong v. United States*, 364 U.S. 40 (1960).
5. *Webb's Fabulous Pharmacies, Inc. v. Beckwith*, 449 U.S. 155 (1980).
6. *Shanghai Power Company v. United States*, 4 Cl.Ct. 237 (1983).
7. *Penn Central, supra*, 438 U.S. 104.
8. Courts about to deny that a regulatory action constitutes a compensable taking of property analogize the complex of rights an individual has in property to a "bundle of sticks" preparing to argue that the government's action only deprived the owner of one or two of the sticks in the bundle, leaving the owner with other valuable rights. *See, e.g., Andrus v. Allard*, 444 U.S. 51 (1979) in which Justice Brennan held that a law that deprived owners of legally acquired protected bird parts of their right to sell those parts, saying that they still had physical possession and title and could give them away or will them and argued that "the denial of one traditional property right does not always amount to a taking" *Id.* at 65. Relying on *Penn Central*, Justice Brennan held that destruction of one major attribute of property, free alienability, is not a taking. "In this case, it is crucial that the appellees retain the rights to possess and transport their property, and to donate or devise the protected birds." (*Id.* at 66.) The Court attempted to distinguish the case before it from *Mahon*, on grounds that the Coal Company, in addition to preventing sale of coal, had to leave the remaining coal in the ground. It is a distinction without meaning. The Coal Company, like the owner of the artifact containing bird parts, had physical possession of and could donate or devise the coal. To the extent that the Court was concerned, for example, about infringing on the authority of government to outlaw something that may be harmful to the general public, there was no problem. There is a distinction between keeping someone from having or selling a dangerous substance or instrumentality from eagle feathers that, after all, represents

nothing more than society's desire to preserve a resource it likes as opposed to preventing affirmative harm to life or health.

9. *Penn Central, supra*, at 130–131.
10. See, *infra*.
11. *United States v. General Motors Corporation, supra*, 323 U.S. at 378, 382.
12. Blackstone, *supra*, *51.
13. See, e.g., Friedman, *A History of American Law* 88–89 (1973); Waterman, Thomas Jefferson and Blackstone's Commentaries, *Essays in the History of Early American Law* 451, 457 (Flaherty, ed., 1959)(original ed., 1765).
14. Blackstone, *Commentaries* *135.
15. Blackstone, *Commentaries* * 135.
16. Blackstone at *138; Locke, *Of Civil Government, Second Treatise*, ch. IX, section 124 (Henry Regnery 1955).
17. September 11, 1776, quoted in 5 *The Founders' Constitution* 312 (Kerland and Lerner, eds., 1987).
18. Blackstone, *Commentaries* *135.
19. *See, also, e.g., Fletcher v. Peck, supra*, 10 U.S. (6 Cranch) at 142 Johnson, J., concurring and dissenting).
20. Hamilton, Federalist No. 12, *The Federalist Papers* 91.
21. 2 Kent, *Commentaries on America Law* 256–257.
22. Jacob, *New Law Dictionary* (9th ed., 1772). *See, also, Grotius, De Jure Belli et Pacis*, bk. VIII, ch. 14, sec. 7 (1625). Grotius's formulation of the power of eminent domain, discussed previously, included both government's right "to use *and* even alienate … property," so long as it ma[de] good the loss to those who lose their property." This formulation also suggests that something less than deprivation of title was sufficient to be a taking.
23. The Northwest Ordinance, *Documents Illustrative of the Formation of the American States* (69th Cong., 1st Sess.) at 47–54, reprinted in Swindler, 1 *Sources and Documents of the United States Constitutions* (1982) [emphasis added].
24. 4 *The James Madison Letters* 478 (March 27, 1792), quoted in Siegan, *Economic Liberties and the Constitution* 58 (1980) [emphasis added]. This language appears in part as well in *Property, National Gazette*, March 27, 1792, in 14 Madison, *The Papers of James Madison* 266 (Riland, ed., 1977).
25. 4 *Letters and Other Writings of James Madison* 174 (1865)(from essay "Property" written in 1792 and published in the *National Gazette*)[emphasis added].
26. *Id.* at 175 (emphasis added).
27. Hamilton, Federalist Paper 68, *The Federalist Papers*; 25 The Papers of Alexander Hamilton 478–479 (Syrett, ed., 1977); *see, also*, Beveridge, *The Life of John Marshall* 416–417 (1916) (Constitution necessary to protect property rights in order to promote and encourage industry).
28. Such as the Northwest Ordinance, discussed in Part I, *supra*.
29. *See, e.g., Hepburn v. Griswold*, 75 U.S. 603, 624 (1870), discussed *supra*.
30. *Fletcher v. Peck, supra*, 10 U.S. (6 Cranch) at 138–139.

CHAPTER 8

1. In the *New Law Dictionary*, for instance, Jacob discriminated between "unlawful takings" and "felonious takings." A felonious taking is a theft, done "with an intent to steal."

2. *See, e.g.*, Johnson, *A Dictionary of the English Language* (2d ed., 1755); Jacob, *New Law Dictionary.*

3. The Statute of Uses, 27 Hen. VIII, c.10 (1536).

4. 4th ed., 1978.

5. Northwest Ordinance, *supra.*

6. *The Vermont Constitution of 1777, Poore, 2 Federal and State Constitutions, Federal Charters, and Other Organic Laws of the United States* 1859 (2d ed., 1878).

7. *The Delaware Declaration of Rights and Fundamental Rules of 1776*, quoted in 5 *The Founders' Constitution* 312 (Kerland and Lerner, eds., 1987).

8. *Vanhorne's Lessee, supra*, 2 U.S. (2 Dall.) at 310.

9. *Id.* Still more can be learned about the meaning of the word "use" by examining the meaning of the word "take." "Take" was no more specifically defined than "use," but the relationship of the two concepts may be instructive. As previously noted, *The American Heritage Dictionary* defines the term "take" as meaning, among other things:

> to get into one's possession ... to seize authoritatively; confiscate ... to accept and place under one's care or keeping ... to appropriate for one's own or another's *use* or *benefit* ... to choose for one's own use; avail one's self of the *use* of ... *to subtract (from)* ... to *use* to one's advantage.

10. Pufendorf, *De Officio Homines et Civis*, Tit. II, ch. 15, Section 4. *See, also*, Pufendorf, *Jurae Naturaeet Gentium*, Bk. VIII, ch. 5, sec. 7 (C. and W. Oldfathers, trans. 1934).

11. *Hepburn v. Griswold*, 75 U.S. 603, 624 (1870).

12. *Samual Johnson's Dictionary* (1775).

13. *Fletcher v. Peck*, 10 U.S. at 135–136. (emphasis added).

14. *See, e.g., Hepburn v. Griswold, supra*, 75 U.S. at 624 (1870).

15. *See, e.g.*, Wright, *The Contract Clause and the Constitution* 4–5 (1938). *See, also*, Nevins, *The American States Before and After the Revolution*, 1775–1789, at 836, 390, 404, 457, 525, 532–533, 537, 549, 570–571 (1924) for a survey of the various laws that concerned the delegates; Chapter 2, *supra.*

16. Hamilton, Federalist Paper No. 7, *The Federalist Papers* at 65.

17. (Madison) *Notes*, at 76.

18. *See, e.g. Poletown Neighborhood Council v. City of Detroit*, 304 N.W. 2d 455 (Mich. 1981) (The government condemned residential property and gave it to General Motors for construction of an auto plant. This was done on the theory that the plant would be good for the local economy).

19. *Id.* at 84.

20. *See, e.g., Hawaii Housing Authority v. Midkiff*, 467 U.S. 239 (1984), in which residential property was taken from its owners and sold to their lessees. The asserted public purpose for this action was to break up the "land oligarchy." More will be said about this case later.

21. *See, e.g., The Bridge Proprietors v. Hoboken Company*, 68 U. S. (1 Wall.) 116 (1963); *Charles River Bridge v. Warren Bridge*, 36 U.S. (11 Pet.) 420 (1837).

22. *See, e.g., United States v. Russell*, 80 U.S. (13 Wall.) 623 (1871).

23. *See, e.g., Charles River Bridge, supra.*

24. *Id.*

25. *Id.* at 537.

26. *Olcott v. The Supervisors*, 83 U.S. 678, 695 (1872).

27. *West River Bridge Company v. Dix*, 47 U.S. (6 How.) at 537 (McLean concurring).

28. Which raises the truly central question in the public use debate, discussed *infra*. Who gets to decide whether a use is properly public?
29. *Hawaii Housing Authority v. Midkiff*, 467 U.S. 239 (1984).
30. *Id.* at 243.
31. 348 U.S. 26 (1954).
32. "The public purpose for which the power is exerted must be real, not pretended." 47 U.S. (6 How.) at 537.
33. 262 U.S. 700, 705 (1923).
34. *Midkiff*, 467 U.S. at 240.
35. *Midkiff*, 467 U.S. at 240 (citing *Berman*).
36. *Midkiff, supra*, 467 U.S. at 242 n.3.

CHAPTER 9

1. 106 U.S. 195 (1882).
2. *Id.* at 217.
3. *Id.* at 220–221.
4. *Frontiero v. Richardson*, 411 U.S. 677 (1973).
5. *Agins v. City of Tiburon*, 24 Cal.3d 266 (1979).
6. *Id.* at 274.
7. *See, First Evangelical Lutheran Church of Glendale v. County of Los Angeles*, 482 U.S. 304 (1987), discussed *infra*.
8. *See, e.g., Mahon, supra*, 260 U.S. at 414.
9. *Id.* at 413 (Emphasis added).
10. *Berman v. Parker*, 348 U.S. 26, 32–33 (1954); *Ruckleshaus v. Monsanto*, 467 U.S. 986, 1016 (1984).
11. *Department of Agriculture and Consumer Services v. Mid-Florida Growers, Inc.*, 521 So.2d 101 (1988).
12. *Mahon, supra*, at 415.
13. *See, e.g., United States v. General Motors*, 323 U.S. 373 (1945).
14. *See, e.g., United States v. Causby, supra*, 328 U.S. 256 (1946).
15. *Agins*, 24 Cal.3d at 275–277.
16. *Id.* at 276.
17. *See, e.g., id.*
18. *Id.*
19. *Id.* at 276.
20. *Agins, supra*, at 283.
21. *Id.*
22. *Id.*
23. *Id.*
24. The Northwest Ordinance, *Documents Illustrative of the Formation of the American States (69th Cong., 1st Sess.)* at 47–54, reprinted in Swindler, 1 *Sources and Documents of the United States Constitutions* (1982) [emphasis added].
25. *See, e.g.,* Blackstone, *Commentaries* *135.
26. *Id.* [emphasis added].
27. *Mahon, supra*, 260 U.S. at 414.
28. Letter from Oliver Wendell Holmes to Harold J. Laski, December 14, 1922, reprinted in, 1 *Holmes–Laski Letters* 462 (Howe, ed., 1953).
29. *Penn Central Transportation Co., supra*, 438 U.S. at 138–139 (Rehnquist, J. dissenting).

30. 483 U.S. 825, 856 (1987).

31. 33 U.S.C. § 1344, *et seq*.

32. *Loan Association v. Topeka*, 20 U.S. (Wall.) 655 (1874).

33. *Nollan*, 483 U.S. at 837 n.5 [emphasis added to *untradeable*].

CHAPTER 10

1. Letter from Oliver Wendell Holmes to Harold J. Laski, January 13, 1923, reprinted in 1 *Holmes–Laski Letters* 473 (Howe, ed., 1953).

2. Constitution, Art. I, Section 8.

3. 369 U.S. 590 (1962).

4. 123 U.S. 623 (1847).

5. *Fletcher v. Peck, supra*, 10 U.S. (6 Cranch) at 133.

CHAPTER 11

1. Bastiat *Selected Essays on Political Economy* 238–239 (1964) (written in 1850).

2. Brutus' Essays, Number VI, *New York Journal*, December 27, 1787, reprinted in the Antifederalist Papers, *supra*, at 285. *See, also,* Letters From the Federal Farmer No. 1, reprinted in the Antifederalist Papers, *supra*, at 259–260.

3. 480 U.S. 470 (1987).

4. 482 U.S. 304 (1987).

5. 483 U.S. 825 (1987).

6. *Keystone, supra*, 480 U.S. at 487.

7. *Id.* at 492.

8. *Agins v. Tiburon*, 477 U.S. 255 (1980).

9. *Nollan, supra*, 483 U.S. at 837.

10. *Nollan, supra*, 483 U.S. at 836 n.3

11. *Goldblatt v. Hempstead*, 369 U.S. 590 (1962).

12. *First English, supra*, 482 U.S. at 321, citing *Mahon*.

13. *See, e.g., Midflorida Growers, supra; Loveladies Harbor*, 21 Cl.Ct. 153 (1990); *Whitney Benefits Corporation v. United States*, 18 Cl.Ct. 394 (1989), *modified* 20 Cl.Ct. 324 (1990), *aff'd* 926 F.2d 1169 (Fed. Cir.), *cert. denied* ___ U.S. ___, 112 S.Ct. 406, 116 L.Ed.2d 354 (1991); *Surfside Colony, Ltd. v. California Coastal Commission*, 226 Cal.App.3d 1260 (1991), *reh. denied and opinion modified*.

14. 53 Fed. Reg. 8859 (1988).

CHAPTER 12

1. The same is true of the term "liberal." *See, e.g.*, F.A. Hayek, *The Constitution of Liberty* 397–411 (1978).

2. Letter No. I, October 8, 1787, *Letters from the Federal Farmer, The Antifederalist Papers and Constitutional Convention Debates* 259"260 (Ralph Ketcham, ed., 1986).

CHAPTER 13

1. *See, e.g.*, McKinley, *The Outlaws of Sherwood* (1988).

2. *Loveladies Harbor, Inc. v. United States*, 21 Cl.Ct. 153 (1990).

3. 33 U.S.C. section 1344.

4. *See*, 40 C.F.R. 328.3(b) (1988).

5. 42 U.S.C. section 4321, *et seq.*

6. 16 U.S.C. section 1531, *et seq.*

7. *Florida Rock Inc. v. United States*, 8 Cl.Ct. 160 (1985); and *Ciampetti v. United States*, 18 Cl.Ct. 548 (1989).

8. *Florida Rock Inc. v. United States*, 791 F.2d 893 (Fed.Cir. 1986).

9. *Id.* at 904, 905.

10. 123 U.S. 623 (1887).

11. 15 Cl.Ct. 381 (1988).

12. *Whitney Benefits Corporation v. United States*, 926 F.2d 1169 (1991).

13. *Whitney Benefits v. United States*, ___ U.S. ___, 112 S.Ct. 406, 116 L.Ed. 2d 354 (1991)(denying review).

14. 791 F.2d 893, 904 (1986).

15. 14 *Chemical Regulation Reporter* 154 (May 4, 1990).

16. 14 *Chemical Regulation Reporter* 288 (May 25, 1990).

17. *See, e.g., Just v. Marinette County*, 201 N.W.2d 761 (1972).

18. *See, e.g., Summa Corporation v. California*, 466 U.S. 198 (1984).

19. *See, e.g.*, California's Permit Streamlining Act, California Government Code section 65950, *et seq.*

20. *See, e.g., Beure-Co. v. United States*, 16 Cl.Ct. 42 (1988); *Ciampetti v. United States*, 18 Cl.Ct. 548 (1989).

CHAPTER 14

1. Bolick, *Unfinished Business: A Civil Rights Strategy for America's Third Century*, 140–143 (1990).

CHAPTER 15

1. *Preseault v. Interstate Commerce Commission*, 494 U.S. 1, 111 L.Ed.2d 914 (1989).

2. *United States v. Whitney Benefits, Inc.*, 116 L.Ed.2d 354 (1991).

3. *Yee v. City of Escondido*, 112 S.Ct. 1522, 118 L.Ed.2d 153 (1992).

4. *Lucas v. South Carolina Coastal Council*, 112 S.Ct. 2886 (1992).

5. *Kaiser-Aetna v. United States*, 444 U.S. 164 (1979).

6. *Yancey v. United States*, 915 F.2d 1534 (1990).

7. 438 U.S. 104 (1978).

8. *Lucas, supra*, 112 S.Ct. at 2894 n.7. [Emphasis added.]

9. *Id.*, 112 S.Ct. at 2998.

10. *Id.* at 2899.

11. *Id.* at 2899 n12.

12. *See*, e.g., *id.* at 2899–2900.

INDEX